the
SURVIVAL of
DOMINATION

the SURVIVAL of DOMINATION

inferiorization and everyday life

BARRY D. ADAM

Elsevier · New York
NEW YORK · OXFORD

ELSEVIER NORTH-HOLLAND, INC.
52 Vanderbilt Avenue, New York, New York 10017

Distributors outside the United States and Canada:
THOMOND BOOKS
(A Division of Elsevier/North-Holland
Scientific Publishers, Ltd)
P.O. Box 85
Limerick, Ireland

Library of Congress Cataloging in Publication Data

Adam, Barry D
    The survival of domination: inferiorization and everyday life.

    Bibliography: p.
    Includes index.
    1. Discrimination—Psychological aspects. 2. Minorities. 3. Power
    (Social sciences) 4. Social structure. I. Title.
HM291.A3   301.15'2   78-17718
ISBN 0-444-99047-X

Designed by Loretta Li

MANUFACTURED IN THE UNITED STATES OF AMERICA

For Mike and Ric

"There actually is a mental experience—fallible indeed, but immediate—of the essential and the unessential, an experience which only the scientific need for order can forcibly talk the subjects out of. Where there is no such experience, knowledge stays unmoved and barren. Its measure is what happens objectively to the subjects, as their suffering."

ADORNO, Negative Dialectics, p. 169–170.

CONTENTS

PREFACE

This study belongs in the larger intellectual tradition devoted to the "problem of order." Traditionally the preserve of Hobbesian political philosophy, the problem of order tended to be phrased thus: how, given the wilful, aggressive, and destructive nature of man, is social order made possible? The response has usually argued for the necessity of social control. The problem has more recently re-emerged in the Marxian tradition. As the "necessity" for social revolution has come to appear increasingly undetermined and contingent, the problem of order arises again. It is no longer founded on an assumed Hobbesian "human nature" but on the realities of class society. Thus: how, given the unequal distribution of social goods, is social order maintained, or how are the dispossessed kept subordinate? This renewed problem of order has occupied twentieth-century Marxian thought in a number of forms. Orthodox schools talk about political suppression, cooptation of labor leaders, and the mass media, relegating the subject to the "black box" of "false consciousness." It remains, in the words of Jock Young,[1] an "idea of a passive, nonreflective individual who is prey without significant defences, to external or internal malignant influences."

---

[1]Young, Jock. 1975. "Working-Class Criminology." In Ian Taylor, Paul Walton, and Jock Young (eds.). *Critical Criminology*. London: Routledge & Kegan Paul.

Attempted here is a phenomenology of everyday life which comprehends the choices made by people within the practical and material constraints of their subordination which, then, re-create or alter that subordination. Evidence from such disparate groups as Jews, blacks, and gay people allows us to understand how inferiorized people cope with living oppressed on a day-to-day basis. The story of how people *survive domination* through resistance, accommodation, and compliance tells us much about how *domination survives* and an inequitable social order is reproduced.

The format of the book reflects the dialectic of inferiorization and response. The first chapters outline the practices of inferiorization creating fundamentally different life-worlds for Jews, blacks, and gay people. This "regressive" dialectical moment manifests itself in the structure of opportunities and its legitimizing ideologies. The "deep logic" of these ideologies is examined in the psychiatric confrontation of homosexuality and in the stereotypic traits attributed in common to each group. The succeeding chapters elucidate the "progressive" moment, that is, the development of strategies to cope with domination. The final chapter contains thoughts on what concepts are adequate to recognize oppression in the manifold places it is found.

Full acknowledgements demand an archaeological tour through the sedimentations of one's own psyche. A complete acknowledgement of one's self-formation would require accreditation of a peculiar matrix of historical conditions, accidents, commitments, and predilections. The "clever" reader does not wait for the author's declaration, but turns immediately to the bibliography to fix him on the intellectual landscape.

I suspect that some of those named here will wonder how their association with me could be related to the work at hand. Certainly none of them is responsible for the use I have turned their ideas and my observations of them.

I am grateful for having studied as an undergraduate under several members of the faculty of Simon Fraser University. The perceptions of Professors Arthur Mitzman, Ernest Becker, and George Smith were always eclectic, yet profound.

The manuscript was written as a doctoral dissertation in the Department of Sociology at the University of Toronto. Professors

Bernd Baldus, Irving Zeitlin, Richard Roman, John Lee, Charles Levine, and Gregory Baum reviewed the work in progress. It could not have been realized without the generous assistance of the Canada Council (grant W753237) and the Robarts Graduate Research Library.

Excerpts have been presented at the conferences of the Canadian Sociology and Anthropology Association meeting at the Université Laval, Québec, and the Gay Academic Union at Columbia University, New York, both in 1976. The section, "Composite Portrait of the Inferiorized Person" appeared in *Gai Saber* 1 (Spring) 72 in 1977.

I owe an immeasurable debt for long months of intellectual and emotional support to Christopher Headon, Robert Pilskaln, Roy Fielding, and Monty Cooper.

The physical production of the manuscript required the combined efforts of Roy Fielding and Gerry King, Miles and Doris Adam, and the University of Windsor library (binding section). The final stage of production was guided with the cooperation and good humor of William Gum of Elsevier North-Holland, Inc.

Barry D. Adam

I INTRODUCTION

Project

Dominated peoples develop a range of behavior patterns to cope with their recalcitrant social environment. The special burdens and restrictions that realize inferiority for people demand special responses. The inferiorized face life possibilities circumscribed by a set of oppressive institutions and practices reserving valued resources for other groups. The struggle to survive, resist, and overcome the processes of inferiorization marks the history of dominated peoples. Our focus is upon the coping strategies employed in *everyday life* to meet the exigencies of inferiorization.

Political histories which select the activities of educated elites, charismatic leaders, and other articulate exponents of the dominated, rarely attempt to grasp the realities of the day-to-day existence of the mass. Such accounts are typically written and consumed by these same elites as a source of inspiration and tested tactics. Yet to understand social revolution most radically requires analysis of these everyday social relationships and their potential for transformation.

Oppression which is imminent in everyday life and necessitates immediate and repeated responses, builds a repertoire of habits and attitudes among its victims. Behavior which is mundane, routine, and taken for granted tends to escape the notice of the more dramatic macrohistories. Yet despite the record of resistance, protest, and discontent evident in the struggle for equality, continuities remain. Most remarkable is the stability of many oppressive relationships. To understand the production and maintenance of social order necessitates focus upon the social accomplishment of inferiorization in everyday life. Socially structured life constraints elicit behavior which adjusts, accommodates, or subordinates itself to adverse situations in the interest of survival and thereby functions to reproduce the constraining order. Much of everyday life cannot but submit to the *rationality* of the given social order.

Over time, defensive tactics evolve into accepted habits. Each generation provides a model for its successor; its wisdom enhances the survival of the next. These behavior patterns molded by the workings of oppression may accumulate about succeeding generations like a deadweight, easing the work of oppressors and serving the more efficient maintenance of the received social order. As Albert Memmi remarks, "The longer the oppression lasts, the more it profoundly affects him [the oppressed]. It ends by becoming so familiar to him that he believes it is part of his own constitution, that he accepts it and could not imagine his recovery from it. This acceptance is the crowning point of oppression."[1] As with the rhinoceros, evolution has provided a protective armor that becomes an ingrown prison.[2]

By selecting three very different minorities as the objects of investigation, the central nexus between social environment and behavior can be laid bare. While the histories of Jewish, black, and gay people remain unique, some commonalities are revealed.

All exist within the general framework of advanced Western capitalist systems and for the most part, within "liberal-democratic" political orders. All three are highly urbanized and exposed to official and social control agents and objectified means of communication—electronic media, publications, the educational system. They are embedded in a milieu which is largely created and defined by an other. Their everyday life is, then, likely to be affected by the larger social order, and only secondarily insulated by community. In addition, they are unlike many ethnic groups whose identity is an institution inherited from and supported by a close-at-hand, self-governing nation. Nor do they enjoy autonomy at home. Their identities, then, rely more directly upon negotiation with local agents of social control and cultural transmission, without mitigating association with a prestigious or powerful nation.

Many of the strategies of inferiorization employed by powerful groups are the same in each instance and create comparable sets of oppressive situations. These situations, in turn, precondition remarkably similar attitudinal and behavioral responses. That such diverse groups respond to their inferiorized status in similar ways militates against naturalistic, biological, pathological, psychiatric, and moral theories that continue particularly to premise accounts of gay people.

Insofar as the workings of domination have been more distinctly perceived in inferiorized groups such as these, the "minority" provides a particularly fruitful level of analysis. The societies examined here construe differentiation between black and white, Jewish and Gentile, homosexual and heterosexual as "significant" or salient and unequally allocate social valuables along these criteria. At the same time, the restriction of life chances does not follow three neat social cleavages. The refraction of oppression by infrastructural and microsocial formations (such as family, occupation, the immediate community, etc.) precondition heterogeneous experiences *within* the selected groups. The comparison of Jewish, black, and gay people affirms the pervasiveness of gradations of oppression and response.

The behavior patterns examined here are by no means the exclusive preserve of these groups. The collective biographies of, for example, some colonized peoples, North American Indians, and women should be amenable to this kind of analysis. Exploration of this theme centers generally on the problem: how are people kept in (subordinate) place?

The present study draws from the history of Jews in Western Europe after their "Emancipation," to the founding of Israel (with notes on studies of the United States from the latter period). Documentation of the black experience stems from their history in United States after their "Emancipation." The history of gay people, though still riven with research lacunae, draws from the two time and place frames.

The selection of indices of everyday life presents special problems of verifiability. In many instances, autobiographical and personal accounts of what anthropologists call "key informers," psychological studies, and philosophical excursus prove most illuminating. Quantifications or demographic profiles of the projects, behavioral orientations, or coping strategies of people prove largely quixotic, though they have been attempted.[3] More fruitful for this endeavor is an "interpretive sociology" which seeks to understand the meaning of the social world for the actor. "We, then, try to understand him in that doing and feeling and the state of mind which induced him to adopt specific attitudes towards his social environment."[4] Adequacy at the level of meaning requires examination of the "in order to" and "because" motives of the actors, which can be organized into ideal types. The adequacy of ideal types depends upon their logical consistency, referability to the subjective meanings of actions for the actors, and comprehensibility for actors in terms of commonsense interpretation of everyday life.[5]

Through historical accounts of approximately the last century of practices of holders of political and economic resources, of social control agents, and of cultural-transmission institutions in the advanced, industrial West, we can come to understand the persistent, socially structured differences which alter the objective life possibilities for Jewish, black, and gay people. Examining how these people make sense of the objectively constricted life possibilities of their social situations throws light upon the mechanisms and perpetuation of domination.

Differing modes of response can be observed according to a rudimentary bifurcation of the histories of inferiorized peoples into (1) periods of "quiescent," structured limitations of life possibilities generally associated with the predominance of the bourgeois classes and capitalist social order, and (2) periods of active persecution and reduction of life possibilities generally associated with the struggle of the threatened precapitalist classes. Of the three modalities of survival strategies proposed, "persecutory" periods appear to allow for "guilt-based" and "withdrawal" strategies, and "quiescent" periods for "withdrawal" and "contraversive" strategies. Response sets of individuals appear further influenced by such intervening conditions as social location within the inferiorized group, parental socialization, social mobility, and the salience of the group within the larger society.

The research literature is, however, a product of the problem: the extensiveness and quality of the research tend to be a function of the prestige of the groups examined. One detects a reluctance on the part of researchers to be "contaminated" by a truly disrespectable group. The development of Jewish studies in the postwar period has made literature on the Jewish experience the "classic" in minority studies. Increasing black militancy has led to an explosion in black studies and sufficient research funding for extensive "hard" (i.e., statistical) analysis. Gay history even today remains suppressed, fragmentary, and the object of manipulation by polemicists.

Survey of the research literature reveals two striking observations: (1) little interdisciplinary communication—there is a tendency to have to "discover America" again and again—and (2) little or no integration of analyses of different dominated groups. For the most part, limited "middle-range" theories, residual categories, or pleas for examination of the topic in its own right, encompass the problem of order. Ethnographic and fragmentary studies are widely distributed through the sociology of deviance, ethnic and race relations, psychoanalysis, philosophy, social psychology, political theory, and orthopsychiatry.

The result has been a plethora of publications in which researchers overlook what they have observed. The lack of integration and typification produces by default a range of naturalistic fallacies. Positing behavior as an "inherent" characteristic—a sort of "human nature"—is the mark of analytic failure. The history of black and Jewish studies abounds with such distortions; research in gay studies has scarcely begun to free itself from them.[6] The confusion has led one recent reviewer of the sociology of the black experience to remark, "The sociology of the black man has not yet begun. Despite more than a century of study, blacks remain a sociological puzzle."[7]

Traditional selections of evidence tend often to perform an unwitting cover-up of the behavior examined here. A certain romantic liberalism[8] runs through the literature, evident from attempts to paper over or discount the very real problems of inferiorization. Some researchers seem bent on "rescuing" their subjects from "defamation" by ignoring the problems of defeatism and complicit self-destruction. Avoidance of dispiriting reflection upon the day-to-day practice of dominated people appears to spring from a desire to "enhance" the reputation of the dominated and magically relieve their plight. Careful observation has been sacrificed to the "power of positive thinking." Albert Memmi, an analyst of colonialism and decolonization remarks,

> As for most social romantics, . . . the victim remains proud and intact through oppression; he suffered but did not let himself be broken. And the day oppression ceases, the new man is supposed to appear before our eyes immediately. Now I do not like to say so, but I must, since decolonization has demonstrated it: this is not the way it happens.[9]

Comparative analysis has been inhibited by the wish to idealize the group at hand. Lengthy "refutations" of "infantilized" or "psychopathological" behavior found in these groups fails to come to grips with the meaning of actions of the young or insane. Analysts indulge in a familiar tactic of status compensation: making distinctions that place the group they are analyzing at a distance from another group which can be stigmatized as yet more inferior.[10] It is a tendency abetted by the dominated themselves.

> The oppressed find the description of their servitude even less bearable, as if the description itself increased their anguish. If necessary they will allow themselves to be pitied, they will allow others to lament with them, but only on the condition that the others pretend to believe them proud and irreproachable; in that way, the inevitable results of their long oppression—their wounds, their inner deformities and destruction—are not closely revealed.[11]

A final caveat: this book is not an attempt at a complete or rounded description of the minority experience. The focus tends to allow the appearance of a monolithic portrait through idealtypification—a reification, which can be dissembled only by keeping in mind the context-fixedness, the diversity, the unevenness of its manifestations and negations.

Dialectics of Freedom and Domination

Terms such as *freedom*, *domination*, and *inferiorization* are by no means self-evident. Most important to bear in mind is the embeddedness of these terms in a historically moving social relationship. Abstraction from dialectical relativity produces brittle, fixed, and particular concepts constructed from positive or "objective" indices. Such concepts are of little use as their contents evolve over time and refer to different sets of conditions and meanings for different groups. *Freedom* and *domination* refer to the contradictory phases of the subject–object dialectic (in Sartrean terms, "progressive' and "regressive" moments). *Inferiorization* can be subsumed as an aspect of the regressive process.

André Gorz provides a cue for an initial locating of freedom in "the power of the individual to shape the condition in which he lives and to change those conditions according to his needs and his desires for self-fulfillment and self-transcendence."[12] The field of action for the individual is the totality of his life. Realization of self is at issue in every sphere—economic, political, aesthetic, erotic, and intellectual.

The possibilities for the pursuit of one's intentions are not given without limit or in a social vacuum. "Every man is defined negatively by the sum of possibles which are impossible for him; that is, by a future more or less blocked off."[13] Domination arises in the ongoing dialectic between this "blocking-off" process and the actions of people. Freedom is the subjective moment: "it is man himself *qua* actor, *qua* unifying labor, in so far as he has hold on the world and he changes it."[14]

Definitions of domination are commonly abstracted from the relationship between commands and obedience[15] or from dramatic incidents and confrontations. Definitions frequently include reference to the attitude of the dominated (e.g., resistance or aspirations). Implicit in this view is a supposed lack of power or domination in the absence of overt conflict.[16] By excluding "authority" from the category of *domination*, the entire problem of the response to domination is suppressed. The artificial abstraction and narrowing of the "political" away from everyday life, microsocial relations, "consenting" relations among individuals and groups, etc., ignores the fundamental and inclusive sociological dimension of domination accomplished as a received structure of access to social goods.

The limitation of life possibilities is not equally experienced by all people. Domination arises in the *differential* distribution of life possibilities.[17] Domination cannot be restricted to instances of open confrontation, commands, or resistance; it lies in the *structure* of concrete alternatives open to individuals. The social cleavages among individuals subject to similar sets of life alternatives form the boundaries of social groups. "Domination" exists in the social structuring of life limitations, by which one group (the dominators) successfully maximizes its life chances by minimizing those of another (the dominated). *Oppression* refers to the systematic abbreviation of possibilities of mastery of most or all facets of life for a specifiable group.[18] It is the experience of the "total institution"[19] in macrocosm.

The attempt, made frequently in ethnic studies, to define dominated groups in terms of hypostatized traits such as skin color, descent, endogamy, self-identification, etc., obscures the fundamental dynamic by which such attributes become necessary or come to be seen as significant.

> Minority groups are characterized by their categorically lowered life chances. Their identifying characteristics whether physical or cultural, serve only as a source of social visibility. It is the relative powerlessness of minority groups that defines their disadvantaged situation, underlying their exclusion from participation in the institutions of the larger society.[20]

Domination cannot be understood outside the dialectical relation in which it exists. As such, it lies within a moving historical context. No absolute standard can be adduced to discover "domination" for all times and all places. Seizure of positive attributes as indicators of domination falsifies its historically embedded existence. As André Gorz remarks, for example, in relation to the perception of poverty:

> Poverty is not the impossibility or difficulty of subsisting (keeping alive biologically); it is the impossibility of living up to the standards of normal life in a given society and enjoying the socially available opportunities, facilities and possibilities of this society. One can subsist quite well without teeth, and the wealthy merchants and aristocrats of the sixteenth century used to lose theirs. But because dentistry nowadays is socially available (i.e., *potentially* available to everyone) a person who can't have his or her teeth seen to is denied a social possibility and is poor.[21]

Even the term *minority* could only begin to be adequate if it were true that majorities rule and minorities do not. It is a term which conceals commonality with dominated majorities (e.g., women, the proletariat). *Race* is a nineteenth-century biological concept whose stress upon posited genetic and inherited traits ignores the historical construction of the idea of race and the social selection of attributes to differentiate people. *Deviance* is a normative term which glosses or suppresses the social construction of stigma and obscures the essential aspect: inferiorization.[22] The reliance here upon the terms *inferiorized, dominated,* or *subordinated* to characterize a group is an attempt to keep clear the political-historical dynamic by which blacks, Jews, and gay people are defined and to bridge the conceptual differences among "commonsense" terms which prevent unified analysis.

The full significance of the central terms of this analysis can be realized only through concrete examination of the relations from which they spring. At this point, the dialectic between domination and freedom, and the process of inferiorization can only be indicated. This preliminary sketch will, it is hoped, provide an orientation toward the logic of analysis and use of terms. Further clarification can only be the function of the development of the text.

Social Construction of Identity

> A *species* comes to be, a type becomes fixed and strong through the long fight with essentially constant *unfavorable* conditions.
>
> —NIETZSCHE[23]

Jewishness, blackness, and gayness can by no means be assumed as self-evident or unproblematic categories. The ongoing social production of Jewish, black, or gay identity continually redefines its membership, its value as a punishable or privileged label, its criteria of recognizability. The distribution of social values according to these identities creates groups, who in turn, may organize sufficiently to negotiate the meanings accruing to them.

The creation of social inequality requires the "discovery" of means by which to distinguish sameness and difference, self and other, among people. A moment's reflection will reveal the extraordinary triviality of traits per se by which disqualification from social opportunities is achieved. A momentous world of meanings accrues about, for example, gender, skin tone, erotic preference, etc., as these qualities are seized upon as bases for social inequality. The minority situation is more a matter of social definition than of social difference.[24] The original social creation of difference may be the product of recent conquest or remote history; once established, as we shall see, an array of social practices and psychological responses contributes to its institutionalization.

Access to social opportunities becomes a function of whichever characteristics have been declared as significant. The privileged develop ideologies and the coercive means to protect the hierarchy of access. The inferiorized are subject to categorical treatment. "The members of this distinguished population segment are 'assigned' to a particular social role and fate."[25] In this sense an *objective* class or *Klasse an sich* comes into existence. In Sartre's words, "it is a material and inorganic object in the domain of the practico-inert insofar as a discrete multiplicity of active individuals produces itself *in it* under the sign of the Other as a *real unity in Being*, i.e., as a passive synthesis."[26]

This disqualification and separation on the basis of specified traits creates a group of individuals sharing a common status. This common status preconditions (but does not determine) the possibility of *recognition* of commonality among affected individuals.[27] There exists an aggregate of differentiated individuals united only by a negative identity. They are a collection of monads existing as an "us-object" reflected by the categorization by others.

It is with recognition of the dialectical production of the group, that James Baldwin termed the Negro an "invention" of whites.[28] As Robert Blauner remarks:

The paradox of black culture is its ambiguous debt to racial oppression. Whereas racism attacks culture at its very roots, and white supremacy in American life and thought has worked tooth and nail to negate the past and present cultural realities of Afro-America, the centrality of racial subjugation in the black experience has been the single most important source of the developing ethnic peoplehood. Racism has been such an omnipresent reality that the direct and indirect struggle against it makes up the core of black history in America.[29]

A "Who am I?" inventory administered to high school students in Pittsburgh, Pennsylvania, not surprisingly found that "blacks identify themselves in terms of race far more often than do whites."[30] The social inferiorization of people according to selected characteristics creates a class *identified* by that characteristic. The salience of such an attribute for the life situation of its bearer can be ignored only at risk.

The consciousness of class arises in the phenomenology of domination. Black or Jewish or gay identity arises from no intrinsic or biologic quality in itself. Intrinsically they are nothing. Only the image of self reflected by *others able to influence or control one's life or survival*, necessarily organizes the self's priorities and orientations. The nature of Jewish identity is particularly instructive. Squabbles among academics and Jews themselves have centered around the issue. First one trait, then another is picked up and discarded as the determinant of Jewishness. Is it religion? tradition? race? ethos? nationality? appearance? Memmi ponders the phenomenology of Jewishness:

> As a Jew I exist more than non-Jews! My uniqueness makes me exist more, because it makes me more cumbersome, more problematical to others and to myself, because my conscience is more painfully aware, because the attention of others is more directly focused on me.[31]

In his essay, "The Non-Jewish Jew," Isaac Deutscher remarks:

> To me the Jewish community is still only negative. . . . Religion? I am an atheist. Jewish nationalism? I am an internationalist. In neither sense am I, therefore, a Jew. I am, however, a Jew by force of my unconditional solidarity with the persecuted and exterminated. I am a Jew because I feel the Jewish tragedy as my own tragedy; because I feel the pulse of Jewish history; because I should like to do all I can to assure the real, not spurious, security and self-respect of the Jews.[32]

In more prosaic manner, Dennis Altman points out the dynamic of gay identity:

> On one level to love someone of the same sex is remarkably inconsequential—after all, but for some anatomical differences, love for a man or a woman is hardly another order of things—yet society has made of it something portentous, and we must expect homosexuals to accept this importance in stressing their identity.[33]

11

Identity is differentiation; a coming-to-awareness of divergence or conflict of interests. The identity of the dominated admits no complacency. It is a necessary alertness and defence. It is problematized—"negative"—because it is continually challenged. Irving Horowitz remarks in *Israeli Ecstasies/Jewish Agonies*:

> When the persecution of the Jews ceases, there will no longer be any need to make portentous inquiries into what it means to be a Jew. But until that long-awaited, but probably never to be realized Day of Judgment, Jewish self-definition will continue, if only as a survival mechanism.[34]

One's identity as Jewish, gay, or black remains dialectically rooted. The Jew, essentially, is the person subject to Jewish *fate*.[35]

The coming to consciousness is the translation of commonality into community. Communicability preconditions the possibility of individuals caught in similar existential situations to form a community. Community implies at least some contact among like-situated individuals over time. Communication sets in motion the reciprocal determination of identity and community. This third or synthetic dialectical phase generated from differentiation of social situations, creates a new dimension in which isolated individuals coalesce through communication. The self comes to consciousness as group self. The communal sense of oneness enhances, and is enhanced by, the amplification of communication into tradition and the written word.[36]

The development of community fundamentally alters identity as an objective attribute of the other. The coextension of the collection of trait-ascribed members and community members ceases. In the interstices exist trait-ascribed members not identified (by self or community members) with the community and non-trait-ascribed members identified (by self and/or community members) with the community. Erving Goffman coined an (unused) term, *homosexualite*,[37] to describe men and women not "objectively" homosexual (i.e., not engaging in homosexual acts) who participate in the gay community. Carol Warren cites the example of a heterosexual woman who presented a gay identity and participated in the gay community.[38] Hereditarily white people may identify and be accepted by the black community.[39] Those willing to accept community identity for themselves may be admitted.

The noncongruence of the two collectivities may be recognized by the dominant group, especially in a highly polarized situation. "Contamination" or "guilt by association" with the inferiorized group may occur. The "nigger-lover" or Semitophile tends to acquire a sociological blackness of Jewishness, regardless of skin color or religious commitment. Civil rights workers in the American South in the 1960s and Gentiles who aided Jews in areas of Nazi domination were quickly accorded new identities by dominators and forced to share the fate of the dominated.

Much of the struggle to come to terms with the meaning of Jewish or black or gay identity revolves about confusion among earlier and later moments of the identity or identification process. The distinction between the regressive, objectivist moment of identification practiced by dominators, and the progressive, subjectivist moment, an ongoing accomplishment of developing community, has engendered distinctive terminologies. The use of the terms *Negro* and *homosexual*, for example, often accompanies "scientific" and reductionist endeavors of nonmembers; *black* and *gay* are historically unfinished cultural terms of self-appellation.[40] *Homosexual* refers (reduces) the person to sexual orientation determined usually by behavioral, judicial, or psychiatric criteria. "The word gay, whose origins are etymologically unclear, is descriptive of the kind of liveliness experienced by the members in this transition (which Berger calls ecstasy); the dropping of the mask, the putting on of the true identity, the ritual celebration of brotherhood enhanced by stigma and secrecy, and the sexuality experienced within this world of meanings."[41] The meanings of "blackness," "Jewishness," and "gayness" are the continuing practice of cultures of poets, artists, writers, and the everyday actions of people. The progressive terminology is employed here to point toward the later, cultural moments of the identification process.

The problems of identification especially disturb the gatekeepers to social opportunities, who rely partly upon legal objectivism to maintain the status quo. Biological-genetic definitions of blackness continually dissolve into absurdity. "Using a sample of over 5,000 Negroes from all over the United States between 1915 and 1926, Melville J. Herskovits estimated that no more than 22 per cent of all persons designated as Negro were of unmixed ancestry.[42] Some

15 percent had more white than black ancestry, 25 percent were approximately of equal proportion, 32 percent had more black than white ancestry, and 6 percent had some combination of black and American Indian. The traditional American definition has been that *any* black ancestry constitutes blackness. On the basis of studies conducted for *An American Dilemma*, Gunnar Myrdal concluded, "The definition of the 'Negro race' is thus a social and conventional, not a biological concept. The social definition and not the biological facts actually determines the status of an individual and his place in interracial relations."[43]

The legal-objectivist identification of Jewishness in Germany in the post-1935 period met similar difficulties. A 1935 German law prescribed a Jew to be any person with three or four grandparents of the Jewish religion, or with two grandparents of the Jewish religion plus current Jewish affiliation of that person or his or her spouse.[44] *"Mischlinge"* included those with some, but less Jewish ancestry or affiliation. In practice, one high Nazi official (complicit in the destruction of the Jews), who had one Jewish grandparent and was married to a woman with two Jewish grandparents, was reclassified by official decree.[45] The social construction of identity was, after a time, enunciated by the courts: "Aryan treatment was to be accorded to persons who had the 'racial' requisites 'but that in cases when the individual involved feels bound to Jewry in spite of his Aryan blood and shows this fact externally, his attitude is decisive.' "[46] Such "Gentiles" were thereby classified as "Jews."

Inferiorization by posited traits proceeds, then, only with difficulty. Visibility becomes a crucial factor in its application. A rank order of visibility may be constructed from almost entirely visible, e.g., women, through to almost entirely invisible (blacks, through to Jews and gay people). Visibility significantly refracts the actual practice of domination. Those clustered toward the invisibility pole of the scale (Jews and gay people) may even be *protected* by the highly obtuse diacritic techniques of dominators. Stereotypes for recognition of such groups may be so wildly inaccurate as to identify successfully only the smallest part of the group. The gay community, for example, is able to develop means of heightening visibility for its members, while diminishing it for outsiders. This is easily achieved when homosexuality is thought to be recognizable by means of a largely unrelated criterion: deviation from sex role.[47]

Social selection of individuals according to the visibility of a proscribed trait produces a hierarchy of inferiorization within the group. "Dark Negroes are in lower occupational and income categories than light Negroes even with relatively high levels of education (some college and high school graduation). Color only washes out as a predictor of occupational-income payoff among the best educated college graduates."[48] Gay people bearing a legal stigma experience heightened visibility. Those with official labels specifying homosexuality, conferred by courts, psychiatric institutions, or the military, report subsequent difficulties. Colin Williams and Martin Weinberg's study of those discharged from the United States' military on the ground of homosexuality found a *majority* suffered subsequent discrimination in employment.[49]

The Inquisition brought with it a new profession of witch-detectors and manuals of witch-detection such as the *Malleus maleficarum*. The frustration of dominators in their wish to keep certain peoples subordinated led to various Church decrees through the Dark Ages and Medieval period, specifying the detection and segregation of Jews and heightening visibility with compulsory yellow badges.[50] The 1935 German laws on Jewish identity engendered specialists in genealogy who would certify racial "purity" for four to seven generations (the latter required for the SS).[51] Psychiatry and psychology have devoted themselves to elaborating techniques for the detecting of homosexuality. "Personality profiles," measurement of pupil dilations, psychoanalytic imputation of "latent" or "overt" homosexual syndromes, continue to serve (no matter how unreliably) specialists bent on eradicating homosexuality in youth, on defaming character in court, and incarcerating gay people in prisons and mental institutions.

Ontogenesis

The genesis of a people is an historical process of many generations. Each new generation must repeat in microcosm the differentiation of self which has created the people of which it is a part. The discovery of *self as devalued other* marks a significant psychological status passage in the life of each inferiorized individual.[52] Autobiographical literature contains testimony of the first recognition of this contradiction.

Blacks in the United States experience the self as racial category very early. "Color becomes an affectively laden concept by the fourth year. Analysis of spontaneous comments provides evidence for this." By the fifth year appears "a clear knowledge that these biological features are connected to social categories."[53] In the words of the landmark study by Kenneth and Mamie Clark: "It is clear that the Negro child, by the age of five is aware of the fact that to be colored in contemporary American society is a mark of inferior status."[54] The assumption of self as black occurs initially between the ages of three and five years, and can be recalled by many in a specific incident.[55]

Jews tend to recall first awareness of Jewishness in a slightly later age frame. Five to eight years of age is reported[56] as the significant period. Memmi remarks, "If one is not always aware from birth of being a Jew, one always becomes so, each in his own way, which adds to the confusion and perplexity."[57]

The "coming out" process of gay people is, on the other hand, primarily a recognition prompted by the sex role expectations of late adolescence and adulthood. The discovery of self as gay occurs over a protracted age span complicated by the fact that the carriers of gay identity are not one's biological parents. Judith Kramer remarks in reference to blacks that "without such conditioning, they would be paralyzed by anxiety, as would anyone else faced with their categorical circumstances for the first time."[58] "Paralyzing anxiety" without a supportive parental and community milieu tends to delay gay identification and make "coming out" a status passage of special salience in the lives of gay people. An average six-year gap separates first homosexual experiences or feelings with self-identification as gay.[59] Entrance into the gay community is, then, by no means automatic, but an extended integration into the horizontal[60] "family" structures that characterize the community.[61] The process is experienced as a feeling "at home"[62] for the first time. The coping strategies which occupy a major part of the stock of knowledge of an inferiorized identity continue to rely almost entirely upon oral transmission in gay culture. The protracted period of gay ontogenesis produces a considerable population "in transition." "At one extreme are those who seek to maintain a self-image of heterosexuality, engaging in homosexual sex furtively, with hostility, and often when drunk;

at the other are those open to both themselves and others about their homosexuality."[63] The gay person must become embedded in a system of social networks such as blacks and Jews are, to a great extent, presented from birth.

II SYSTEMATIC RESTRICTION OF LIFE CHANCES

Historical Outline: Jewish

Pre-nineteenth-century Jews existed as "foreigners" under the various monarchies of Europe, living only by the arbitrary will of the crown despite many centuries of habitation. Myriad restrictions confined Jewish populations to overcrowded ghettos away from other inhabitants. Social intercourse was strictly regulated. Exit and entrance to the ghettos was subject to curfew and body taxes. Only a very few occupations were permitted to Jews; landowning was denied. Insulation from the outside culture allowed considerable internal autonomy tolerated by the ruling aristocracy and the churches; even taxes were imposed at the community level.

Medieval restrictions permitting only such trades as moneylender, merchant, and peddler ironically prepared the Jews for the dissolution of the feudal order, as this "interstitial" economic form grew to predominance with the rise of capitalism. The eighteenth century saw the selective emancipation of a very few Jews as European courts sought the favors of financiers. Most disabilities encumbering Jewish life were lifted by the Austrian Edict of Tolerance of 1781–82. "Emancipation" which removed most special limitations, provided civil equality and citizenship for the first time tended to follow the rise of the bourgeoisie in Europe. The

French Revolution brought the most complete civil emancipation for Jews. Religion was reconstituted into the "private" sphere with nineteenth-century liberalism; everyone was to assume the rights and obligations of the nation. The Napoleonic conquests at the beginning of the nineteenth century incorporated the ethics of the bourgeois state into the legal systems of most of Western Europe. Through the introduction of the Napoleonic Code, Jews acquired civil freedoms denied in the feudal order. Official restrictions increasingly gave way to social discrimination.

Yet the struggle between the feudal aristocracy and established churches with the increasingly powerful bourgeoisie was not resolved with France and Napoleon. Though the ghettos permanently dissolved in France, the Netherlands, and Denmark, the Congress of Vienna eclipsed the new gains by reimposing the old order in Italy and many of the German states. National unification in Italy in 1861 and in Germany in 1871 later removed official restrictions.

Civil equality wrought profound changes in Jewish life. It brought new participation in national cultures and economies, questioning of religious orthodoxy, struggles to assimilate national and religious identities. Moses Mendelssohn inspired "Enlightened" Jews to embrace national culture and reconceptualize Jewishness as a private confession compatible with the modern world. Conversion to Christianity figures as one resolution to the conflict of identities in a number of prominent instances, including later generations of Mendelssohn's own family.

The consolidation of the German states under the Prussian monarchy and land-owning aristocracy did not augur well for Jews whose fate had become too closely associated with the fortunes of the new bourgeoisie and, in particular, the German Liberal Party. Though by no means privileged as a whole, the new visibility of Jews in professions and finance permitted widespread identification of them with the growing bourgeoisie and nineteenth-century liberalism. Rising nationalism and the race theories of social Darwinists coalesced in anti-Semitic movements of the 1870s and 1880s. Academic spokesmen of the old order such as Eugen Dühring and Heinrich von Treitschke published anti-Semitic tracts. Adolf Stöcker's anti-Semitic Christian Social Party drew support from traditional agrarian and artisan classes who felt themselves "squeezed" by large-scale capitalism. In 1892, the governing Conservative Party adopted an anti-Semitic plank, confirming existing policies of exclusion in the civil service, judiciary, and academe.

Arthur De Gobineau's 1855 *Essai sur l'inégalité des races humaines* presaged the appearance of anti-Semitic publications and the Action Française in France in the 1880s, which similarly perceived Jews as the symbol of the new order. The conviction of a Jew, Alfred Dreyfus, of treason in 1894, drew the battlelines between the Dreyfusards, republicans, liberals, the bourgeois, and the anti-Dreyfusards, monarchists, clerics, and conservatives. Dreyfus's exoneration in 1906 marked the victory in France of the forces that Jews had come to symbolize and to whom the fate of real Jews had become closely linked.

For Jews in Eastern Europe, by contrast, the onerous restrictions of the feudal order endured under Russian czardom. With a reactionary monarchy firmly entrenched in the late nineteenth century, repressive policies were effected with particular ferocity. Laws decreed in 1882 further concentrated Jews in a few urban ghettos in western districts of the Empire. Jewish presence in universities and professions was radically reduced. The pogroms of 1903 and 1904 erupted with official tolerance. Charges of ritual murder circulated at the turn of the century in Russia, Hungary, and Germany.

Nationalism and the dream of escape founded the Zionist movement in 1895–97. Emigration increased with the promise of tolerance in the New World.

Outside intervention deposed but failed to eliminate the aristocracy and its army, the land-holding Junkers, and the new monopoly capitalists, allowing the Social Democrats to preside uneasily over the Weimar Republic of post-World War I Germany. The reactionary coalition gained power in 1933 with the National Socialist program to abolish the preceding century, a program of neomedievalism which found the Jews guilty for the ills of the new era. An immediate boycott of Jewish commerce accompanied purges of the civil service, educational institutions, the professions, and cultural institutions. The *Kristalnacht* of 1938 marked the final seizure of Jewish economic life. By 1942 Napoleon's work had been reversed. Most of Europe had fallen under a regime that was to exterminate four and one-half million Jews.[1]

Jews in the United States found a social order constructed on capitalist and liberal-democratic principles. Without powerful, indigenous precapitalist classes to dislodge, the United States did not suffer the conflict which continually embroiled Jews in Europe. Without a long history of ghettoization dissolved by a strengthening bourgeoisie, Jewish fate was not tied symbolically or materially to the fortunes of that class. In the United States, Jews were not a people distinctly apart from the national culture, but immigrants in a nation of immigrants. Anti-Semitism proved of residual consequence in United States history. Racism overshadowed other ideologies of subordination.

Historical Outline: Black

The United States' Civil War brought judicial civil liberties to a people confined to slavery. Unlike European Jews who had been largely excluded from the feudal economic system, the Africans imported to the United States' South provided the labor power of a plantation economy. "Emancipation" proved short-lived. State governments imposed by the North brought brief participation of blacks in government and small entrepreneurial industry. The "Black Codes" which reimposed legal disabilities were, at this point, struck down by the federal court. Failure of the Radical Republican program to redistribute land left the land-owning aristocracy intact. By 1872, the last of the Confederate leaders were amnestied; four years later, the "Reconstruction" era had ended as the last of the Radical Republican state governments had been ousted by the indigenous elite.

The counteroffensive against the new liberal-democratic system and black emancipation proceeded with a systematic reign of terror to reimpose black subordination. White supremacist organizations such as the Ku Klux Klan employed murder, fraud, and intimidation to disenfranchise blacks. A rising crescendo of lynching claimed more than 1,400 lives in the period 1882–92. E. Franklin Frazier remarks that the subsequent decline in lynchings occurred with increasing black acquiescence to the oppressive system. Limitations became institutionalized in disenfranchisement through poll taxes, literacy tests, "grandfather" clauses, and property qualifications. Between 1896 and 1900, for example, black voter registration fell from 130,344 to 5,320 in Louisiana. Jim Crow laws sanctioned by the federal court segregated public transit, railways, schools, and recreational facilities.

Permitted only a brief respite from an oppressive regime and without capital, the black population found its social mobility blocked. Unlike the many European Jews, who with capital and extended periods of legal rights, attained middle- or professional-class status, blacks in this period were bound to peonage, or increasingly to the Northern industrial labor market. At the turn of the century, the white-sponsored voice of black people, Booker T. Washington, advocated work and self-sacrifice for blacks. White biological and social sciences declared black inferiority inherent. The church propounded racial doctrines developed during the slave era "that the Negroes were the accursed of God, either the descendants of Cain or else of the 'snake' (nachash) who tempted Eve and who was 'really' the Negro."[2] Divine approval sanctioned the status quo; "For reasons unknowable to man, the idea ran, an infinitely wise but inscrutable Creator had ordained and created separate and easily distinguishable races. Each He endowed with qualities and capacities befitting its role in the providential design, and each had developed in conformity with His plan.[3]

Black restiveness manifested itself in the Niagara Movement founded in 1905, which after four years, led to the National Association for the Advancement of Colored People, a civil rights organization pledged to abolishing segregation, and to equal educational opportunities, voting rights, and the enforcement of the Fourteenth Amendment and the Fifteenth Amendment.

The return of soldiers at the end of World War I to the unemployment of the growing ghettos culminated in the first urban riots of 1917–19. In this period, the meteoric career of Marcus Garvey crystallized the dream of escape in a nationalist "back-to-Africa" movement, which foundered upon Garvey's imprisonment in 1925. Garveyism, like Zionism, rejected attempts to integrate into an inhospitable social environment, choosing national separation in order to realize freedom. Garveyites first employed the term *black* as a prideful self-appellation.

Like the issue of Jewish rights in late nineteenth-century Europe, imputation of sympathy with black causes remained highly discrediting. To renounce the degraded symbolic value of blacks was to question white hegemony. Robert Brisbane points out the moral logic of the 1928 federal election campaign where Republicans accused the Democratic candidate of having a black secretary and plans to appoint black people to federal posts. The Democrats replied that their candidate, while governor of New York, appointed blacks only as "porters, janitors, and charwomen," charging the Republican candidate with having "at one time become friendly with and even danced with a Negro woman."[4] Hoover termed the accusation "most indecent and unworthy." In 1944, Myrdal observed: "Any white man can strike or beat a Negro, steal or destroy his property, cheat him in a transaction and even take his life, without much fear of legal reprisal."[5]

The Roosevelt administration's "New Deal" response to the Depression brought with it a liberalized Supreme Court which rendered a series of civil rights decisions at the end of World War II and in the early postwar period. In 1944, the exclusion of blacks from primary elections was disallowed. Universities and buses were ordered desegregated. Fair employment practices commissions were appointed in several states. In 1954, the landmark "Brown" decision ordered school desegregation.

The trend toward postwar judicial emancipation remained ineffective without popular movements to end de facto social discrimination. Large-scale black organization developed in 1955 around a move in Montgomery, Alabama, to integrate public transit. Federal intervention to enforce civil rights decisions and the growing black movement under the stewardship of Martin Luther King, Jr., acted to realize integration in schools, universities, transportation, restaurants, and accommodation. Campaigns such as these and the voter registration drive of the early 1960s met considerable opposition, including obstructionist state legislation, vigilante resistance, and assassination of leaders and workers. Alabama succeeded in banning the NAACP for two years for refusing to supply membership lists to the state government.

A more militant trend became evident with Malcolm X. Widespread urban rebellions broke out increasingly from 1964 to a peak of 125 cities in 1968, spawning the more radical Student Nonviolent Coordinating Committee and the Black Panther Party.

The statistical portrait of black social status in the 1960s and 1970s indicates that the struggle against white hegemony remains far from won. The unemployment rate of blacks runs twice that of whites. Blacks' median income is three-fifths that of whites. More nonwhite high school graduates hold blue-collar jobs than white.[6] Black people are overrepresented in operative, service, laboring, and domestic occupations; underrepresented in professional, technical, managerial, entrepreneurial, selling, skilled, clerical, and agricultural occupations.[7] And, "More than one-half of the urban blacks live in tracts in which over 90 percent of the population is black."[8]

Though as many white adolescents as black admit to having committed delinquencies, blacks are arrested more than three times more frequently than whites.[9] Higher arrest rates are matched by higher conviction rates, with special sensitivity to the race of the victim. Black crimes against whites yield the longest sentences, followed by white against white, black against black, and white against black. "Assault convictions in state court resulted in imprisonment for 74% of the blacks and 49% of the whites and 54% of the blacks and 40% of the whites who were convicted in federal court."[10] Executions could not be more indicative of inequality of life chances in the most absolute sense. "Of the 3,859 persons executed for all crimes since 1930, 54.6 percent have been black or members of other racial minority groups. Of the 455 executed for rape alone, 89.5 percent have been nonwhite."[11] The commutation of death sentences runs at 11 percent for blacks and 20 percent for whites.[12]

Historical Outline: Gay

The medieval order made little allowance for gay life, condemning homosexuality through Church doctrines against the "crime against nature." With marriage highly influenced by kinship and economic factors, sexual-emotional preference found expression in sub rosa social institutions of the mistress, prostitute, and homosexual relations—largely a male prerogative. The military and clergy provided alternatives to traditional family relationships with all-male institutions. Medieval historiography tended to focus upon these arrangements among the small, literate aristocracy. English diarists, however, report the existence of gay bars frequented by working-class clientele in large cities in the eighteenth century.

Industrialization brought rapid growth to the cities, often rupturing traditional family relations. The privatization of sexuality, like religion, in the liberal philosophy of the growing bourgeoisie brought the decriminalization of homosexuality after the French Revolution. The Napoleonic Code emancipated gay people as well as Jews through much of Europe. By the 1860s, articulate spokespersons such as Jean Baptiste Schweitzer, John Addington Symonds, and Karl Ulrichs had appeared in England, Germany, and Hungary.

The gay sensibility became increasingly prominent in national cultures of the last decades of the nineteenth and early twentieth centuries. Most notable were the Oxbridge group in England of which Oscar Wilde is most celebrated, the (Stefan) George-Kreis in Germany, Walt Whitman and, later, Gertrude Stein, in America, and a rich French tradition (uninterrupted by the purges which plagued the other cultures) including Rimbaud, Verlaine, Proust, Cocteau, and Gide.

The reassertion of reactionary trends in the late nineteenth century acted against the gay renaissance associated, like increased Jewish visibility, with liberalism and the bourgeoisie. While German unification brought Jewish civil emancipation, homosexuality, however, was recriminalized as the imposition of the Prussian penal code nullified Napoleonic reforms in other German states. In 1885, a similar measure revived the dead-letter antihomosexual statute in Great Britian. Oscar Wilde was condemned to two years in prison in 1895 and the gay intelligentsia silenced or driven into exile. As one London newspaper editorialized the day after Wilde's conviction:

> England has tolerated the man Wilde and others of his kind too long. Before he broke the law of his country and outraged human decency he was a social pest, a centre of intellectual corruption. He was one of the high priests of a school which attacks all the wholesome, manly, simple ideas of English life, and sets up false gods of decadent culture and intellectual debauchery.[13]

The symbolic sacrifice of one of its leading artists and most prominent homosexuals legitimized the suppression of gay organization in the Anglo-American world for several generations.

In Germany, a movement for gay emancipation formed in 1897 called the Scientific-Humanitarian Committee which launched a petition campaign, succeeding in winning the support of the Social Democrats. Yet homosexuality proved a convenient charge, when a Social Democratic newspaper sought to discredit the government. From 1906 to 1909, such charges led to purges in the aristocracy, civil service, and military. During the Weimar Republic, some thirty gay periodicals appeared and the gay movement enjoyed Communist support until the end of the Leninist period, when the Scientific-Humanitarian Committee and Wilhelm Reich's Sexpol movement fell from favor.

The accession of the Nazi Party to power led to the immediate suppression of organized gay life and the destruction of the Committee's Institute for Sexual Science with a public burning of its books. The systematic extermination of gay people began with the "night of the long knives" when Hitler eliminated his rival, Röhm, and several thousand others, charging homosexuality. More than 200,000 died under a diet-and-work regimen designed for extermination.

The postwar period, however, did not bring emancipation for gay people, who were denied compensation for their camp experiences. In the United States, the McCarthy investigations of "un-American" activities purged suspected Communists and gay people from the civil service, cultural institutions, and the airline industry. Small-scale witchhunts recurred to terrorize gay people. John Gerassi documents the moral crusade of an American town in the 1950s, which led to numerous arrests, evictions, dismissals, and prison terms of five years to life, for vaguely supported accusations of consensual homosexuality.

Psychiatric, social, and biological sciences declared homosexuality a hormonal imbalance, genetic disease, "mental illness with psychoses or feeble-mindedness," the result of "alcoholic indulgence," or brain damage.[14] The churches traditionally stigmatize gay relationships as sinful and continues to form a major oppositional block to gay rights.

Small gay societies for mutal support and legal reform formed during the late 1950s and 1960s. In 1969, the "Stonewall Rebellion," where New York gay people collectively resisted a two-day police assault, marked the beginning of the modern gay liberation movement.

In many instances, gay people have yet to achieve the civil rights that have been gained by Jews and blacks. Anglo-American law attempts to prohibit gay existence under a number of provisions— "lewd and obscene conduct," "solicitation," "gross indecency," "the infamous and abominable crime against nature" (!), "buggery," and so on, according to jurisdiction. A majority of the United States continue in 1978 to prosecute homosexual acts with penalties ranging to life imprisonment. That these laws continue to exact a toll has been documented by Walter Barnett.[15] As late as 1976, the United States Supreme Court sanctioned criminalization of consenting sexual relations, rejecting the right-of-privacy argument embodied 150 years ago in the Napoleonic Code.

Saghir and Robins' interviews with members of homophile organizations reveal that 37 percent had suffered arrest under antigay statutes. Entrapment accounted for 24 percent. In addition, "while a similar proportion of homosexuals and heterosexuals were arrested for nonsexually related offences, homosexuals tended to be imprisoned and put on probation more often."[16] A number of professions, including law, medicine, education, psychiatry, and ministry; military, civil, and foreign service; and "high-security" positions retain explicit prohibitions against the admission and licensing of gay people.[17] The military imprisons and expels gay members, adding legal stigma to their lives.[18] Marcel Saghir and Eli Robins found among the members of their sample that "in only [sic] 30% the reasons for being fired were directly or indirectly related to homosexuality."[19] Weinberg and Williams found 30 percent reported on-the-job problems related to homosexuality, but a smaller 16 percent job loss rate.[20]

Municipal regulations proscribe residence in many areas to all but the heterosexual nuclear family unit. The homophobia of landlords is not countered by law. Segregation and concentration of gay people is accomplished (1) socially, by police intolerance of "vice" except in specific areas of cities, and (2) individually, through official confinement of gay people to prisons and mental institutions.[21]

Structural Constraints

The liberal, individualist ideology of the nineteenth-century bourgeoisie sought to integrate all people under the mantle of civil equality. The medieval meaning of the Jewish, black, or gay person was that of a creature apart, feared, shunned—another order of being. The competitive labor market of the strengthening capitalist economic system created a negative common equality for all the dispossessed. The ground was laid for the idea of civil equality in a "public" sphere, weakening the moral divisions among people of the feudal period and "privatizing" religious, cultural, and erotic distinction.

Though the capitalist order rapidly developed its own systematic inequality, dislodging the traditionally privileged aristocracy in favor of the bourgeoisie, civil emancipation failed to eliminate precapitalist criteria for the distribution of resources. Privatization of social differences (or assimilation) was sought by pariah groups as the means to social equality. The post emancipation historical record demonstrates that the brief period of pre-twentieth-century competitive capitalism created a new alignment of privilege but failed to benefit the mass, including traditional outcast groups. (Jews, however, were most favorably placed during this period and some succeeded to wealth.)

Beneath the oscillations of repression and tolerance suffered by these groups can be detected a consistent and continual limitation of life possibilities structured on a group basis. During periods of relatively quiescent, structured practices of inequality, official agents of social control tend to be especially attentive in depriving inferiorized people of liberty and neglectful of protecting them from violence. Official blindness toward and "neglect" to prosecute crimes against a specific people creates a "free-fire" zone in which that group becomes a sanctioned object of aggression. Such people function socially as "lightning rods" for discontent and aggression, syphoning away potentially threatening accumulations of unrest against the established order. At the same time, the inferiorized themselves are more frequently subject to arrest, police harassment, and conviction by the courts.

The ability to earn a living is curtailed through inaccessibility to institutions facilitating employment, including schools, labor unions, professional associations, and by discriminatory hiring. Where some basis of economic support is achieved, remuneration tends to be lower, job security less likely, and advancement limited. Political access remains the monopoly of "respectable," i.e., noninferiorized people.

Other limitations are frequently imposed by restriction of place of residence, criminalization of sexual relations between specified classes of people, and exclusion from public parks and recreational facilities. Communication and cultural expression remain circumscribed by censorship of the public media by government, owners, or media personnel who define the boundaries of "good taste." "Subversive" or "immoral" ideas and people are similarly controlled through the certification of instructors and adoption of textbooks in educational institutions.

At other times, inferiorized peoples are forced to cope with active campaigns of persecution beyond the pervasive minimum level of restriction. The late nineteenth century saw post-Reconstruction campaigns of the Ku Klux Klan against blacks in the United States, anti-semitic movements in Europe, and a symbolic crusade against gay people in Britain. The Nazi period carried out systematic pogroms against Jews and gay people. The McCarthy investigations purged gay people in the United States. In addition to structured constraints, persecutory campaigns frequently entail the legal creation of categories of nonpersons, expulsion from employment, segregation in labor camps, prisons, and mental institutions, and ultimately annihilation.

Every person experiences a social world which is imperfectly amenable to his or her will. The study of subordinated people should provide insight into the existential situation of every person insofar as everyone must learn to cope with scarcity. Examination of the methods of social limitation and the pervasiveness of their application provides some sense of how a group lives in a world *alien* to its needs and capabilities.

The Reality Principle governs the lives of the inferiorized more repressively. They more frequently find themselves the *object* of social forces, than their originators. They more likely meet frustration in realizing their wishes in action, thereby experiencing a truncation of their being as *subjects*. This desubjectivization process preconditions the development of self, the perception of the social world, and estimation of personal effectiveness and capability.

Cultural Transmission

Educational institutions, churches, the mass media, the publishing industry, and other agents serve as conduits of cultural reconstitution, by continually reproducing the language and symbolic universe of a society. The systematic selection of attributes of inferiorized peoples for public presentation by agents of cultural transmission constructs an image which rationalizes inferiorized status for both privileged and inferiorized groups. The suppression of the hermeneutic tradition of a group and substitution of negative or distorted presentations of the group-self inhibit communication and thus consolidation among group members, and provide an impoverished resource for the development of self as a subject in the world.

The transmission of systems of meaning across generations occurs through a multiplicity of agents. At the most basic level, cultural transmission is the practice of language. It is people speaking to one another, parents to children, individuals to peers. The accumulation of knowledge is an accretion of tried methods for living, an enrichment of perception, a developing power over given reality. Increasingly complex societies develop special carriers of tradition; the received wisdoms of the common stock of knowledge become less common in distribution and accessibility. Educational institutions, the electronic media, churches, and social environments increasingly differentiated by class, locale, gender, occupation, etc., come to distribute ideas unequally.

At issue here are the interests of groups vested with the official production and distribution of ideas. Whose experience is institutionalized in official definitions of reality? How are moral categories developed which serve the interests of some at the expense of others? What functions do widely distributed and conventionalized idea systems fulfill in relation to the structure of domination? Is there evidence to suggest that pervasive ideologies serve to obscure or suppress certain stocks of knowledge in order to lubricate the wheels of domination? How does officially propagated "knowledge" demarcate the lives of those alien to its symbolic universe?

A comprehensive survey is by no means possible, nor the focus of the present inquiry. In looking over the structuring of limitations in the symbolic sphere, the *totality* of the many-faceted aspects of inferiorization can be indicated. The logic of the dominated world-view cannot be comprehended without recognition of the mechanisms of hegemonic constraint.

Inferiorized people discover themselves as symbols manipulated in the transmission of the dominant culture. Their "objective" identity lives beyond their control; the image of self, institutionalized by cultural agents, exists alien to their own experience and self-expression. The ongoing, emergent lives of a people are confronted by a "representation" which exists only as an object for the other.

The Jew can find himself in the classics, popular and children's literature, as the representative of the cruel, wicked, and treacherous persona.[22] Dickens defended his use of the Fagin stereotype as a literary symbol given by hermeneutical history and employed by Shakespeare. In other spheres, he is absent. Memmi found among even those of his professors who were Jewish, a pervasive fear and embarrassment concerning any mention of Jewishness as a historical, cultural, or personal entity. Even those few members of the inferiorized group permitted into institutions for cultural transmission present only the official view at the risk of dismissal.

"Larrick ... studies all trade books published for children in 1962, 1963, and 1964. Of the 5,206 books published in that period, only 6.7% contained one or more Negroes. The majority of the books portraying Negroes, however, place them outside the United States or before World War II. Fewer than 1% of all the children's books told a story about American Negroes today."[23] The black student is likely to encounter black people in school books only as primitives and barbarians.[24] Black authors are separated from the younger generation by a white education system. At best, they are credited only with the ability to write within the "folk" tradition.

Gay people can find nothing of their tradition in the educational system. They are permitted in schools only as the symbol of perversion in "guidance" textbooks.[25] "Censorship is blatantly and covertly practiced by otherwise reputable scholars who chant the cliché about mere literary imitation; by translators who make erotic innuendo appear to be spiritual admiration; by editors who omit offending passages from anthologies."[26] A brief survey of university textbooks in "abnormal psychology" reveals only the old panoply of unfounded myths presented in the guise of science[27]: homosexuality results from seduction by adults[28]; it is feminization or transvestism in males[29]; gay people are dichotomized into sex roles (active and passive)[30]; homosexuality is a hormonal imbalance[31]; it is the fear of women[32]; it is a bad habit[33]; it is failure to learn heterosexual "skills".[34] Accounts are punctuated by "sad tales" of "perversion" or "degeneration"[35] with Freud's "Letter to an American Mother" *minus* the opening lines: homosexuality "is nothing to be ashamed of, no vice, no degradation, it cannot be classified as an illness."

The process is reproduced by the publishing industry and electronic media. The inferiorized person tends to be portrayed with discrediting affiliations—in terms of crime, immorality, disorder, or ugliness. Failing this, he or she may be abstracted from the inferiorized group and rehabilitated through suppression of the knowledge of his or her group membership. In either case, moral boundaries remain inviolate. Peretz Bernstein characterizes Weimar Germany:

> Where some Jewish action is, according to the accepted norms, too obviously valuable, it is either divested of its Jewishness, or qualified as an inordinate exception from a rule which is thereby the more clearly abused.[36]

> One helps oneself to the fiction that not the Jewish but the Dutch flowerbed has produced Spinoza; Mahler becomes an Austrian composer, Heine a German poet, Bergson a French philosopher, Disraeli an English statesman. . . .[37]

In like manner, Socrates, Michelangelo, da Vinci, Tchaikovsky, Gide, and Whitman are divested of homosexuality to rescue them for respectability.

If the inferiorized are to be publicized at all, their appearance is confined to the composite portrait of disrespectable traits.[38] Pity or contempt is elicited as the audience's response. Jewish "comedy," for example, thrives on self-derision in the media.[39] Frazier remarks:

> In every representation of the Negro, he was pictured as a gorilla dressed up like a man. His picture was never carried in the newspapers of the South (. . .) unless he had committed a crime. In the newspapers the Negro was described as burly or ape-like and even Negroes who looked like whites were represented in cartoons as black with gorilla features.[40]

The conspiracy of silence surrounding the gay world was broken only by pitiable and demeaning portrayals such as *The Boys in the Band*. Altman observes:

> No film depicting homosexuals as anything but pitiful and scarred or at least pathetic and ridiculous has come out of Hollywood, and where necessary the movies falsify history to preserve accepted notions of morality.[41]

The strangulation of gay writing is accomplished through routine expurgation and bowdlerization by publishers of depictions of gay love.[42] Suicide has long been the prescribed "final solution" to literary homosexuality. Divine justice is wreaked upon the gay character through prolonged misery, castration, beatings, or death.[43] Newspapers continue to ban advertisements for publications of the gay community, in the name of the family.[44] Gay people attain media publicization as sex criminals; the public expression of affection between same-sex pairs remains strictly forbidden.

The institutions which predominate in the public distribution of ideas ultimately produce the communication medium itself: language. The selection and combination of images become routinized; the value and significance of words acquire the indelible mark of their habitual contexts. The molding and coloring of words occurs in a political milieu; generations of distortions definitively shape perception mediated by linguistic categories. Subordination becomes inherent in labels; the names of social groups may become insults in themselves. Court suits have been launched for libel due to (mis)application of group names to individuals.

Awareness of the social production of words and symbols becomes lost. The moral vector embedded in their meanings impels the movement of thought long after the origin of the distinction has disappeared. Herbert Marcuse explicates the development of one-dimensional language: "The meaning of words is rigidly stabilized. Rational persuasion, persuasion to the opposite is all but precluded. The avenues of entrance are closed to the meanings of words and ideas other than the established one—established by the publicity of the powers that be, and verified in their practices.[45] The voice of the dominated is heard only through the rhetoric of derogation. "Thus the process of reflections ends where it started: in the given conditions and relations."

Naturalism and Therapeutic Ideologies

Of all vulgar modes of escaping from the considerations of the effect of social and moral influence on the human mind, the most vulgar is that of attributing the diversities of conduct and character to inherent natural differences.

—JOHN STUART MILL

The language of naturalism functions as an effective device in closing the universe of discourse to alternative constructions of reality. The outright surveillance of the conduits of cultural transmission by inferiorizing groups becomes decreasingly necessary as the conceptual apparatus itself develops defenses against threat. The "therapeutic" endeavor arises as a modern manifestation of older forms of social control. Therapy develops as a social practice to maintain the boundaries of the established symbolic universe, reified through the language of naturality.

The term *natural* innoculates against reason or critical inquiry. The biologization of social phenomena shrouds them in a casing of immutability and permanence. The declaration of natural order, instinct, or biological "fact" enhances the opacity of the hypostatization. From the standpoint of "natural order," the social theorist can render inconvenient evidence into the ontological darkness of the "unnatural," the "deviant," and the "pathological." The language of deficiency and failure applies to that beyond the pale of "normality." Naturalistic reasoning evolves from theology into the "scientific" proliferation of "illnesses," mental or otherwise.

The naturalist argument functions as a motivated "forgetting" of the social-historical origins of human institutions.

Official campaigns of suppression directed against the inferiorized extend the logic of biologization. The subordinated *themselves* become diseases! Anti-Semites never tired of characterizing Jews as insects or bacteria. Martin Luther declared Jews to be a "plague, pestilence, and pure misfortune." Christian Social deputies elected to the Reichstag in the nineteenth century referred to them as "cholera germs." The National Socialists were to insist that Jews and gay people were vermin, bacteria, and lice.[46]

Benjamin Rush, reputed father of American psychiatry, did not hesitate to name blackness a disease derived from leprosy, when one of his slaves developed a skin disorder lightening his color.[47] Various other diseases appeared in order to explain the behavior of blacks. In 1851, Samuel Cartwright found "two new diseases peculiar to Negroes: one, which he called 'drapetomania' was manifested by the escape of the Negro slave from his white master; the other, which he called 'dyaesthesia Aethiopis,' was manifested by the Negro's neglecting his work or refusing to work altogether."[48] Cartwright's recommendation for cure was whipping and paternal surveillance. Homosexuality joined the ranks of diseases in Nazi Germany[49] and in modern France as a "social plague"[50]; homosexuality continues to be defined as a disease in much of modern psychiatric writings.[51]

The naturalization of the status quo manifests itself in academic treatment of the etiology of the problems of the inferiorized. Measurement of the social world of the dominated is framed by a normalized world of the privileged. Differences become interpreted as deficiencies, if not as moral depravity, when compared to this "normal" world. Normality is negatively indexed by the scientific selection of the causes of inferiorized status. Deviation from the norms of patriarchal society, for example, figures prominently in the theories of minority ills. Incursions into the domain of male privilege, it is alleged, set the stage for ruin. Women who have escaped the confines of "expressive," nurturing, and servile roles are identified as the culprits for "motivational" pathologies in men.

The proverbial Jewish mother is conjured forth as a domineering, close-binding, and pathogenic figure. Black inferiority is imputed (by the Moynihan Report and its sociological derivatives[52]) to female heads of families who fail to prepare black men for the right of male privilege. Psychiatrists complain that the social equalization of women presents a growing population of "emasculated" men, and therefore, so the argument runs, homosexuals.[53] The reasoning identifying the mother as the progenitor of female homosexuality becomes more convoluted. Lesbianism itself is symptomatic of the "failure" to confine women to woman's role. After all, writes one psychiatric expert, lesbians are "the familiar type of women who ceaselessly complain of the unfairness of women's lot and their unjust ill-treatment by men."[54]

Indeed, the psychiatric treatment of gay people exemplifies the technique of ideological control. The relationship of analyst and gay client reflects in microcosm the larger conflict between the system of ideological and coercive control and gay people in general. The refutation of biopsychiatric theories on their own grounds need not preoccupy us here.[55] The tenacity of such dubious and contradictory ideologies arises in their convenience for therapeutic control programs. Moral guardianship is accomplished through the following process: (1) dogmatic positing of natural order, (2) invalidation of the experience of the dominated, (3) induction of guilt, and (4) punishment of "wrong ideas."

Despite the appearance of so-called liberal trends in some psychiatric thinking, the writers examined here clearly continue to exercise influence upon the therapeutic professions, the treatment of homosexuality in related social sciences, and popular opinion. The American Psychiatric Association retreated from the "sickness" doctrine in 1974 by removing "homosexuality" per se from the list of illnesses. This revised index to styles of "emigration" from official reality permits and encourages the control program on a "voluntary" basis. Maurice Feldman and M. J. MacCulloch, for example, insist their "therapy" is administered "voluntarily" when 42 percent of their subjects appear before them because of "an order of the court, as a sequel to court appearance, or prior to a court appearance."[56] The submission to aversion therapy is named "voluntary" by carefully ignoring the social hegemony of courts, welfare, and health officials, parents, peers, and clergy, who condemn and coerce people into it.

The psychiatric literature sometimes explicitly posits a natural order: "We assume that heterosexuality is the *biologic* norm and that unless interfered with all individuals are heterosexual"[57] or "Homosexuality is pathologic. It is not a natural biologic phenomenon. . . . Through treatment, the normal heterosexual direction of the sexual drive can be re[sic]established. These assumptions provide the therapeutic framework within which the therapy is conducted. They must be reiterated again and again throughout the therapy."[58] Assumptions translate into norms through the rhetoric of "basic instinctual drives."[59] Where the phenomenon refuses to conform to the categorical Procrustean bed, it is the phenomenon that must be altered to "fit." Reality is reformed in the image of assumptions which must be "reiterated again and again."

The experience of the homosexual patient is to be systematically invalidated. The analysand is taught to distrust his or her own feelings and experience in an effort to annihilate his or her own reality. Adoption of the perspective of a dominant other usurps the self as center of own experience. As Charles Socarides argues, the therapist insists that what the analysand "says and does as regards his homosexual behavior really makes no sense."[60] The therapist adds one more voice to the chorus proclaiming the analysand's illegitimacy. His or her own self-expression and wishes are read only symptomatically. The therapeutic program contains the client's pursuit of happiness and freedom within a rhetoric derogating the meaning of that pursuit and the reality of his or her sense of fulfillment. Socarides, for example, translates a wish for friendship into the jargon of failure: "The homosexual claims that his motivation is to 'find a friend' but this is merely a rationalization for the overriding and imperative need for neutralization of his anxiety through homosexual orgastic contact."[61]

Guilt is the sine qua non of psychological control.[62] Electroshock therapists consider "self-insecure" personalities (i.e., those with "inner feelings of anxiety, guilt, inadequacy, and inferiority"[63] to be "good" candidates for therapeutic coercion. Where the dominated person has inadequately internalized a sense of inferiority, the therapist reinforces the ideological hegemony. The problems of the homosexual in psychotherapy are collectively reduced to a single demon. Playing on the fears, prejudices, and contempt purveyed by homophobic society, the psychiatrist summons forth the spooks of the homophobic conscience. Pronouncements about the alleged loneliness, sordidness, and instability of the gay world fetishize the theme of homosexuality as evil. The presented choice is Manichean:

> Instead of union, cooperation, solace, stimulation, enrichment, healthy challenge and fulfillment, there are only destruction, mutual defeat, exploitation of the partner and the self, oral-sadistic incorporation, aggressive onslaughts, attempts to alleviate anxiety and a pseudo-solution to the aggressive and libidinal urges which dominate and torment the individual."[64]

Every difficulty is essentialized as a product of homosexuality. The psychiatrist holds out a heterosexual Eden, where supposedly there exist no problems of adjustment due to class backgrounds, sexual objectification, waning interest by one partner, strength and dependency needs, disillusion, etc.[65]

The psychiatric morality drama induces guilt when it is not yet present. The analyst writes, "Homosexual behavior throughout adolescence in the absence of anxiety, guilt or conflict together with perverted [sic] fantasies is an alarming sign. It is imperative to initiate therapy in order to *create a conflict* for the patient by driving a wedge between the id representative and ego. In many cases the homosexual symptom is ego-syntonic, especially at this stage of life."[66] In other words, the young man or woman who has contentedly begun to enjoy his or her own senses and those of another, must be made to feel anxiety, guilt, defeat, torment, bad conscience.

The liberal, salutary jargon of Lawrence Hatterer scarcely veils the control program:

> A patient is usually highly unaware of the degree of his guilt, denial, and self-punitive activity related to his past and present homosexuality. Bringing to the surface his underlying reaction to society's attitudes and the elaborate defenses built to protect himself from social injury is extremely helpful in breaking through his resistance. A therapist must let the patient know that his reactions and defences are understandable, and not at all unrealistic in light of American society's homoerotophobia. Neither the law nor society's attitude toward homosexuality is likely to change in the near future.[67]

(Feldman, who reiterated the faith in the solidity of social condemnation to justify his own coercive tactics was to face an invasion of gay liberationists at a professional conference a few years later.[68])

Hatterer insists that his patients regularly play tapes of his "wisdom" to themselves. Without repetitive indoctrination, they may "revert" to their own impulses and learn to trust their own spontaneous feelings toward other people. They may "emigrate" from official reality, discovering its inappropriateness for their own experience of the world.

This is no easy task. Persuasion is notoriously unreliable. The therapeutic establishment does not hesitate to reach into a well-developed arsenal of coercive techniques.[69] Feldman and MacCulloch recommend electric shock for its efficiency, precision, and manipulability and provide a detailed description of the machine and affixation of electrodes.[70] Indeed,

> . . . it seems mandatory, both on economic and on ethical [sic] grounds, to use a treatment which will enable the greatest number of patients to be treated successfully in any given unit of time. . . . Learning techniques may be automated so that they require little more than general supervision by a junior psychologist or even a suitably trained nurse.[71]

The academic literature is replete with "experimental" applications. A noted bibliography on homosexuality lists academic articles recounting the application of LSD, testosterone, drugs destroying sex drive, castration, insulin shock, and aversive therapy drugs resulting in death.[72]

It is noteworthy that the goal of coercive therapy is rarely enunciated. "Cures" may be proclaimed upon the repression of homoerotic expression or isolation from the gay community. "Cures" are most generally declared when a homosexual has sexual intercourse with the other sex.[73] "Success" is reported by one psychiatrist after a twenty-two-year-old man with a homosexual fantasy life but no sexual experience, declares himself "sexually neutral" after six weeks of aversion therapy.[74] Others find "progress" in a patient who reduces his (homo)sexual behavior and moves into depression.[75] Another castigates a man whose primary erotic-emotional orientation is toward a male friend. The man subsequently developed a relationship with a woman and, in the psychiatrist's words, "he has not fallen in love and was able to express only a rather remote kind of affection for this girl."[76]

Feldman and MacCulloch grant themselves "success" for self-reported decrease in homesexual fantasy and practice, not requiring heterosexual activity and entirely ignoring subsequent isolation of their subjects from any other person.

With few exceptions, the "cure" criterion seems to be quite literally "fucking" women. Charles Moan and Robert Heath congratulate themselves on this 1972 experiment.[77] Their subject is a twenty-four-year-old homosexual man with highly disturbed relationships with men and women. Paranoid thinking with hypochondriasis is combined with "marked apathy, chronic boredom, lack of motivation to achieve and a deep sense of being ineffectual, inadequate, worthless and inferior. . . . He does have a three-year history of drug abuse, which ran a course punctuated by alcohol, amphetamines, barbiturates, major and minor tranquilizers, the sniffing of chemical agents and solvents, marijuana, and nutmeg. Addiction and preference were for amphetamines." He continually considers suicide.

Moan and Heath decide his problem is homosexuality (!) and treat him by implanting electrodes in the brain. (Medical charts are provided for imitation.) A prostitute is hired and introduced into the laboratory. They couple and "then, despite the milieu and the encumbrance of the electrode wires, he successfully ejaculated." The prostitute is dismissed and the patient in the following eleven months "reports that homosexual behavior has occurred only twice, when he needed money and 'hustling' [prostitution] was a quick way to get it when he was out of work." The scientists announce a "cure" because of a subsequent short relationship with a married woman and add, "He still has a complaining disposition which does not permit him readily to admit his progress." They continue, "Plans for such treatment programs are under way by the Tulane staff and will be activated in the near future."

A majority of gay people (over half of gay men and more than three-quarters of gay women) have had heterosexual experience.[78] Some degree of heterosexuality is clearly the norm in the life histories of gay people. According to Saghir and Robins:

> The most frequently encountered emotional reaction following heterosexual involvement is that of indifference. It is not an aversion, nor a conscious fear of heterosexuality, for most homosexual women and men find no emotional aversion and feel no trepidation in becoming

involved heterosexually. The determining factor in the subsequent avoidance of heterosexual involvement is the lack of emotional gratification and true physical arousal with opposite-sexed partners.[79]

These therapists suppress the opportunity for a genuine I–Thou relationship in the interests of mechanical relations with the socially approved gender or withdrawal from sexuality. These therapists appear content to have a man who relates sexually to men in a superficial and objectifying manner, learn to relate to women in the same manner. Known as the "Playboy" therapy, the patient learns to masturbate to plastic images. Says Hatterer to a homosexual patient: "I've known a lot of patients who've been successful doing similar kinds of things. You should get a subscription to Playboy."[80] Impoverished relationships between people whereby the other is used as a means or object, continue untouched by attempts to alter choice of gender. The induction of heterosexual behavior in people whose emotional-spiritual orientation is toward those of their own gender appears likely to exacerbate superficial relationships alienated from the wellsprings of psychic gratification. Kurt Freund observed that men who have contracted marriages out of therapeutic prodding "seemed to be very happy for about a year but, in the course of time, the heterosexual adjustment usually deteriorated and they were left with a virtually non-functional marriage and greater problems than those which they had had prior to therapy."[81]

It is beyond the scope of this work to analyze the alienation of people, the objectification of the other, anatomical fetishism, displaced aggression, and so forth, evident in the psychiatric writings. If the interest of psychiatrists were in rehumanizing instrumentalized relationships among people, instead of participating in the manipulation of them, their analysis would begin here. If therapists were interested in benefiting the gay people who appear before them, they would face the special problems of relationships subject to total negotiation without socially given roles solidified by tradition, kinship, and law.

The psychiatric literature provides a compendium of the responses to domination; it is a vast document of the contempt internalized by an inferiorized people from a society which stands opposed to its self-realization. The "cure" is the disease. Acting as an agent of inferiorization, the therapeutic establishment cannot but compound the malaise of the oppressed. "Cure" may never have been the objective of the therapists; insistence upon sometimes brutal "therapeutic" techniques does successfully perform one social function. Exploitation of the oppressive ideologies internalized by the oppressed themselves, contributes to the maintenance of a relatively quiescent and manipulable population.

Composite Portrait of the Inferiorized Person

> The mythical portrait of the Jew paves the way for and adds the finishing touches to his actual oppression. It is the symbol of his oppression; its preliminaries and its crowning point: the myth justifies the oppression in advance and makes the consequences lawful.
>
> —MEMMI[82]

Jewish, black, and gay people face an alien image purported to represent themselves in the wider culture. In comparing the stereotypes assigned to such outgroups as Jews in medieval Europe with blacks and gay people in America, each group seems, at first glance, uniquely characterized: Jews as greedy and rich, gay people as effeminate men or masculine women, blacks as shiftless and lustful. The complete incongruity of the stereotype to the real lives of the people to whom it is applied becomes evident with cursory observation.

The traits attributed to these groups reveal striking similarities upon closer examination. The interchangeable aspects of these images lead one to suspect the irrelevance of assigned traits to any characteristic peculiar to the people they purport to represent. In comparing stereotypes, a "portrait" of the inferiorized person draws into view. The coherence of "logic" of the stereotypes can be understood only as the artifact of the dominant majorities. The traits assigned in common to such diverse groups united only in their status as subordinated people, can be read only as symptomatic of the superordinate imagination. The common portrait retains the role of *foil* to ideals of health and the good. As these standards of "official reality" evolve, the composite portrait accommodatingly adjusts in order to negatively index the norms of propriety, decency, conventionality, right. Official communications agents comply in propagating the product.

The composite portrait is founded on three axioms: the inferiorized are (1) a "problem," (2) all alike, and (3) recognizable as such without exception.[83] This consistency and totality is postulated for the series of beliefs outlined in the following subsections.

They Are Animals

Inferiorization is accomplished with placement of people into subhuman categories. Medieval debates centered around the question of whether, like animals, Jews, sodomites, or savages could have souls. The sentiment is concretized in the charge: they smell! The primacy of smell as a criterion of distinction from animals has been noted by Max Horkheimer and Theodor Adorno: "The multifarious nuances of the sense of smell embody the archetypal longing for the lower form of existence, for direct circumambient nature, with the earth and mud. . . . Hence the sense of smell is considered a disgrace in civilization, the sign of lower social strata, lower races and base animals."[84] Smell is repeatedly attributed to Jews in the Middle Ages[85] through to the modern era.[86] Hitler wrote in Mein Kampf of his "discovery" of Jewish smell following his reading of anti-Semitic pamphlets distributed in the streets of Vienna.[87] References to the smell of blacks recurs frequently in North American literature.[88]

"Brutishness" is claimed for the reputed instinctiveness[89] and "horrific impassiveness towards suffering"[90] in blacks. The "higher" passions are thought, therefore, to be excluded from their experience. Slaves were sold without regard for family ties because, it was argued, black sexuality could not include love.[91] Psychiatric ideologies deny the possibility of love to gay people, echoing popular opinions that homosexuals are given to "mindless animal promiscuity."[92] The subhumanity of homosexuals is imputed "scientifically" in terms of "immature," "regressive," or "atavistic" stages of development.

"Uncivilized" behavior is believed to be characteristic of all three groups. They are "unrefined, ill-mannered and unclean."[93] They are unethical, unscrupulous, and deceitful.[94] As perceived by white children, "Negro children are described as bad, ill-mannered, naughty, disobedient, dirty, careless, in sum everything that the white child struggles so hard *not* to be."[95]

They Are Hypersexual

Otto Fenichel remarks that in the ancient world, foreigners were considered *sacer*, a word signifying simultaneously holy and cursed. The outsiders contained by society represent a similar uneasy fusion for the majority. Minority members are suspected of special powers. The oppressor is convinced of their enormous hidden powers for vengeance. The symbol of the libidinal "underworld," the subordinated are never adequately repressed. In earlier times, witchcraft was "discovered" among them; in a secular age, these special powers become primarily sexual. The confining of sexuality to procreation and the family in "civilized" society manufactures the illusion of sexual liberation in its social foil. The subordinated are made to bear the social anxiety concerning sexual repression: "Society can conceive of no more powerful menace to its culture than would arise from the liberation of the sexual impulses."[96] The socially privileged launch periodic campaigns against the symbols of sexuality as part of the general struggle against "vice," "lewdness," and other signs of sexuality not contained by social institutions. Yet as sexual symbols, black, Jewish, and gay people acquire an inordinate attractiveness: they are *sacer* as the personification of erotic ambivalence.

The early linkage of Jews with witchcraft[97] accompanied popular mythologies of Jewish infanticide, sadism, and bloody rituals.[98] Luther was convinced of the irresistible Jewish ability to corrupt and seduce Christians. Indeed, in medieval literature, the Jew

> . . . has monstrous sexual powers; and his sexual powers transform him into an ogre threatening the sexual life, the existence, and very soul of his helpless primordial son. Each—the Jew as much as the Devil— runs insanely about the countryside mutilating or castrating little boys and leading Christian youths into vile debauchery. And each wantonly seduces or rapes beautiful Christian virgins.[99]

Nazi ideology perpetuated the theme. The same sexual paranoia is evident in Hitler's images of Jewish "white slave traffic" and in this fantasy from *Mein Kampf*:

For hours the black-haired Jew boy, diabolic joy in his face, waits in ambush for the unsuspecting girl whom he defiles with his blood and thus robs her from her people.[100]

"Excessive sexuality"[101] endures as a trait attributed to Jews by anti-Semites.

White fascination with black sexuality is well known. Early twentieth-century sociology generally argued that "Black morality (read: Black sexual conduct) was hopelessly unrestrained."[102] The fixation upon reputed black promiscuity continues with the social scientific essentialization of black problems in "family breakdown." Lynching was traditionally justified with the contention that "many Negroes were literally wild beasts with uncontrollable sexual passions and criminal natures stamped by heredity."[103] The ideology of black hypersexuality was absorbed into American psychiatry.[104] The belief materializes in the black penis, to which widespread conviction assigns a remarkable size.[105]

Colonizers have thought colonized peoples to have a special propensity toward rape.[106] Rape fantasies have been especially predominant in the racist ideology of the American South.[107] The anxiety manifests itself in rape laws which prescribe death. In practice, the law is univalent. In Florida, for example, 54 percent of black men convicted of raping a white woman are executed, while no white man convicted of raping a black woman has been executed.[108] The rape specter is summoned forth with the first signs of black restiveness. As the move to integrate public transit got under way with Martin Luther King, Jr., a leading Alabama politician "charged that the main goal of the NAACP was 'to open the bedroom doors of our white women to the Negro Man.'"[109]

Anthropological evidence suggests that homosexual men have frequently been cast into the role of shaman or witchdoctor—a being with special powers including supernatural understanding.[110] The high estimation of homosexual witchcraft among "primitives" is matched inversely by the pervasive fear of gay sexuality in the modern period. The assumed extraordinary sexual appetite of gay people is thought to require special prohibitory legislation in many jurisdictions. Without controls, the argument runs, the youth of the nation will be molested, if not "converted." Gay people were banned from employment in the United States' federal government in the McCarthy period, when one congressman described homosexual orgies and "palatial surroundings where these people worship at the fleshpots and cesspools of immoral sex demonstration."[111] Eugene Levitt and Albert Klassen report that 59 percent of a nationwide United States survey agree that "homosexuals have unusually strong sex drives." "Thirty-five percent agree strongly with the proposition that frustrated homosexuals seek out children for sexual purposes."[112] Convinced that gay workers are sure to seduce fellow employees and schoolchildren, employers and school boards deny them the means to earn a living.[113]

An axiom of psychoanthropological theory asserts that the existence of strong taboos against certain behavior implies a strong tendency or desire of a people to perform that behavior. The control measures taken to quell the hypersexuality imputed to the inferiorized conceal a symbolic countertrend. The dominated are secretly glamorized; forbidden sexuality offers special "promesse de bonheur."[114] The equation of uninhibited sensuality with blackness appears, for example, to enhance the image of black masculinity among certain male subcultures.[115] The moral outrage which condemns gay sexuality as "too easy" or "promiscuous" conceals resentment of imputed sexual freedom.

The heightened attractiveness of black, Jewish, and gay people[116] may be contained by a liberal, "sophisticated" society through the collective adoption of some of its members as "pets." As Hannah Arendt writes, observing turn-of-the-century French society: "They did not doubt that homosexuals were "criminals" or that Jews were "traitors"; they only revised their attitude toward crime and treason. . . . The role of the inverts was to show their abnormality, of the Jews to represent black magic ("necromancy"), of the artists to manifest another form of supranatural and superhuman contact."[117]

They Are Heretics and Conspirators[118]

The role of Jews as heretics in Christian society is perhaps self-evident. The possibility of "moral contamination" of those faithful to the established moral order provoked persistent anxiety in the medieval Church. Containment of the infidels to segregated areas of cities and close supervision of Jewish intercourse with the local population countered this threat to the "natural" order.[119] As the fount of social evil, Jews found themselves, for example, held responsible for causing the Black Death by poisoning wells in the fourteenth century.[120] In the secular age, heresy against the Church reemerges as heresy against the state, i.e., treason. It is no surprise that Dreyfus, the man who became the *cause célèbre* of late nineteenth-century France, stood (falsely) accused of treason. The press did not hesitate to vilify all French Jews with the charge in the wake of his conviction.[121] Treason became a stock indictment in the National Socialist barrage against the Jews. In the United States in 1950, a public survey asked people to "recognize" persons who had been accused of spying. "Scattered through the list were the names of six imaginary persons—three Jewish sounding ('Max Finkelstein,' 'Isaac Shapiro,' 'Samuel Levinsky') and three others ('Daniel Carpenter,' 'William Brooks,' 'Robert L. Phillips'). The nonentities with non-Jewish names, taken together were 'remembered' by 3 percent of the sample, those with Jewish names by 20 percent, or more than six times as often."[122]

The charge of heresy, however, has been by no means the preserve of groups defined by religion. As early as 1240, an English law provided: "Those who have dealings with Jews or Jewesses, those who commit bestiality, and sodomists, are to be buried alive, after legal proof that they were taken in the act, and public conviction."[123] Derrick Bailey speculates that the early Albigensian heresy, credited with sexual practices forbidden by the Church, established the link between heresy and sodomy.[124] The Albigensians or "Bulgarians" became embodied in English law as "buggery." The term outlawed not only sexual relations between men (women were omitted) but included sexual relations between Christians and Jews.[125] Sexual heretics, with other heretics, were to fall prey to the fires of the Inquisition. Modern exclusion of gay people from diplomatic service continues as a standard practice against their supposed susceptibility to treason, despite the absolute lack of evidence to support the belief. Fear of heretical influence can be detected in the modern opinion poll where 55 percent of the public agree, "Homosexuality is a social corruption that can cause the downfall of a civilization."[126] The fear of "moral contamination" by sexual heretics is clear in this 1975 statement by Canada's largest newspaper rationalizing its censorship practices: "Advertising of homosexual organizations where the purpose of the advertising is to recruit or convert [sic], for example, promoting circulation subscriptions to periodicals which they may publish is not acceptable."[127]

Special powers and heresy as qualities of outcast groups intersect psychologically in the fear of conspiracy. Hidden international conspiracies of Jews arise periodically in the anti-Semitic mind. Luther proclaimed: "They want to rule the world."[128] French parliamentarians during the Dreyfus period demanded protection of French society against the takeover by an alien race.[129] The notorious, fabricated *Protocols of the Learned Elders of Zion* were taken up by the Nazis to demonstrate conspiracies threatening "civilization."

Rumors of conspiracy circulated constantly among whites in Southern slave society.[130] The rise of black militance in the United States provoked a rash of "conspiracy" trials, a charge familiar to the labor movement.

Conspiracies to subvert "culture" are attributed to the three groups. Jewish domination of the arts and press was a persistent Nazi theme.[131] Homosexual conspiracies in the arts are "exposed" periodically.[132] Rumors of an international conspiratorial "Homintern" circulated in the 1950s, an echo of the 1906–1908 scandal in Germany.[133] The prejudiced person is convinced that black people are "taking over."[134]

Dominators characterize their suppression of inferiorized groups as "defense." Paranoid hyperbolization of "secret" or mysterious "powers" and organizations summons forth the demons to be destroyed. Real people divested of even the limited powers assumed by members of privileged groups must face a formidable arsenal at the disposal of the privileged elite.

> An anti-Semite could not stand to see Jews tortured if he really saw them, if he perceived that suffering and agony in an individual life— but this is just the point: he does not see Jews suffering; he is blinded by the myth of the Jew. He tortures and murders the Jew through these concrete beings; he struggles with dream figures, and his blows strike living faces.[135]

They Are Overvisible

All three groups have a reputation for offensive flamboyance. Characterizations of these groups never fail to include claims about gregariousness and garrulousness.[136] They are "loud," pushy, aggressive, careless, extroverted.[137] The charge is accepted by the inferiorized in an acute embarrassment which arises when they perceive their compatriots acting overvisibly. Black people report feeling uncomfortable in the presence of blacks who become "noisy and boisterous around white people."[138] Gay men frequently practice a studied disassociation from "effeminate" men in a social setting with heterosexual onlookers. Memmi expresses the same anxiety in reference to Jews: "To dress in bright colors was Jewish. To speak too loudly, to call out, to gather in the streets was Jewish.[139] The typified black and drag queen is "flashy" and rude. The public image insists on ugliness: the black man as gorilla, the Jew as vulture, the homosexual as "fairy" or "diesel dyke."

Stember found an overwhelming public tendency toward overestimation of the Jewish population in the United States.[140] It is indicative of a syndrome of perceived overvisibility of the subordinated group. Its very existence is interpreted as offensive, "too much," "obsessive," "loud," etc. Despite limited numbers, the "failure" to be totally invisible provokes the resentment of the larger society. The theme is preserved even in the legalization of homosexuality. The universal stipulation "in private" is prescribed by statutes stigmatizing visibility as "gross indecency" or "lewd and obscene conduct." The perception of the subordinated as overvisible is reminiscent of Hindu caste regulations which prescribed that an Untouchable could not raise his or her voice "because the sound of his voice falling on a caste Hindu's ear was deemed to be as polluting as his touch" or that he or she could in no way adorn himself or herself.[141]

A final contradictory subtheme can be detected. Despite the imputation of special powers and conspiracy, of suspected megalomanic tendencies and pervasive ability to corrupt and contaminate, the inferiorized are subject to an opposing image complex in the composite portrait. They are, it seems, weak and incompetent, yet moronically cheerful. Scientific studies have repeatedly attempted to link low intelligence with inferiorized groups. Academic "proof" of Jewish stupidity was presented in 1925.[142] The black IQ controversy rages to this day. Attempts to link homosexuality with imbecility persist.[143] The association between male homosexuality and weakness, passivity, or incompetence pervades Western values. The social construction of homosexuality as failure is so extensive, that Lionel Ovesey identifies a "pseudohomosexual" syndrome among men who show no signs of homoeroticism, yet fear they must be homosexual. "The equation is the following: I am a failure = I am not a man = I am castrated = I am a woman = I am a homosexual."[144] An experiment performed by T. Weissbach and G. Zagon in 1975, where a videotaped man was labeled "homosexual" to one group of viewers but not labeled to another, found that viewers indicated the "homosexual" subject to be more "weak, feminine, emotional, submissive, and unconventional."[145]

Exclusion of the subordinated from the economic system leads to fantasies, on the one hand, of parasitism and laziness,[146] and on the other, of cheerful carefreeness (the Sambo image).[147]

The composite portrait of the inferiorized person functions dialectically to convince the majority of its own identity as the "good." In terms of the phenomenology of mind, "the unessential consciousness [the bondsman] is, for the master, the object which embodies the truth of his certainty of himself."[148] Erik Erikson remarks in the same vein:

> Psychoanalysis shows that the unconscious evil identity (the composite of everything which arouses negative identification—i.e., the wish not to resemble it) consists of the images of the violated (castrated) body, the ethnic outgroup, and the exploited minority. Thus a pronounced he-man may, in his dreams and prejudices prove to be mortally afraid of ever displaying a woman's sentiments, a Negro's submissiveness, or a Jew's intellectuality.[149]

The insight recurs to members of inferiorized groups pondering the genesis of their own identities and to their observers:

> If the Jew did not exist, then he would have to be invented.   [Memmi][150]

The negro, then, is the white man's fear of himself. [Mannoni][151]

People invent categories in order to feel safe. White people invented black people to give white people identity. . . . Straight cats invent faggots so they can sleep with them without becoming faggots themselves. [Baldwin][152]

Unlike [sic] other minorities, we [gay people] lie within the oppressor himself, and our very invisibility, the fact that we represent a human potential that has been realized, makes the need to draw the line against us that much sharper. [Altman][154]

Popular Ideologies

The systematic selection of negative and distorted images of inferiorized peoples by agents of cultural transmission clearly affects the wider population. Public opinion surveys reveal persistent stereotypes relatively stable both in content and over time.[155] The image is almost universal. The study of anti-Semitism by Bruno Bettelheim and Morris Janowitz found no statistically significant differences among stereotype-holders according to age, education, religious denomination, political affiliation, formal family composition, class or occupational status.[156] Social distance scales developed from surveys in the present-day United States show residual anti-Semitism (exclusion from marriage but tolerance as neighbors or more distant social contacts); significant anti-black prejudice (exclusion from marriage or the status of "close friend" and tolerance of social contact in church and school); and great homophobia (exclusion from church, school, and neighborhood; tolerance only at community and nation level, with slightly greater tolerance of lesbians).[157] In the latter case, "more than 80 percent prefer not to associate with them."[158] Indeed, Levitt and Klassen found an "overwhelming objection to homosexuals' dancing with each other in public places—55 percent strongly object and nearly three-quarters have at least some objection. Nearly one-half (46 percent) do not agree that homosexuals should be allowed to organize for social and recreational purposes (31 percent object strongly), and 43 percent would not permit bars serving homosexuals (27 percent feel this strongly)."[159]

In interpersonal relations, these social distance statistics translate into a hierarchy of deference, whereby the standards of conduct of the dominant group prevail even when as few as one representative is present in a social gathering of inferiorized members. Deference expressed in demeanor and forms of address is required of the black toward the white.[160] The presence of heterosexuals in a group of gay people tends to constrain all to observe dominant norms of linguistic and personal interaction.[161] This resembles the linguistic stratification of Canada, where, until recently, the presence of English-speakers in a Francophone group prompted the use of English.

Hierarchy itself nurtures oppressive ideologies. Inferiority ipso facto becomes read as its own justification. "In the United States a relatively illiterate, criminal, diseased, base, poor, and prostituted colored people serves by comparison as proof to the world that Negroes do not deserve the social opportunities available to whites."[162] The dominant ideology offers everyone a set of "rationalizations"[163] to "explain" his or her own inferior status in terms of personal inadequacy plus "compensation" in the form of symbolic superiority over some other group. Robert Lane found that among members of the working class, status tends to be accounted for in terms of "failure to continue one's education due to lack of family pressure ('they should have made me'), or youthful indiscretion, or the demands of the family for money, or the depression of the thirties."[164] He speculates that "lower status people generally find it less punishing to think of themselves as correctly placed by a just society than to think of themselves as exploited, or victimized by an unjust society." Each consoles himself or herself with his or her even minimal status superiority over some other. Racism presents symbolic status to the degraded by identifying a more degraded group than one's own. Memmi delineates the psychological ground of racism of the *Dominated Man*: "Racism offers everyone the solution that suits him best; he need only find someone smaller, more humiliated than himself, and there he has his victim, the target for his scorn and prejudice. Racism is a pleasure within everyone's reach."[165] This "poor man's snobbery"[166] channels discontent away from the larger structure of oppression, toward the more oppressed. "The racist instinctively chooses the oppressed, heaping more misfortune on the unfortunate."[167]

The modern Prince ranges his subjects upon a status hierarchy with numerous gradations to distribute subtle or symbolic values according to rank. Seeing themselves only in comparison to others in their immediate world, the subjects do not occupy themselves with the larger relations between subjects and Prince. The frustrated, the resentful, the dominated themselves fall prey to the logic of status differentiation.[168]

The socially produced "fact" of inferiority comes to a life of its own. Inferiorized status collects devalued attributes which reinforce and legitimize the initial inequality. The salutary language of religion and medicine "assures" the victim of his or her essential depravity in the name of his or her "own good." The dominator "does not punish his victim because his victim deserves to be punished; he calls him guilty because he is *already* punished or, at best, because he, the accuser, is preparing to punish him."[169]

Every act of the dominated person falls under suspicion. "His virtues, if he has any, turn to vices by reason of the fact that they are his; work coming from his hands necessarily bears his stigma."[170] The logic of oppression draws a protective cloak about itself; the dominated become locked in their very being, into the constraint structure.

III OPPRESSION AND CONSCIOUSNESS

Atomization and Insecurity

> To the isolated, isolation seems an indubitable certainty; they are bewitched on pain of losing their existence, not to perceive how mediated their isolation is ... Stubbornly the monads balk at their real dependence as a species as well as at the collective aspect of all forms and contents of their consciousness.
>
> —ADORNO[1]

The systematic restriction of life chances shapes a distinctive world for inferiorized people. Cultural negation interferes with or eliminates the transmission across generations of the group's common stock of knowledge, namely, methods for living in a difficult social setting and interpretations of the group's particular social condition. Such political-economic and ideological practices have a general structural (or "destructuring") consequence, the atomization of inferiorized groups. In conjunction with the methods of social control applied generally to almost all social members, such macrosocial structures condition the existence of inferiorized peoples, introducing an additional insecurity or "surplus" social anxiety to their lives.

Medieval ghettoization insulated Jews from atomization and provided a medium for transmission of cultural traditions. The community fostered in the ghetto buffered the negative identity purveyed in the environing societies. Jews marginal to the medieval ghetto structure of Jews attempting to "integrate" in the post-Emancipation period, experienced the atomization and insecurity more characteristic of black and gay people. Memmi reports, for example, that Tunisian Jews experience a similar rootlessness and anxiety.[2]

The inferiorized are much less likely to discover each other when faced with systematic obstructions to the means of cultural transmission. Blocked access to communications channels hinders the development of the primary condition for formation of community: communicability. Inferiorization entails atomization; the dominated are kept largely unaware and unable to collectivize.

"Self-consciousness exists in itself and for itself, in that, and by the fact that it exists for another self-consciousness; that is to say, it is only by being acknowledged or 'recognized.'"[3] The development of self is thereby inhibited by (non)accessibility to acknowledging others; and all but precluded by a cultural milieu which refuses to recognize its existence. The dominated person finds "himself" reflected in literary traditions, the electronic media, formalized education, and so forth, either not at all or in a highly distorted and "unhealthy" manner. She or he suffers an impoverished identity, by being removed from others who are identical.

The inferiorized person is written out of history. That person has no tradition. He or she learns the meaning of his or her existence at best from immediate groups—perhaps family, peers, friends, enclaves of compatriots. He or she learns how to live, how to survive and find happiness from an oral tradition, from the streets, from immediate associates. The institutionalized culture may be experienced as remote, irrelevant, ideal, or suspect in its "naive" values.

The consequent sense of identitylessness in blacks is starkly evident in the titles of books of major black writers, e.g., Ralph Ellison's Invisible Man, James Baldwin's Nobody Knows My Name.[4] Malcolm X preferred the leap into the unnamed unknown rather than keep a name inherited from dominators. In James Baldwin's words: "There was not, no matter where one turned any acceptable image of oneself, no proof of one's existence. One had the choice either of 'acting just like a nigger' or of *not* acting just like a nigger—and only those who have tried it know how impossible it is to tell the difference."[5] These are people with forced amnesia, atomized by a received cultural nothingness. Each "is imprisoned in the objective reality of his society, although that reality is subjectively present to him in an alien and truncated manner."[6]

Suppression of the cultural traditions of inferiorized peoples compounds the more general structures preserving order through atomization. The ideology of individualism nurtured by the competitive, capitalist labor market retards consolidation. Survival demands a sharpened egocentricity which greatly facilitates social control by preempting identification with like-situated others. Like the middle-class liberals confined to concentration camps, some inferiorized members may become successfully convinced that "what was wrong was that *they* were made objects of a persecution which in itself *must* be right, since it was carried out by the authorities. The only way out of this particular dilemma was to be convinced that it must be a 'mistake.' "[7] Grievance is thereby successfully localized and contained. Domination is experienced as an individual affliction.

Male sex role ideology, which embodies the competitive egocentricity of the capitalist market system, further militates against the solidarity of the homoerotic bond which threatens the atomizing methods of domination. It is not accidental that the psychiatrist attempts to disrupt homosexuality among men by amplifying rivalry, recommending the induction of "aggressive and self-assertive urges in competition with male figures."[8]

With atomization comes heightened insecurity. The inferiorized are presented with a social environment where insecurity is normal. "Normal" expectations fail the test of experience. The rules of "common," "respectable," middle-class interaction prove inadequate to everyday life.

The inexorable essence of the minority experience is disjuncture. The normal procedures of others are not reasonable expectations for minorities. Dominance is expressed at all levels with practice of "interruption" in what would otherwise be considered a single action or process. The relationship between means and ends is so tenuous for members of minority groups that one does not necessarily follow from the other; going to school, for example, does not guarantee getting a job. Such a breakdown in instrumental relationships and normative expectations disorders the reality that others take for granted, and psychic disruption results from this disconnection between means and ends. A sense of inner chaos may accompany social deprivation and derogation; there is then confusion about the self and its situation.[9]

The sense of confinement or the experience of limitation is contained etymologically in the very origins of the terms *Angst*, *angoisse*, *anguish*, which spring from the word for narrowness. Psychological projective tests administered to black children reveal greater worry and anxiety. "Black children perceive their environments as more threatening than do white children."[10] Lack of control over one's future and the unreliability of the social world contribute to a general attentiveness, restlessness, anxiety, fear.

The gay person "does not know what to expect from his family, from his employers, from his friends; he does not know what the gay world will be like when he goes into it; he has no cues from the mass media (such as the heterosexual does) on how he is to operate."[11] "The election of a new mayor or the appointment of a new police chief or even precinct captain can alter the homosexual's situation overnight. . . . changes in expressions of official morality can also be accompanied by changes in a variety of private sanctions (blackmail, extortion, 'queer baiting') on the part of other citizens toward the homosexual."[12] The approach of an election or public event (for example, the 1976 Olympic Games in Montréal) is heralded by a "clean-up" of such "undesirables."

In sum, the consolidation of oppressed individuals into community is retarded through exclusion from major communications systems—educational institutions, book publishing, electronic media, etc. The alienation of man from man in the capitalist economy engenders an ideology of individualism which in turn, contributes to perpetual arrest in a state of atomization. There is evidence to suggest that the objective insecurity of inferiorized status is mirrored in a heightened sense of insecurity or anxiety.

Distribution of Restricted Life Chances

The uneven distribution of life chances contributes to the diversity of responses to domination. "Middle-level" social institutions mediate the hegemonic structure sketched in the preceding section. The practice of domination is refracted according to social location of the recipient, providing different possibilities for individual members of inferiorized groups. Every dominated person experiences a different situation; each is located uniquely in time and place and as an element of social networks. The unequal application of restrictions creates strata of vulnerability to oppression within subordinated groups themselves. Differences in the distribution of oppression vary according to two major sets of conditions: (1) the larger social-historical environment in which the group finds itself, and (2) the group's internal structure. Commonalities in the experience of oppression are shared by individuals located in the same time and place.

The severity and totality of restriction change from generation to generation. Aggression against a subordinated group can move from "passive," structured restrictions to "active" campaigns of destruction.

Possibilities for escape or mitigation of domination vary. Groups with an adequate economic base, geographical remoteness, or easy emigration have greater opportunities for simple withdrawal from persecution. The three groups examined here do not experience the relentless transhistorical and totalistic oppression of, for example, medieval serfs, Indian lower castes, or African slaves.[13] Inequalities and inconsistencies in the application of restriction rupture hegemony and permit the perception of alternatives among the subordinates. There is, perhaps, an "oppression threshold" below which, resistance is effectively suppressed. As Michael Mann remarks in reference to the working class: "the conception of alternative is almost absent where workers' experience is most *total*, that is among the unskilled workers whose passive alienation spills over into their whole life. The most alienated workers are not the most revolutionary, for the necessary confidence in their own *power* is lacking."[14]

Acquiescence in the form of apathy, despair, and estrangement is confirmed among the poorest blacks.[15] Ghetto riots occurred in cities where nonwhites were more likely to have a higher income.[16] Jewish, black, and gay people experience an (objectively) more restricted set of freedoms and a (subjectively) more anxious world. The totality of that experience is not, however, so extensive as to preclude resistance.

In addition to macrocosmic conditions variably influencing the oppression of the entire group, refraction of the practice of domination occurs according to individual relationships to the whole. Individual responses over time vary with changing historical treatment of the entire group and according to personal "social location," i.e., location within the group. "Groupness" is no thing, but an ongoing, historical accomplishment. The movement of a collection of individuals toward community restructures the relations among members in the group and between the group and the larger society. Collective strategies to deal with systematic restrictions increasingly displace specifically individual ones. The historical stage of groupness exercises an influence upon the distribution and experience of domination.

Phylogenetic groupness is paralleled by a synchronic dimension. At any given time, a more highly developed core community and "counterreality" can be distinguished from less integrated members, outward toward atomized potential members subordinated to the official reality paradigm. Individual responses to domination, then, must be viewed within the contexts of the historical development of the group and individual centrality or remoteness to the group core.

Individual perceptions and actions change according to location on the synchronic continuum, i.e., with increasing integration into the community. In addition, individual centrality in the group cannot be assumed as fixed, but evolves diachronically. Personal development, in many instances, recapitulates group development, as the individual moves from isolation to association.

Reified instruments for the quantification of "self-concept," "self-hatred," and other measures of responses to domination consistently produce nonsense by failing to account for the movements of ontogenesis and phylogenesis. This means more concretely, that group structure and development, and individual adaptations to domination are influenced by residence in a neighborhood where one's own group is predominant or a minority, type of occupation and mobility, age and ties to the nuclear family, size of urban population and presence of own group therein. Gloria Powell,[17] for example, cites a study which found higher self-esteem among black inhabitants of a city in the United States South, compared to a city in the North. The relationship springs clear, when it is noted that the Southern city contained a large black population, with a black university and professional stratum, a militant student population, and an active desegregation program. The Northern city, by contrast, had a small ghettoized black population living amid a conservative Protestant majority, with an antipathetic city government.

Ambiguous Identity

Both the practice and the experience of domination assume peculiar forms for those "interstitial" individuals, who experience ambivalent or ambiguous identities at the margins or "boundary" between dominating and dominated groups. Light-skinned blacks, Christianized Jews, and bisexuals are often presented with an erratic or mixed pattern of restriction and respond with heightened anxiety and conflicting or unstable behavior modes. The life plans acquired through identification with each group often conflict. The behavior patterns provided with each identity may coexist in separated psychological compartments or present schizoid inconsistencies. With "one foot" in the realm of privilege, conformity and compensation for the inferiorized aspect becomes especially tempting. "Uncle Toms" are more likely in this stratum; acceptance is thought to be within reach.

The phenomenon has been observed in the colonial situation. The mixed Malagasy-French "display the celebrated racial inferiority complex in its purest form with its fantastic compensations in the form of vanity."[18] Gertrude Williams provides this account of colonial India in 1928:

The most pathetic of India's minority groups are the mixed bloods. . . . They speak in a metallic falsetto with a curious singsong accent. They always wear European clothes. . . . They are ostracized by both English and Indians. They in turn look down on the Indian with a scorn that is acid with hatred. . . . for it is their Indian blood that is their curse. They fawn upon the English and make pitiful advances to them. They speak of England as "home" though they may never have been there, and they are forever vainly trying to include themselves with the British.[19]

Ambiguous identity appears to be a social location highly amenable to choice of the acquiescent or conforming mode of coping with domination.[20] Memmi notes the mimetic efforts of North African Jews.[21] "In a desegregated classroom, light-skinned Negro children, who are in a more marginal position, show particularly strong white preference."[22] Status anxiety and liberal-accommodative attitudes among light-skinned blacks have been observed elsewhere.[23] Lower self-esteem, ambivalence, and greater participation in anonymous, furtive sexuality is reported among bisexuals.[24] Proportionately twice as many bisexuals as men who identify themselves as gay report guilt, shame, or anxiety regarding their homosexuality.[25] In Johnston's words, "Bisexuality is staying safe by claiming allegiance to heterosexuality."[26] Marginal to the supportive bonds of the group, whether superordinate or subordinate, those of ambiguous identity tend to be more susceptible to accommodative or "masochistic" responses to domination. Marginality tends to be reinforced as members of the subordinated group come to reject them as "unrealiable" in dyadic or group relationships.

The role of the ambiguously identified is especially interesting in the evolution of civil rights advocacy. The first movements sought "liberal" patrons from the dominating class. The early presidents of the National Association for the Advancement of Colored People, for example, were white. German Jewish associations in the 1880s sought Gentile sponsorship, believing public credibility possible only with such "disinterested" patronage.[27] The early Mattachine society defined itself as concerned about homosexuality, but launched a court suit for defamation when it was suggested that Mattachine members were homosexuals.[28]

The second-generation leadership tends to be drawn from the interstitial sector, a move accompanied by a shift from a stance of petitioning and pleading to liberal-assimilationist ideologies. The guarantee of endorsation of dominant values remained an apparent prerequisite for the right to be heard. This guarantee was met by adoption by the leadership of some symbol of the privileged realm. Among black leaders, a white wife (as George Schuyler complained); among nineteenth-century Jews, endorsation of Christian values; among homosexual or bisexual leaders, a wife (and children) served as tribute. Scarcely a volume published on homosexuality during the 1950s and 1960s omits conspicuous acknowledgments or dedications to the wife and children of the volume's author.[29] The prominence of leaders identified with established religion at this stage is noteworthy. Only with the third generation of civil rights advocacy does a radical analysis and militance among these groups bring leaders shorn of the symbols of conventional respectability.

Minority Salience, Class, and Mobility

Being an inferiorized member in one's immediate, everyday social world tends to increase the sense of importance of that identity and heighten exposure to the dominant system. Ghettoization, then, insulates inferiorized individuals to a certain extent from the strain imposed by the dominant group. Morris Rosenberg found, for example, lower "self-esteem" among high-school students who were members of a religious group which comprised less than one-quarter of their neighborhood.[30] Barry Wellman found greater identification of self in terms of race among black high school students in integrated schools.[31] Integration into the community of inferiorized people clearly becomes more likely where concentrations of such people are close at hand.

Upward mobility similarly tends to increase marginalization. Frazier's perceptive analysis of the black bourgeoisie[32] demonstrated the tendency to emulate the values of dominators as anticipatory socialization to aspired privilege. Attainment of higher status tends to remove the individual from group members concentrated in the lower echelons and heighten exposure to dominant ideologies, provoking some degree of rejection of other inferiorized members. Seymour Parker and Robert Kleiner found "Negroes in the higher status positions tend to have values more similar to those of the white middle class, stronger desires to associate with whites, more internalization of negative attitudes toward other Negroes, and relatively weaker ethnic identification, than individuals in lower status positions."[33] The tendency is confirmed in studies of black children.[34]

The rejection by the upwardly mobile second generation of its Jewish heritage has been widely observed.[35] Weinberg and Williams found a parallel greater concern with passing and lower self-acceptance among gay men in higher occupational strata.[36] This phenomenon merits comparison with the theory of the labor aristocracy.

Parental Authoritarianism

The family, as the primary socialization agency, decisively molds the child's apprehension of and orientation to the social world. The basic political relationships within the family frequently provide the models upon which the individual relies when faced with macrosocial domination. Fundamental attitudes toward domination established in the relationship between the powerless child and the child's powerful parents condition his or her later response to inferiorization by the larger society. Personality syndromes of this nature influence the subject's later social location and movement within the evolving dominated group. Marginality tends to be reinforced by a predisposition to uncritical submission to power. Accommodative and acquiescent modes of coping with domination are more prevalent among people from families structured in the "authoritarian" manner. The paradigm is elucidated by Freud:

> If the father was hard, violent and cruel, the super-ego takes over those attributes from him and, in the relations between the ego and id, the passivity which was supposed to have been repressed is reestablished. . . . A great need for punishment develops in the ego, which in part finds satisfaction in ill-treatment by the super-ego (that is, in the sense of guilt).[37]

Studies in child psychology confirm the dynamic. Coopersmith found that "children with low self-esteem are more likely to claim that their parents emphasize and prize accommodation. . . . [i.e.]

such characteristics as obedience, helpfulness, adjustment to others, kindness, good grooming, and cordial relationships with one's peers."[38] Cameron found that children with "unusual reliance on others for approval and/or assistance, and conformity to the demands and opinions of others" perceived their parents as more strict and demanding of obedience. These parents more often condoned spanking, prohibiting the expression of anger toward them, and selected their children's friends.[39] Similar relationships are confirmed by Rosenberg.[40]

Studies in *The Authoritarian Personality* found:

> Prejudiced subjects tend to report a relatively harsh and more threatening type of home discipline which was experienced as arbitrary by the child. Related to this is a tendency apparent in the families of prejudiced subjects to base interrelationships on rather clearly defined roles of dominance and submission in contradistinction to equalitarian policies. In consequence, the images of the parents seem to acquire for the child a forbidding or at least a distant quality. Family relationships are characterized by fearful subservience to the demands of the parents and by an early suppression of impulses not acceptable to them.[41]

Conventionality and behavior "helpful in climbing the social ladder" is highly esteemed and demanded of children in this socialization pattern.

The children caught within this family structure tend to develop low self-esteem, a sense of anxiety and insecurity. In other words, the sense of self as subject diminishes, establishing a primarily submissive response to domination. Among the inferiorized, where identification with dominators entails the adoption of a plan which (we have seen) negates their own existence, an insoluble contradiction is introduced into the psyche. The Oedipal conflict is replicated in the personal solution to group conflict. Emanuel Berger's general finding that self-acceptance is correlated with acceptance of others is replicated in specific studies of inferiorized individuals.[42] Irving Sarnoff found "anti-Semitic Jewish subjects are likely to be insecure, chronically anxious individuals who have been severely rejected by their parents. They tend to dislike themselves as a result of having been the objects of parental dislike and disapproval. . . . In becoming anti-Semitic, these Jews may be vicariously appropriating the power position of the majority-group and simultaneously achieving a vehicle for perpetuating the negative images of themselves and their parents."[43]

Bruce Maliver believes that Sarnoff's findings are not paralleled in black people, though he found a greater "negative percept of father" and greater fear of rejection by adults among blacks who reject blacks.[44] Tests of black schoolchildren have found significant correlations between parental and children's attitudes, suggesting that "social distance attitudes towards one's own group, for example, Negro, as well as towards fictitional groups, for example, Piraneans are significantly related to a generalized personality predisposition or response set which involves the rejection of people in general."[45] Richard Trent found among black schoolchildren, that "if a child does not accept himself as a person of worth and value, he may tend to perceive groups, including his own, in a derogatory and hostile fashion. . . . Children who were *most* self-accepting expressed significantly more positive attitudes toward both Negroes and whites than did children who were *least* self-accepting."[46]

The authoritarian parent has become a stereotype in the psychiatric literature devoted to homosexuality. The mother is characterized as "dominant, aggressive, hostile, binding but hypercritical"[47]; or again, hostile, detached, dominant, and exploitative.[48] Both parents are portrayed as "domineering, masculine-oriented, demanding, emasculating, and expressing hostility toward and devaluating women in general" and so on.[49] Irving Bieber et al. remark that "hostility emerged as the most conspicuous trait" among the fathers of homosexuals.[50] As with Jewish and black people, gay people suffering from self-hatred, lack of self-esteem, feelings of inadequacy, and so forth, tend to present a similar family syndrome. Not surprisingly, gay people who have internalized the self-negating contradiction, experience emotional trouble and tend to select themselves for psychiatric assistance. Not the genesis of homosexuality but the genesis of inadequate, self-defeating strategies for coping with inferiorization among gay people can be associated with the authoritarian family pattern. The fact that only gay people who experience such an inability to navigate in their social worlds appear before psychiatrists[51] perpetuates the psychiatric confusion of identifying the authoritarian family type with all gay people.

Caveat: Self-Esteem as a Psychological Construct

After the problem of self-rejection in subordinated peoples became prominent in the late 1940s with the publication of Jean Paul Sartre's *Anti-Semite and Jew* and Kurt Lewin's "Self-Hatred Among Jews," the topic began to appear increasingly in the behavioral sciences. Transmuted into the objectivated categories of experimental social science and shorn of the political context in which the phenomenon arises, the question reappeared as the measurement of self-esteem in minority groups. Translation into questionnaires spawned a new scientific entity viewed as a personality construct. Methods by which people deal with subordination evolved in the scientific literature into a hypostatized syndrome of ideas and attitudes. By the 1970s, the analysis had become arrested in an ill-defined psychological state divorced from the original problem and abstracted from the situation which made it meaningful. When the concern had been drained of meaning by positivist distortions and mangled by the romantic liberalism which found it an embarrassment at best, the *American Journal of Sociology* in 1971–72 published a series of articles as a form of obituary on the question of "self-worth" among black people.[52] The phenomenon was relegated to absurdity by the "nonsignificant" results of statistical research.

These surveys produced contradictory, "ambiguous," and "nonsignificant" results by:

1. Suppressing historical and regional differences. By failing to take into account the movement of phylogenesis, i.e., the embeddedness of community formation and solidarity in concrete historical and regional conditions, such differences were "flattened out."[53]
2. Failing to note individual locations within the group structure and movements in these locations. Crain and Weisman observe, "There is more 'spread' in the distribution of self-esteem scores for blacks, and blacks tend to have either very low or very high self-esteem."[54] By "freezing" individuals at different stages in their personal evolutions and failing to

consider their marginality or their centrality in the group, the dialectical movement from internalized oppression to emancipation is "averaged" and "balanced out." A minimal first step toward remedy would be to examine the participation of individuals in the community, e.g., reading the community press, living and working in community environments, going to community churches, supporting community civil rights and political organizations, etc., relative to "self-esteem."[55]

3. Relying on questionnaires which range from one or more questions vaguely inquiring into general sense of well-being to probes into physiological and psychosomatic states—all of which purport to measure "self-esteem."

Jerold Heiss and Susan Owens, for example, make a quixotic attempt to dismiss self-rejection among the subordinated by "showing" no "significant" differences in "self-esteem" between blacks and whites. Besides committing oversights 1 and 2, they claim to measure "self-esteem" by the vague and almost meaningless query: "Now I would like you to rate yourself as above average, about average or below average, on some things that you do and some things that you are. First, would you say that as a son (daughter) you were [sic] above average, about average, or below average?"[56] Robert Crain and Carol Weisman question in the same vein, asking similar self-evaluations in terms of trustworthiness, willingness to work hard, intelligence, mechanical ability, athletics, conversation, appeal to women or men.[57] Many borrow from Morris Rosenberg. Sample self-rating criteria are the statements "I feel that I have a number of good qualities," "I take a positive attitude toward myself," "I certainly feel useless at times."[58] Weinberg and Williams use Rosenberg's questions to quantify "self-acceptance" and also test for stability of self-concept, depression, psychosomatic symptoms of anxiety, anxiety associated with subordinated status (homosexuality), interpersonal awkwardness, faith in others, loneliness, and having seen a psychiatrist.[59] Others draw on Dwight Dean's scale of powerlessness and normlessness (sample: "We are just so many cogs in the machinery of life. . . . I often wonder what the meaning of life really is")[60] or Thomas Langner (sample: "In general, would you say that most of the time you are in high [very good] spirits, good spirits, low spirits, or very low spirits? Have you ever had any fainting spells? My memory seems to be all right [good].").[61] Some tests would require universal and chronic depression in the groups measured in order to indicate "low self-esteem." Rosenberg and Simmons state, "Our measure carefully seeks to exclude judgments about any specific characteristics of the self; race, for example, is not made salient."[62]

Measures of "general self-esteem" by vague indices often run aground in a conceptual fog. All assume a common absolute standard of esteem and anxiety. Questions addressed to individuals about general psychological states ignore the general level of anxiety tolerance of the group of which the individual is a part. Personal evaluations may be made in a context where heightened insecurity is normal.[63] In addition, when "the discrepancy between self and self-ideal is [frequently] used in psychological research as a measure of self-esteem," E. Earl Baughman finds higher self-esteem among blacks.[64] Yet there is evidence to suggest that the process of inferiorization entails curtailed expectations (or lowered self-ideal standards) among the subordinated.[65]

Psychologization of the progressive moment of the dialectic of domination neutralizes or fixes the regressive moment. In other words, exclusive focus upon psychological states fraudulently equalizes their macrosocial preconditions. John McCarthy and William Yancey, and Morris Rosenberg and Roberta Simmons, for example, conclude that whites are not "significant others" for blacks,[66] as if the latter were able to simply choose to ignore the white hegemony in earning a living, going to school, reading or watching television, consuming, and other daily activities.

Finally, we cannot ignore the *situationality* of the phenomenon. Porter suggests a degree of disjuncture between personal self-esteem and racial self-esteem;[67] orientations toward own's immediate world are, in practice, particularized in time and place. The historical embeddedness of every social interaction permits inconsistency between "general" and specific response-strategies to domination according to the salience of group identification in the conflict. Sense of personal efficacy (an element in the "self-esteem" construct) varies with the social situation. Meaning structures develop autonomously as a complex of "sedimented and situationally conditioned explications which are composed in part from individual and in part from socially transmitted 'traditional' solutions of problems."[68] Individuals may draw from a repertoire of logically nonintegrated acquiescent and resisting strategies of behavior. Historical events in the conflict between own and other groups, as well as personal confrontations may explode some orientations forcing reliance upon heretofore "latent" structures. Heightened conflict or similarity of response among group members, may provoke greater consistency in orientation toward subordination. Conflict between disparate meaning structures "only occurs if it turns out that those elements in a situation that have been taken to be relevant in a taken-for-granted way up to now do not suffice for mastery of the situation, thus making it necessary for such elements as until now appeared as 'less' relevant to be drawn on."[69] The compartmentalization of meaning structures functions psychologically to "freeze" or neutralize internalized social contradictions and constitutes a major (pseudo)solution to the experience of inferiorization.[70]

In attempting to restore the fundamental problem in its totality, positivist social psychological studies remain useful only insofar as they successfully indicate the dynamics of the oppressed consciousness, viz., acceptance of the rationality of the established system, compartmentalization of the construction of reality purveyed by dominating institutions, (de-)subjectivization of the subject, belief in one's own (in)effectiveness, and perception of the legitimacy of the given opportunity structure. Research interest in the "self-esteem" of minorities makes sense only in relation to the mechanisms by which dominating groups preserve inequality and reproduce behavior functional to the status quo.

Politics of Guilt

Nothing is more customary in man than to recognize superior wisdom in the person of his oppressor.

—de Tocqueville[71]

A continuum of responses to domination can be constructed parallel to the continuum of locations of the individual in his isolation or integration into community. We begin at the first instance of the third dialectical moment, i.e., at the collection of atomized, powerless individuals, and move through the evolution of responses to domination changing with the development of community. The isolated, constrained subject caught in a hegemonic structure of limitations cannot but orient himself or herself within the given order to be able to survive. Behavior running contrary to and thus transcending the oppressive rationality remains the prerogative of later instances of the third dialectical moment, i.e., with the communication and association of individuals over time, enabling the social construction of a counterreality.

The confrontation of the subject with a seemingly intractable and omnipotent environment constitutes the primordial relationship of man to the "elements." Survival requires understanding of the natural order sufficient to permit anticipation for conformity to its laws. Disregard or rebellion against the movement of the seasons, agricultural cycles, and the migration of animals, jeopardizes life itself. Punishment is exacted through famine. Thus sophisticated calendars appear among the earliest of human technologies; a device to rely upon as a strategy for assured existence.

The alleviation of suffering through success in coping with natural events convinces men of order itself: "The primitive— ...—cannot conceive of an unprovoked suffering; it arises from a personal fault (...) or from his neighbor's malevolence. ... Against this suffering, the primitive struggles with all the magicoreligious means available to him—but he tolerates it morally because it is not absurd.[72]

The *Antigone* enunciates the basic tactical guide to existence: "Because of our sufferings we acknowledge we have erred."[73] Navigation through the opaque, but *ordered* natural environment recognizes suffering as the criterion of failure or nonconformity.

The paradigm of this first, most primitive survival mechanism, traceable from earliest times to the behavior patterns of modern inferiorized groups, is contained in the Book of Job. Job is, as it were, a well-socialized individual, "perfect and upright, and one that feared God, and eschewed evil" (Job 1: 1). He becomes the object of a series of natural calamities which, we are told, follow from a conspiracy between God and Satan, designed to test Job's single-minded submission to omnipotence. Job proves himself fanatically loyal to the principle of self-abasement before superior power. After God recites a lengthy catalogue demonstrating his vast powers (Job 38–41), Job avows: "I had heard of thee by the hearing of the ear, but now my eye sees thee; therefore I despise myself, and repent in dust and ashes" (Job 42: 5–6). The theme is echoed in Psalm 51: 17: "The sacrifice acceptable to God is a broken spirit; a broken and contrite heart."

In the face of an apparently irresistible environment, man can only turn inward to find maneuverability; adjustment to the (often hidden) demands of the immovable order increases the chances of survival. Interpretation of the suffering imposed by violation of natural necessity as personal inadequacy permits hope for its alleviation. Rectification of personal failure remains within the competence of the individual. Suffering is made meaningful in a closed system of responses. Commenting upon the ancient Hebrews, Freud remarks, "When the great Father hurled visitation after visitation upon them, it still never shook them in this belief or caused them to doubt His power and His justice; they proceeded instead to bring their prophets into the world to declare their sinfulness to them and out of their sense of guilt they constructed the stringent commandments of their priestly religion."[74] This turning inward and discovery of personal inadequacy typifies guilt. Guilt, being rooted in the experience of personal limitation has been characterized by modern existentialists as a human universal. Writes Maurice Merleau-Ponty, "All personal guilt is conditioned and overwhelmed by the general and original culpability with which fate burdens us by causing us to be born at a certain time, in a certain environment, and with a certain face."[75] The characterization of guilt as universal obscures the politics of suffering and the concomitant maintenance of surplus guilt as a mechanism assuring submission to authority. The oppressed subject tends to reflect guiltily upon his biography when presented by his systematically constricted life chances. Fanon writes, "All those white men in a group, guns in their hands, cannot be wrong. I am guilty. I do not know of what, but I know that I am no good."[76] Huey P. Newton observes that the black man

faces a hostile environment and is not sure that it is not his own sins that have attracted the hostilities of society. All his life he has been taught (explicitly and implicitly) that he is an inferior approximation of humanity. As a man, he finds himself void of those things that bring respect and a feeling of worthiness. He looks around for something to blame for his situation, but because he is not sophisticated regarding the socioeconomic milieu and because of negativistic parental and institutional teachings, he ultimately blames himself.[77]

Blacks who appear in psychoanalysis display symptoms of this deeply instilled guilt. William Grier and Price Cobbs report the case of a man whose success became sabotaged by neuroses, "as if the proper place in life for him was as ineffectual, defenseless, castrated man, and that his brief period of competence was but a temporary violation of the natural order of things."[78] "Black women," they continue, "have a nearly bottomless well of self-depreciation into which they can drop when depressed. The well is prepared by society and stands waiting, a prefabricated pit which they have had no hand in fashioning."[79] The psychiatric literature testifies to the same syndrome among gay people.[80]

Mark Zborowski found a tendency among hospital patients afflicted with painful illnesses to ruminate about personal failings as if to interpret their pain as atonement for some hidden guilt.[81] Irving Janis observes the guilt reaction of a woman who interprets impending surgery as a mutilation for past misbehavior.[82] Concentration camp victims tend to acquire profound guilt about events over which they had absolutely no control: "They persist in accusing themselves, frequently without justification. They are unable to resolve their dilemma of doubt, self-accusation, and shame."[83] Stanley Rosenman details the effects of a tornado and an air crash on different American communities. Natural catastrophes came to be interpreted as "deserved." In addition to "the actual bereavement, terror, and loss which he [the disaster victim] sustains directly because of the disaster's fury; . . . [is] his abject need for further self-harassment to alleviate the biting pangs of an irrational and unwarranted guilt. All too often, a dejected apathy—defense against, expression of, and atonement for, the guilt—debilitates the individual long after the disaster has passed, lacerating anew his unhealed wounds, and unnerving him for any effort at improvement of his situation."[84] Suffering indicates guilt to third parties as well.[85] The escalation of German persecution of the Jews through the 1930s increased the willingness of Americans to attribute fault (or guilt) to the Jews for their plight.

Suffering, then, permits the growth of guilt. But suffering is distributed differentially, and guilt functions repressively to maintain those who suffer *within* the system of domination. Guilt is the crampedness of the powerless subject in dialectical relation with the powerful object. It is the symptom of the aborted project and frustrated intention. "This *instinct for freedom* forcibly made latent—we have seen it already—this instinct for freedom pushed back and repressed, incarcerated within and finally able to discharge and vent itself only on itself: that, and that alone, is what the bad conscience is in its beginnings," wrote Nietzsche.[86]

The production of guilt through the practice of domination is illustrated most clearly in studies of Chinese "thought-reform" of the 1950s. Robert J. Lifton elaborates the inferiorization mechanism in its pure form:

1. Those to be "reformed" are at first separated (atomized) and placed in a total institution (prison).[87]
2. Over a period of months, prisoners are subjected to unpredictable fluctuations in punishment and leniency,[88] high-stress interrogation, and material deprivation producing a state of heightened insecurity and anxiety. An omnipresent system of wardens, educators, and interrogators directs a ceaseless attack upon the prisoners' identity with accusations of criminal activities and states. They are essentialized as enemies of the people, imperialist spies, etc. The prisoners become complete dependents; their masters assume a paternalistic role over them. "After two or three months of this treatment, the prisoner is greatly fatigued, undernourished, and physically ill; he is highly confused, has confessed a great deal of material, and may no longer be able to clearly demarcate the boundaries of truth and fiction. He is guilt-ridden, demoralized, and depressed, frequently to the point of being suicidal or experiencing transient psychotic symptoms."[89]
3. The relentless material and ideological hegemony practiced as active persecution in a total environment produces, in a relatively short period, a sense of inferiority in the prisoner. Such stringent objective oppression soon begins to mold the subject as Being-in-the-world. By this time "he is so per-

meated by the atmosphere of guilt that external criminal accusations become merged with his subjective feelings of sinfulness—of having done wrong. Rather than experiencing resentment, he feels that he must deserve this punishment. *His pervasive pain is experienced as guilt anxiety."*

4. The successful induction of guilt entails learning of modes of accommodation to the ruling order. Confession functions as a ritual to expiate guilt.[91] Identification with the aggressor may become so complete that the jailers permit the prisoner to help "reform" other prisoners.[92]

The guilt response to domination begins to develop a logic of its own. Learned through painful eons of struggle with dominating environments, it emerges as an ingrained, reflexive mechanism to cope with lack of freedom. Divorced from the natural context, the guilt response operates as "second nature." Civilization, Freud believed, ". . . obtains the mastery over the dangerous love of aggression in individuals by enfeebling and disarming it and setting up an institution within their minds to keep watch over it, like a garrison in a conquered city."[93] Not only aggression, but action per se—the everyday praxis of the subject—becomes subjected to this internalized garrison. Social order is assured. "As long as things go well with a man, his conscience is lenient and lets the ego do all kinds of things; when some calamity befalls, he holds an inquisition within, discovers his sin, heightens the standards of his conscience, imposes abstinences on himself and punishes himself with penances."[94] People develop an uncanny facility of simultaneously containing and perpetuating the original suffering through replaying the guilt mechanism. The circuitry of the guilt response culminates in *masochism.*

Masochism exists in reification of the dominator and repetition of the guilt response. Masochism requires unquestioning faith in the immovable powerfulness and lawfulness of the environing order. "The masochistic character has a strong, idealistic conception of the justice governing the world. He is convinced that you have to suffer, if you sin, and that you will be rewarded, if you are good."[95] The masochist is so "good" (i.e., perfect in his conformity to the rationality of oppression) that he anticipates the punishment of deviance or rebellion by imposing it. People learn that the reward for conformity to natural law is survival and alleviation of suffering. The masochist, in secret contract with the reified order, imposes its sanctions to atone for his or her inadequacy or inferiority or guilt and thereby experiences momentary release from its tyranny. The masochist's own temporary happiness is offered as a sacrifice to the omnipotent other in return for (hoped-for) beneficence in a "permanent exchange" fantasy.[96] "By ordering his own punishment the masochist has made himself the master of his destiny."[97] The masochist's resolution of the contradiction between the negating other and the struggling self is to "buy off" the reified other in order to permit the brief realization of his own will. "The masochist regards the law as a punitive process and therefore begins by having the punishment inflicted upon himself. Once he has undergone the punishment, he feels that he is allowed or indeed commanded to experience the pleasure that the law was supposed to forbid."[98] The masochist does not enjoy pain. The self-negating policies he adopts from his oppressor are played out to *permit* (if only momentarily) expression of his own subjectivity. His self-negating projects are aimed ultimately toward self-affirmation. "Masochism is a perpetual effort to *annihilate* the subject's subjectivity by causing it to be assimilated by the other; this effort is accompanied by the exhausting and delicious consciousness of failure so that finally it is the failure itself which the subject ultimately seeks as his primary goal."[99]

Because the masochist presupposes "divine justice" in the oppressive order that he seeks to mollify, his self-negating behavior produces uncertain results. In sexual masochism, the pain paid as tribute to the punishing other permits release (orgasm). The guilt mechanism can operate to completion within a single psyche. The psycho-scenario breaks down in social masochism. The promise of release (freedom) is predicated on an imputed or invoked contract with the "they" to provide reward for obedience. The masochist may subsequently search extensively for "signs" of "cosmic" approval.[100] The operation of the guilt mechanism is ultimately stalled in the tension of waiting, which may come to underlie the total life experience. The protest or overturning of the Law accomplished intrapsychically by the sexual masochist remains arrested in the ideal realm for the social masochist who requires history to respond to his aspiration for release. Gilles

Deleuze concludes, "Formally speaking, masochism is a state of waiting; the masochist experiences waiting in its pure form."[101]

The masochist, then, is caught in a pseudosolution to the conflict between self and dominant other. His or her self-negating sacrifice is met at best by the *hope* for liberation. His or her identification with the aggressor resolves itself into self-defeating behavior. "Here the individual feels he is doing the 'right thing,' pleasing the sadistic partner whose love he craves, and, in addition, hopes to gain approval by emulating the aggressive trends of the partner even to the point of losing his own identity."[102] The individual who employs the masochistic "solution" to domination, imposes the work of the oppressor upon himself or herself and waits for divine succor. Dominators encourage the myth of future bliss, especially through religion to support the masochistic "solution" in the perpetuation of the dominating order.

Guilt-based responses to domination are evident in inferiorized groups. The classic instance of masochistic repetition can be drawn from the victims of Nazi concentration camps:

> One of the games played by the guards was to find out who could stand to be hit longest without uttering a complaint. This game was copied by the old prisoners, as though they had not been hit often and long enough without needing to repeat this experience as a game.[103]

The traditional Hebraic response to oppression is characterized by E. O. James:

> The tribulations of the Jews during and after the fall of Jerusalem in A.D. 70 led to the Rabbinic interpretation of self-inflicted suffering as an atoning sacrifice in the expiation of national guilt.[104]

Memmi remarks, in relation to European Jews:

> The Jew rejects himself to ward off the rejection of others, and in so doing he confirms their rejection and consents to the condemnation and the sanctions which they exact.[105]

Hortense Powdermaker comments upon the psycho-logic of sycophantic behavior among American blacks:

> The masochist and the meek, unaggressive Negro derive a similar kind of pleasure from their suffering. For the Negro as well as for the ma-

sochist there is pleasure in appeasing the guilt feeling; for each there is the pleasure derived from the belief that through his suffering he becomes superior to his oppressors; and finally, for each the suffering is a prelude to final victory.[106]

Psychiatrists confound the same behavior among gay people with homosexuality itself. The clinical literature abounds with documents of internalized self-contempt among gay people, leading some writers to associate homosexuality with unconscious or conscious guilt, self-damaging behavior, and clinical masochism. Masochism appears among gay people as a coping strategy to domination, a response much aggravated in the clinical setting by an oppressive therapist. It is not remarkable that the most homophobic and tyrannical of psychiatrists most often discover evidence of masochism in their gay clients.[107]

Phenomenology of Life Limitations

To the single individual, of course, distribution appears as a social law which determines his position within the system of production within which he produces, and which therefore precedes production. The individual comes into the world possessing neither capital nor land. Social distribution assigns him at birth to wage labour. But this situation of being assigned is itself a consequence of the existence of capital and landed property as independent agents of production.

—MARX[108]

The guilt-based, masochistic response to domination requires perception of the dominating other as omnipotent and immovable. Social domination is conceived in the same manner as domination by the natural environment. The activity of the subject turns upon itself as it turns away from the constraint structure accepted as given. The dialectic between the subject and the quasiobjective environment is, in this mode, frozen: the social constraint structure is reified into a fixed, inevitable system. The subject falls into the masochistic orientation, turning upon himself or herself to cope with domination.

Each new generation finds itself in a pre-given social world inherited from its fathers. The powerlessness of the child leaves accommodation the only workable orientation to the given political reality. The initial ad hoc strategies of coping with reality become regularized and habituated. The guilt-based response is primary or "natural" as the individual learns how to survive in a world where resources are held by adults. Subordinated people experience the same socialization pattern, but attain fewer of the freedoms of "adulthood."

John Hammond remarks in reference to the early English working class: "They took the world as they found it."[109] When questioned about their condition, Baldus encountered this reply from an African slave: "Why must one obey the Fulbe? We have found it that way. It has been this way since the time of our ancestors, and it can never disappear. We have found it that way, and that is the way we carry it out."[110]

The increasing complexity and opacity of modern society enhances a reified image of the social order for the individual.[111] The evolution of the web of existing interhuman relations develops the appearance of irresistible naturality.[112]

The subordinated person finds himself or herself enmeshed in a world not of his or her own creation which stands alien and limiting. Georg Lukács remarks of the "natural attitude":

> In terms of his consciousness the single individual is a perceiving subject confronting the overwhelming objective necessities imposed by society of which only minute fragments can be comprehended. . . . when the individual confronts objective reality he is faced by a complex of ready-made and unalterable objects which allow him only the subjective responses of recognition or rejection.[113]

Here arises the "reified consciousness" characterized by tacit acceptance of the given structure of closed possibilities. The reified consciousness emerges with the delimitation or desubjectivization of the subject. The process tends to be accompanied by vicarious participation of the subject in the power of his dominators and adoption of their ideology. The reification process sets the stage for the masochistic response to domination. Describing the black person's encounter with the white world, Frantz Fanon relates:

When the Negro makes contact with the white world, a certain sensitizing action takes place. If his psychic structure is weak, one observes a collapse of the ego. The black man stops behaving as an *actional* person. The goal of his behavior will be The Other (in the guise of the white man) for The Other alone can give him worth.[114]

In Heidegger's terms, the subject is "thrown" into the "they." The reified consciousness, understood phenomenologically, exists passively:

The *Dasein*, although it exists essentially for its own sake (*umwillen seiner*), has nevertheless not itself laid the ground of its *being*. And also, as a creature 'come into existence,' it is and remains, *thrown*, determined, i.e., enclosed, possessed, and compelled by beings in general.[115]

Understood in an historical vacuum, the exponents of Heideggerian philosophy proved unable to distinguish between "authentic" and "inauthentic" existence in their own lives. Yet the distinction strikes upon the divergence between the reified and free consciousnesses. Reembedded in the social-historical context, Heidegger's phenomenology of inauthenticity accurately portrays the experience of the reified consciousness. In his own words, "The "they" itself Articulates the referential context of significance."[116]

The desubjectivized subject without conscious decision, becomes subsumed in the rationality of domination. The guilt-based response provides an orientation to the world which is experienced as "adequate" and which nevertheless abnegates the subject's potential for freedom.

The projection of its ownmost potentiality-for-Being has been delivered over to the Fact of its thrownness into the "there."[117]

The supposition of the "they" that one is leading and sustaining a full and genuine 'life,' brings Dasein a *tranquillity*, for which everything is 'in the best of order' and all doors are open. Falling Being-in-the-world, which tempts itself, is at the same time *tranquillizing* [*beruhigend*]. ... When *Dasein*, tranquillized, and 'understanding' everything, thus compares itself with everything, it drifts along towards an alienation [*Entfremdung*] in which its ownmost potentiality-for-Being is hidden from it.[118]

Everyone is the other, and no one is himself. The "they," which supplies the answer to the question of the "who" of everyday Dasein, is the "nobody" to whom every Dasein has already surrendered itself in Being-among-one-other [sic] [Untereinandersein].[119]

The inferiorized person is especially vulnerable to the development of reified consciousness. The social constraint structure appears particularly formidable and encompassing for him or her. Those peripheral to the community of subordinated members or the products of authoritarian families are highly susceptible to the apparently hegemonic influence of the social order. The bourgeois world-view possessed by superordinate social groups has its counterpart among the inferiorized. In Horkheimer's characterizations: "The whole perceptible world as present to a member of bourgeois society and as interpreted within a traditional world-view which is in continuous interaction with that given world, is seen by the perceiver as a sum-total of facts; it is there and must be accepted."[120]

Power is experienced as an "other," as "the beyond," as "that which lies remote" from the perceiver.[121] The reification of power outside oneself founds the guilt-based orientation. This "inauthentic" existence strives contradictorily to rescue the active, moving subject from environmental limitations by affirming those limitations. The subject is alienated from his or her own subjectivity and is unable to discover himself or herself in his or her own world. The following psychoanalytic description of the clinical masochist retraces the philosophical history of the "unhappy," "alienated," "inauthentic," or "reified" consciousness:

> Genuine or autonomous feelings are, for the most part, deadened or muted in masochistic persons. Life is generally experienced as occurring outside their orbit, as not to be responded to but to be reacted to in submission, at times to the point of self-extinction. The center of gravity is found outside themselves or is centrifugally directed.[122]

This orientation to the world remains arrested in the parent–child relation, where the absolute dependent, the child, petitions the parents for "gifts." Happiness, solace, contentment are thought to flow magically from omnipotent sources.[123] The process of de-subjectivation is described precisely in Hegel's phenomenology of the unhappy consciousness:

Through these moments—the negative abandonment first of its own right and power of decision, then of its property and enjoyment, and finally the positive moment of carrying on what it does not understand—it deprives itself, completely and in truth of the consciousness of inner and outer freedom or reality in the sense of its own existence for itself. It has the certainty of having in truth stripped itself of its Ego, and of having turned its immediate self-consciousness into a "thing," into an objective external existence.[124]

Or in the words of Leon Salzman: "The masochistic values can ultimately be reduced to needing no one—a supreme isolation and separation without, however, the usual despair which accompanies such a movement."[125]

Psychological analysis describes the content of the everyday operation of the reified subject in his social world. The investigations of Adorno, Frenkel-Brunswik, Levinson, and Sanford into the authoritarian personality reveal the most common or "ideal typical" manifestations of the reified consciousness in the modern world. The delineation of this personality syndrome is particularly instructive in understanding the guilt-based response to domination, and thus, the general phenomenon of self-negating behavior in inferiorized people. Widespread among members of superordinate and subordinate groups, the authoritarian personality functions as an order-preserving social member. *In nuce*, the following traits are indicative of the authoritarian personality:

- rigid adherence to conventional, middle-class values,
- submissive, uncritical attitude toward idealized moral authorities of the ingroup,
- tendency to be on the lookout for, and to condemn, reject, and punish people who violate conventional values,
- opposition to the subjective, the imaginative, the tender-minded,
- the belief in mystical determinants of the individual's fate; the disposition to think in rigid categories,
- preoccupation with dominance–submission, strong–weak, leader–follower dimension; identification with power figures; overemphasis upon the conventionalized attributes of the ego; exaggerated assertion of strength and toughness,
- generalized hostility, vilification of the human,
- the disposition to believe that wild and dangerous things go on in the world; the projection outward of unconscious emotional impulses.[126]

The sensitivity to group pressure of the authoritarian personality and others of low self-esteem is confirmed in psychological and psychoanalytical observation.[127]

The authoritarian syndrome is clearly linked to the rejection of self and fellow inferiorized members. Jews expressing anti-Semitism on questionnaires tend to score high on the Fascism scale (used as an indicator of authoritarianism).[128] Black self-disparagement appears similarly linked to authoritarianism.[129] Gary Marx found an inverse correlation between scores on the Fascism scale and black militancy (seen as self-affirmative).[130] Black people scoring high on the Fascism scale are much more likely to defend segregation and condemn the NAACP, while admitting hatred for their own group.[131] The discovery of repressed homosexuality among authoritarian subjects suggests *not*, as many have surmised,[132] an inherent link between homosexuality and authoritarianism, but a definite relationship between the *repression* of homosexuality and the reified consciousness. The *rejection* of homosexuality in self and others among authoritarians is congruent with their general rejection of everyone believed to represent weakness, inadequacy, or moral unconventionality. Adorno et al. remark:

> We observe in Mack, therefore, attempts to conceal weakness by verbal denial and by presenting a *façade* of toughness, to get rid of weakness by projecting it onto other people, chiefly outgroups, and then condemning them on this score, to overcompensate for weakness by strivings for power and status and to allay the sense of weakness by aligning himself with powerful individuals and groups.[133]

Among homosexuals self-rejection and the guilt-based response to domination occur in the same manner as in the other groups. The undialectical, hyperpsychologized perspective falsely identifies the artifacts of oppression with the "nature" of homosexuality.

IV STRATEGIES COPING WITH DOMINATION

Mimesis

> This consciousness was not in peril and
> fear for this element or that nor for this or
> that moment of time, it was afraid for its
> entire being; it felt the fear of death, the
> sovereign master. It has been in that ex-
> perience melted to its inmost soul, has
> trembled throughout its every fiber, and
> all that was fixed and steadfast has quaked
> within it.
>
> —HEGEL[1]

Some precautions must be recalled in categorizing actions people use to deal with social restrictions. Generalizations about
"basic personality types" of entire peoples appear popular among
some psychologists. This exceedingly treacherous endeavor ab-
stracts action from its social contexts. The reified consciousness
must be understood in relation to the macrosocial and microsocial
conditions adduced in Chapter III. Lifton, for example, enumerates
the factors for vulnerability to Chinese thought-reform as: "a strong
and readily accessible negative identity fed by an unusually great
susceptibility to guilt, a tendency toward identity confusion (especially that of the cultural outsider), a profound involvement in
a situation productive of historical and racial guilt, and finally,
a sizable element of totalism."[2]

The behavior patterns presented in this chapter cannot be attributed to all members of inferiorized groups at all times, nor even consistently to given individuals over time. We have begun at the first instance of the third dialectical phase with the response of atomized individuals subject to hegemonic limitation. This behavior, sometimes taken for granted, sometimes thought to be "peculiar," "unnatural," or "neurotic," both responds to and contributes to the logic of domination. In moving toward the coalition of individuals and the rupture of hegemony, the contingency of "basic personality types" becomes clear. The moving historical situation elicits new patterns of behavior demonstrating the fluidity of the postulated "personality." Strategies coping with domination dissolve into methods to alter or resist domination.

The masochistic response, for example, tends toward objectivity in its repetitive reappearance. It is an "essence . . . which lies concealed beneath the facade of immediacy, of the supposed facts, and which makes the facts what they are. It comes to be a law of doom thus far obeyed by history, a law the more irresistible the more it will hide beneath the facts, only to be comfortably denied by them.[3] Reflection upon this "law of doom" and comprehension of the practice which realizes it permit the possibility of its transcendence. Neither universal nor inevitable, it is a "law" only insofar as it operates preconsciously. "Objectivity is the self-objectification of human society at a particular stage in its development; its laws hold good only within the framework of the historical context which produced them and which is in turn determined by them."[4]

Consideration of the behavior of subordinated people is apt to degenerate into squabbles over words. Stanley Elkins' characterization of behavior among American slaves as "infantile,"[5] provoked storms of protests for several years. Kenneth Stampp, for example, retorted, "Those who consciously and purposefully acted the part of Sambo, thereby reducing sources of friction and putting limits on what would normally be expected of them, were in no sense being childish or infantile; rather, their behavior was rational, meaningful, and mature."[6] Stampp reads an insult into the word *infantile*, and implies that the behavior of children is neither rational nor meaningful. Anxious to relieve a maligned people of a stigma, Stampp fails to recognize the commonalities in the behavior of children and slaves, both of which are produced by "normal" means of socialization. "Humanitarians" are quick to "exonerate" the inferiorized of certain behaviors, as if they reflected ultimately upon their humanity or humanization. In what sense, was "Sambo" like behavior "rational"? It was "rational" as an "understandable" response to domination, just as "infantile" behavior in children is a "rational" response to adult hegemony. It was "irrational" (judged by critical reason) in its functionality for the established system of domination. The desire to divine the motivations of the dominated, in order to postulate a "real" and unsullied person beneath the visible level of apparent behavior or "just acting," arises from the belief that they are in need of moral rehabilitation.

The language of "diseases" and "pathologies" tends to suffer from similar conceptual myopia. "Diseases" divorced from their dialectical embeddedness become conceptual monstrosities. "Diseases are not entities: the classification of diseases is purely a matter of convenience: what are known as diseases are the result of what happens when the organism comes in contact with inimical agents."[7] The competent physician, then, treats the offending organism, rather than the symptoms. Debates over the "neurotic" character of behavior tend to founder on this issue. Behavior directed toward the neutralization of menace appears among the subordinated and among "neurotics," producing a similar set of symptoms in each. The term *neurosis* has unfortunately acquired a moral connotation. The psychological physician is wont to treat the "offending" symptom instead of the social root.

> The idiosyncratic narrowed world of the neurotic is not the product of man's instinctual heritage but rather an invention designed to cope with the existing limitations of contemporary social reality. Constrictions and limitations exerted by the force of contemporary institutional forces serve to effectively narrow the scope of man's world. The neurotic stance that we shall witness is simply an exaggeration of the one in which modern man in general no longer originates or acts but merely reacts or adapts to an oppressive situation.[8]

Or in the words of Grier and Cobbs:

> To regard the Black Norm as pathological and attempt to remove such traits by treatment would be akin to analyzing away a hunter's cunning or a banker's prudence. This is a body of characteristics essential to life for black men in America.[9]

Mimetic behavior which falls into the guilt-based response modality appears most frequently and clearly under extreme conditions of oppression. Anna Freud analyzed the phenomenon in her study of a confrontation between a schoolboy and his stern master. The schoolmaster had been offended by the boy's "making faces" while being disciplined. Freud remarks:

> The boy's grimaces were simply a caricature of the angry expression of the teacher and [that] when he had to face a scolding by the latter, he tried to master his anxiety by involuntarily imitating him. . . . Through his grimaces he was assimilating himself to or identifying himself with the dreaded external object.[10]

The social situation of the inferiorized duplicates the parent–child relationship; generations of dependence may "freeze" this mode of behavior. Mimetic adoption of dominant values and manners appears among the subordinated. The politics of socialization become clear in the life of a total institution:

> Only a small number of the prisoners, perhaps not even one, was able to escape a certain measure of identification with the SS. . . . (1) [That] for all of us the SS was a father image, of such ambivalence, however, that the intensity varied from one instant to the next, (2) [That] through repression, which was an essential of adaptation, "identification with the aggressor" occurred.[11]

Like children, concentration camp internees, slaves, and those in mental institutions are forced to conform to a highly regulated regime. Food, accommodation, and clothing are authoritatively regulated. Sleeping and eating are routinized. Financial responsibilities and sexual opportunities are all but eliminated.[12] Constrained by the official regimen, survival demands some degree of psychological adjustment. "It seems that the majority of the old prisoners had realized that they could not continue to work for the Gestapo unless they could convince themselves that their work made some sense, so they had to convince themselves of this sense."[13] Lower castes in India, slaves, and mental patients[14] face a similar lack of options. In accounting for the support for the caste system expressed by Untouchables, Anant speculates:

Dependence on the parents is displaced later to higher castes for whom Sudras work and get grain in exchange for their services. Strong identification with the authoritarian father seems to be transferred to strong identification with the aggressor (the higher castes). The conformity to the norms and standards of caste hierarchy, viz., the identification, gives the individual an emotional security which he does not want to lose.[15]

In the same manner, "to obtain the only security available to them, both the slave and the child repress consciously or unconsciously, their hatred for the object which restricts their desires and freedom."[16] Legal emancipation alone fails to eliminate dependency habituated through generations of domination.[17] That some of the behavior patterns associated with children should appear among the dominated is, then, not surprising.

Conformity to a regimen imposed by a dominating other over time results in detectable psychological "fallout." Reduction in "cognitive dissonance" entails reproduction of the behavior required by dominators:

The satisfaction with which some old prisoners enjoyed the fact that, during the twice daily counting of the prisoners, they really had stood well at attention can be explained only by the fact that they had entirely accepted the values of the Gestapo as their own. . . . Often the Gestapo would enforce nonsensical rules, originating in the whims of one of the guards. They were usually forgotten as soon as formulated, but there were always some old prisoners who would continue to follow these rules and try to enforce them on others long after the Gestapo had forgotten about them.[18]

Dominators survey the inferiorized for behavior complementary to their own ends.[19] Some of the more highly socialized members, whose adoption of dominant values is most complete, may be sponsored to a slightly more privileged status, giving them an apparent investment in the established system and added incentive to conform. A small class of apologists and converts develops, who thereby assist dominators in the preservation of the status quo. Constant awareness of the precariousness of their new status often prompts converts to the extremes of conformity to the values of their masters. Among the colonized, "the recently assimilated place themselves in a considerably superior position to the average colonizer. They push a colonial mentality to excess, display proud disdain for the colonized and continually show off their borrowed rank, which often belies a vulgar brutality and avidity. Still too impressed by their privileges, they savor them and defend them with fear and harshness; and when colonization is imperilled, they provide it with its most dynamic defenders, its shock troops, and sometimes its instigators."[20]

In the concentration camps, the "Kapo" was the convert coopted to perform the work of the oppressors: "Both outwardly and inwardly he has identified himself with the SS, as he reveals in his behaviour, his clothing, his bawling, his beatings, his treatment of the weak, his shameless 'organizing,' his cruelties on the pattern of the SS, his demand for discipline and obedience."[21]

The zeal of the convert testifies to his inability to eliminate his core identity as a member of a subordinated group. He struggles against his excompatriots to expunge his own too real primary identity. Recruited usually from the interstitial group of those with ambiguous identities, the convert presents a chronic threat to the inferiorized community.

Jews have suffered from former members eager to prove their conversion to the Christian world. The sixteenth-century pogrom of the Frankfurt ghetto was led by an ex-Jew who convinced the authorities of a secret conspiracy within the ghetto.[22] In the 1860s, an ex-Jew, Jacob Brafman, worked as a Russian police spy, reporting a world Jewish conspiracy aimed at the exploitation of the Gentile world.[23] "His *Book of the Kahal* was issued at public expense and sent to all Government officials as a guide in their relations with the Jewish population."[24] It served as a source of legitimation for periodic pogroms. William Marr's 1873 *Der Sieg des Judentums über das Germanentum* became an influential anti-Semitic tract.[25] Otto Weininger, a nineteenth-century German Jewish philosopher, wrote anti-Semitic diatribes later adopted by Alfred Rosenberg, chief racial theorist of the National Socialists.[26] The Nazi party and Action Française counted (ex-)Jewish members in the early stages.[27]

The political and academic establishments recruit converts to play the role of "representative spokesmen" for inferiorized groups. Booker T. Washington became much celebrated and widely heard by white audiences for glorifying manual labor for blacks and promising "the most patient, faithful, law-abiding, and unresentful people that the world has seen."[28] Myrdal noted that "statements that interracial relations are good [thus] belong in the South to the etiquette of Negro college presidents, principals and teachers of Negro schools, and all other Negroes enjoying upper or middle class status."[29] Instructors who first introduced black history into schools met with dismissal from black administrators in the early stages.[30] Upward mobility sponsored for token blacks creates a small class of "achievers" endorsing the Horatio Alger myth.[31]

Homosexuals in positions of influence similarly may seek to protect themselves by excluding their fellows. "Closet queens" often present themselves as the first to endorse the homophobic ideology. Merle Miller relates how as editor of a city newspaper, he indulged in "queer-baiting" to conceal his own homosexuality.[32] Gay psychiatrists and academics may espouse "deviance" theories preserving the hegemony of therapeutic ideologies.[33] A classic instance is Edward Sagarin, who, under a pseudonym, broke the silence concerning homosexuality in the United States by writing the first widely circulated book from a homosexual viewpoint. Later awarded a Ph.D. in sociology, his anti-gay polemics proliferated in scholarly journals, authoritative and popular anthologies, under his own name, articulating the predominant "liberal" editorial standard: ostensible tolerance combined with gratuitous moral condemnation. Conversion to heterosexual identity from bisexual marginality through marriage permitted cooptation by the agents of oppression.[34]

Escape from Identity

The person who discovers himself or herself as a member of an inferiorized group[35] is presented with a "composite portrait"[36] which purports to define him or her. The portrait is accompanied by a range of social penalties[37] guaranteed to produce a more difficult and insecure life than could be expected by membership in a more highly valued category. This discovery is usually prompted by attacks (direct or anticipated) menacing one's overall chances for survival and well-being. The first impulse, not surprisingly, is to move toward escape. Inferiorized identity appears as an iron cage negating one's freedom, constraining one's subjectivity or self-expression. The inferiorized person perceives an initial choice: (1) acceptance of categorization as an inferiorized member with the composite portrait of undesirable traits, or (2) rejection of or lack of recognition of self in the composite portrait, with lack of identification with the inferiorized group. This pseudochoice locks the subject into a social conundrum, leading to one of two debilitating results, and frequently, oscillation between the two: (1) guilt, self-hatred, and masochistic responses, or (2) flight from identity, denial, or "bad faith." As this initial "choice" exists as an insoluble contradiction, the "choice" is as such only attempted. The contradiction resides within the subject, who may ambivalently present one, then the other, complex of coping strategies.

The social presentation of this initial pseudochoice assures maintenance of the status quo. The former "choice" successfully personalizes failure;[38] the latter successfully isolates the individual from others presented with the same fate. Atomization of the inferiorized occurs in either instance. Society presents the subordinated subject with a false choice leading to a cul-de-sac, then stigmatizes the trapped and frightened person for his or her sense of trappedness and fright. The internalization of the contradiction manifests itself as "neurotic," "for neurosis is after all only a sign that the ego has not succeeded in making a synthesis, that in attempting to do so it has forfeited its unity."[39] Those who have foundered upon this no-win paradox, fall into the mental contortions from which, for example, psychiatry derives its image of the homosexual. In Memmi's words, "Yes, the Jewish condition was an *impossible condition*. . . . I define an impossible condition as a condition which can have no solution in its actual structure."[40]

Flight from identity, then, constitutes another major complex of strategies coping with inferiorization. "The first act of bad faith is to flee what it can not flee, to flee what it is."[41]

Among Jews, conversion to Christianity figures as a widespread legal refuge from stigma in nineteenth-century Germany.[42] In the early post-World War II period, many American Jews tended to express a flight from identity. When Hook surveyed his students, about a possible "magical" transformation of identity (phrased in terms of reincarnation), "the overwhelming majority of Jewish students did not want to be born again as Jews but as something else—'no religion,' 'agnostic,' 'pagan,' 'Protestant' (mostly Unitarians with a few scattered Episcopalians), 'nothing that would be be a burden or be discriminated against'—were some of the typical responses. Not a single Gentile student ever wanted to be born Jewish."[43] Greenberg found a similar response revealing a marked "effort to conceal one's identity, to de-emphasize 'Jewish' characteristics, and finally to sink into the obscurity of the majority group."[44] Name-changing has been an especially prevalent practice among American Jews to dissociate themselves from a Jewish past. Again in the early postwar period, almost half of name-changers appearing in court were Jewish.[45] Sartre's classic *Anti-Semite and Jew*[46] delineated the Jew in "bad faith." "Like every other neurotic, the Jewish anti-Semite feels that he can solve his difficulty only by ceasing to be himself, by concealing his identity from himself as well as from the outside world—or by running away."[47]

Frazier reported in 1940: "many lower-class [black] youth say frankly that if they were born again they would prefer to be white."[48] Studies of black mental patients note the centrality of the bad-faith mechanism to the dynamics of neurosis. Morton Chethik et al., in working with "disturbed" black children found a tendency to bolster self-esteem through assumption of white identity. One boy was convinced: "I'm a nigger and a Reed. My family is black and so am I. I'll end on Skid Row. I'll go back to what I was before, a big fat black pig."[49] Among paranoids, there is a tendency to construct a mythical white autobiography and focus upon blackness as a dastardly plot or trick engineered by parents, the Ku Klux Klan, etc.[50]

The phenomenology of "bad faith" among gay people is perceptively described by Warren: "He is taught that homosexuality is bad and so are homosexuals, *but* he is taught to recognize homosexuals by lurid signs such as extreme effeminacy or a fiendish, warped, or debauched appearance (thus he is not equipped to recognize actual homosexuals). These rather confusing elements that make up the societal stereotype of homosexuals actually provide a homosexual actor with ways out of self-labelling as a homosexual. . . .

ELDON: I had been told by my mother that all fairies as she called them were very light and small and I was big and muscular so I knew I wasn't one. . . .

DRUMMOND: As far as I knew homosexuality was a horrible thing, and I knew sex with Gerald was fantastic so I knew I couldn't be homosexual. . . .

BRUCE: I was engaged to be married, so every time me and my college roommate made it we said 'Boy was I drunk last night' and left it at that.[51]

Jill Johnston comments, "The internalization of the taboo was so great that you didn't think you were what you wanted or were doing."[52]

Surveys of gay people reveal some flight from identity. Saghir and Robins found considerable self-reported guilt and fear, decreasing with age from 46 to 29 percent for men and from 29 to 10 percent for women.[53] Weinberg and Williams found 22 percent willing to agree, "I wish I were not homosexual" and 14 percent willing to obtain "psychiatric treatment."[54] The "magic pill" question (which asks if the respondent would consent to a certain, quick, and painless transformation to heterosexuality if it were possible) yields 13–19 percent acquiescence among military men, 9 percent for female and 22 percent for male urban homophiles, and as high as one-third in a small Iowa college town.[55]

Marriage can provide social advancement and flight from identity for each group.[56] Among married gay people, well over 90 percent cite social acceptance, domestic reasons, or family pressure as reasons for (heterosexual) marriage.[57] Marriage here functions as a legal refuge from inferiorized identity.[58]

The false choice accepted by the subject in his initial apprehension of the world functions then as a "false consciousness" or "bad faith" subordinating him to the rationality of domination. It is interesting that black people found in mental institutions more frequently endorse the American myth, that "if a man works hard, saves his money, and is ambitious he will get ahead," than do other blacks.[59] Adoption of the dominant values that assert an open opportunity structure to American society clearly fails in practice. The inadequacy of methods of living purveyed by bourgeois society to the objective structure of life possibilities for inferiorized people manifests itself as neurosis, when these values are adopted by them. Nietzsche's metaphoric characterization of the bad-faith contradiction illustrates most succinctly the experience of adopting the socially presented composite of negative values in one's own identity: "he loads too many *alien* grave [*schwere*] words and values on himself, and then life seems a desert [*Wüste*] to him."[60]

The subordinated transcend this pseudosolution only by learning the inadequacy, inapplicability, or hypocrisy of the received stock of knowledge to their own social situation. The nexus between identity with subordinated compatriots and "identity" presented by official agents of cultural transmission must first be exploded. The fate represented by the composite portrait must not be permitted to foreclose identification and consolidation with like-situated others. Solution requires the resubjectivization of the subject, that is, rejection of the regressive identity for a perpetually created, emergent, progressive practice. The basic axioms of the "natural attitude"[61] must be problematized and reality restructured in order for the subordinated to comprehend their situation.

Social Withdrawal

> He has learned that modesty, silence, patience are proper to misfortune, because misfortune is already a sin in the eyes of men.
>
> —SARTRE[62]

Social withdrawal provides a coping strategy, which no longer requires a personal escape from identity, but externalizes identity conflict into the immediate social world. Inferiorized persons, then, develop repertoires of behaviors employed for specific audiences, shifting from one behavior set to another as the occasion demands. Goffman's dramaturgical view of "stigma" is most appropriate for this style of coping response, a style which presumes the social conventions of "liberal" societies (see the section above entitled "Structural Constraints"). Social withdrawal, then, presumes the possibility of alternative, in-group, or community audiences that permit a wider range of personal expression (or deviation) than the larger society.

Transcendence of bad faith (as sketched above) permits the first move toward reconciliation with identical others. Abandonment of isolation accompanies recognition of identity. The first step toward coalescence of subordinated persons comes about as the individual accepts his or her commonality with like-situated others. Thrown into communication with them, the individual may discover his or her identity with them. A halt to the flight from identity permits contact with compatriots.[63] A dialectical movement toward integration commences as current community members and the potential community member discover each other.

This first collectivity tends to withdraw from an inhospitable social environment. Consolidation of inferiorized members implies, at this point, some degree of disengagement from other social groups. Both the intolerance of dominating groups and mutual gravitation of subordinated members promotes concentration in some areas, absence in others. Legal and economic constraints may force segregation; the inferiorized become confined to a few specific spaces.

The ghetto represents exclusion from freedoms of superordinate groups and may be experienced as confining and stifling. At the same time, it is "a haven of refuge in unfriendly surroundings."[64] Commenting on the ghettoized Jew, Wirth states, "Without the backing of his group, without the security that he enjoyed in his inner circle of friends and countrymen, life would have been intolerable."[65] Social withdrawal creates a "home territory . . . where the regular participants have a relative freedom of behavior and a sense of intimacy and control over the area."[66]

The ghetto exists both as a response to domination and as a first assertion of community.[67] The sense of guaranteed freedom within the subordinated community is suggested by a phrase used by gay people: "coming out of the closet." "Coming out" expresses the sense of liberation from isolation in a small, fixed space,[68] which is the process of coming "in" to the community.

Social withdrawal and beginning coalition require some degree of "tolerance" from the dominating society. Ruthless persecution and total vigilance by dominators maintain the atomized state and allow, for the most part, only the mimetic and guilt-based responses as survival tactics. Withdrawal and (incipient) formation of a community require a rupture in the oppressive hegemony; they entail either limited civil rights and toleration or a symbiotic relationship with superordinate groups where the inferiorized are seen perhaps as "useful" if inferior. The development of enclaves is precluded by the totalitarian state but becomes increasingly possible with the rise of "bourgeois" or "liberal" socioeconomic formations. Domination evolves into new forms; outright destruction tends to give way to exclusion.

Withdrawal carves out an exception to the prevailing rationality; it does not challenge or negate it. The dominated assume a "low profile" to avoid the attention of dominators. Compliance remains the first strategy in placating the powerful other. Raul Hilberg remarks, "The Jews attempted to tame the Germans as one would attempt to tame a wild beast. They avoided 'provocations' and complied instantly with decrees and orders. They hoped that somehow the German drive would spend itself."[69] Withdrawal or avoidance of confrontation contributes toward a strategy of submergence or invisibility. Black parents recommend it to their children to cope with harassment.[70] W. E. B. DuBois outlined a bitter compendium of black compliance: "servility and fawning, gross flattery of white folk and lying to appease and cajole them . . . submission to insult and aggression; exaggerated and despicable humility."[71]

The ghetto frames the everyday life of inferiorized people, limiting even their expectations and aspirations. Life within this set of restricted possibilities draws back from the taken-for-granted privileges of superordinate groups. The ghetto curtails expectations just as the mental institution contains the lives of its inmates: "the sampling of the outside provided by the establishment is taken by the inmate as the whole, and a stable relatively contented existence is built up out of the maximum satisfaction procurable within the institution."[72] An ideology which personalizes failure legitimizes the limitation of life possibilities. Inferiorization enforces the unhappy belief among its objects that their degradation is somehow "deserved."[73]

"Passing" presents an escape from identity which is not bad faith, but duplicity. It is an escape from identity more for the other than for the self. Allegiance to dominant norms is paid by "lip service"; a compliant facade is adopted to facilitate social interaction. The actor is likely to be somewhat integrated into the subordinated community; his denial of identity continues on a part-time or ambivalent basis. To other inferiorized people, the actor reveals a more "authentic" identity, discarding a pseudo-identity constructed for superordinate audiences. The former identity is experienced "at ease;" the latter as inhibited—an act. The assimilated Jew, passing in Weimar Germany "trembles for the revelation of his real origin; he keeps himself under constant observation lest he betray himself by a word, a gesture, a look; his life has no more than one aim and purpose: successful camouflage."[74]

Light-skinned black people who pass, face the same insecurities. Assumption of Latin American or Arab identity[75] requires defenses against discreditation. Camouflage becomes a consuming orientation.[76] Whether discovered or undiscovered, these black people develop a humble or at best "cool" role for white audiences.[77]

Early gay organizations significantly called themselves "Mattachine," adopting the name of "the Italian jester, acrobat, mimic who pleased crowds but kept his truer feelings out of sight."[78] Though the incongruity of the stereotype to gay people allows almost all to pass successfully,[79] the anxiety of possible discreditation remains as with the other groups.[80]

Ambivalent or inadequate playing out of the inferiorized role provokes uneasiness or suspicion among superordinate observers. Many (including researchers) complain of the "dishonesty" or "unreliability" of Jewish, black, or gay people, sensing the artificiality of behavior presented to them.[81]

Exposure may be vigorously resisted. The family of Léon Blum, the French Socialist leader, sued Larousse for printing Blum's original family name, Fulkenstein.[82] Attribution of a black inheritance to (ostensibly) white people or homosexuality to (ostensible) heterosexuals has led to similar court action for defamation.[83] The passer thereby admits his "real" identity as a defect.

German liberalism convinced many Jews that Jewishness belonged in the private sphere; "assimilation" (i.e., adoption of dominant norms) in the public sphere.[84] Gay and black people earn some degree of grudging tolerance by confining their particular identities in the private sphere *even when these identities are known*. Liberal societies produce another manifestation of ghettoization compared to the feudal form. Liberalism tends to ease passing as a total concealment of identity, by ghettoizing identity in the "private" sphere. The public sphere requires the presentation of Gentile, white, and heterosexual masks.[85] Nonhegemonic or "liberal" oppressive societies *permit* social withdrawal into a nascent community and a private identity, but also *require* that withdrawal, demanding continued invisibility. Dominant norms must be accepted in letter if not in spirit.

Psychological Withdrawal

A cautious, low profile conservatism among the inferiorized aims toward decreasing visibility and "compensating" for a disfavored identity. Compensatory conservatism may partake of the duplicity of "passing" and present mimetic behavior, while retaining elements of the masochistic "exchange fantasy" which offers self-limiting behavior for the promise of toleration. "Overvisible" behavior[86] among fellow members is strongly condemned, because, as the argument runs, it is the "loudmouthed" black, the "pushy" Jew, and the "swish" homosexual who give the rest a "bad name."

People exposed to chronic physical and psychological stress frequently experienced a dissociation from their hostile environment, seen as apathy or cynicism. Studies of former prisoners of war, for example, reveal "withdrawal from involvement with the environment and a constriction of overt behavior and emotional responses."[87] Ghettoization develops as a strategy coping with domination in the personal as well as the social sphere. Spontaneous emotions, actions, and wishes are "ghettoized" within the mind. The "low profile" attitude demands a guardedness or apparent impassiveness toward outside threat. The heightened insecurity of the inferiorized situation shapes a seemingly stoical response.

Among slaves, "where labor was sometimes exploited ruthlessly and punishments were brutal . . . the slave was profoundly apathetic, full of depression and gloom, and seemingly less hostile than indifferent toward the white man who controlled him."[88] The effort to minimize the hazards of a high-risk environment stifles active outreach. In highly oppressive situations where alternatives are most severely reduced, "lethargy, submission, and passive sabotage are more typical than aggression"[89] as reactions to frustration.

Statistical epidemiology of mental illness tends to be inconclusive because of variations produced by different allocation of funds for mental health care in various jurisdictions, local and historical definitions of "insanity," disparity of health care reaching different social classes, and opacity of categories describing disorders. A possible linkage between inferiorization and mental states characterized by severe withdrawal suggests itself. The neutralization of anxiety produced by inferiorization through alcohol and other drug dependencies merits further investigation.

Heightened insecurity provokes increased wariness. A problematized social environment obviates complacency. Observers have tended to label this special sensitivity "obsessive concern"[90] or "paranoia." Freud believed homosexuality and paranoia to be intrinsically linked. Blindness to social oppression allows the attribution of "persecution complexes" to gay people in psychiatry. All three groups discussed here have been periodically labeled "paranoid."[91]

Withdrawal may present even a kinesic manifestation. The restrained, "cramped" style of the ghetto Jew has been observed.[92] Bieber et al. speculate that the so-called effeminate appearance of some gay men arises from their "constricted" and "inhibited" mannerisms.[93] Its resemblance to "femininity" raises the question of the origin of "feminine" behavior among women as perhaps part of the stance of a powerless subject who learns the mannerisms of petitioning and acquiescence.

Success in carving out even a restricted life space tends to inspire caution among the inferiorized. Rather than resist a known evil which nevertheless tolerates one's survival, there arises a tendency to "leave well enough alone." Withdrawal fails to threaten the oppressive order; the larger social structure remains as it is. This passive conservatism receives further impetus from a tendency to conform rigorously to the dominant rationality as if to compensate for a nonrational identity. The effort to prove one's "normality" leads to meticulous fulfillment of all other demands of the established social order. Nineteenth-century Jews became preoccupied with "proving" their patriotism (while being suspected as traitors) by leaping into nationalist movements.[94] Those intent on being "good Germans," "good Frenchmen," and "good Americans" denounce Jews who fail to adopt wholeheartedly behaviors demanded by superordinate groups. "The immortal, the nonconformist, the radical, the intellectual, the crooked, the overreligious, the atheistic, these Jewish types and others, it is felt, provoke the Gentile and endanger the position of those Jews who conform."[95] Jews during the 1950s espionage trials in the United States fervently believed in the Rosenbergs' guilt and the necessity of the death sentence to demonstrate that Jews too follow the rules— only more so.[96] Fearful conservatism accompanies the withdrawal strategy. "Perhaps better manners on the subway would mitigate anti-Jewish feeling; perhaps if Jews did not appear in public at all . . ."[97]

Compensatory overconformity prompts the black man to seek esteem in displays of "masculinity" and conspicuous consumption.[98] Frazier observes, "By echoing the opinions of the white community the intellectual leaders of the black bourgeoisie hope to secure the approval and recognition of the white propertied classes with whom they seek identification."[99] Among gay males the collection of status symbols and rigid adherence to norms of masculine conduct manifest compensatory conservatism. Altman remarks, "It is a strange paradox that homosexuals, who suffer from the opprobrium of 'respectable' society, are often its most stalwart defenders."[100]

Generally widespread methods of demonstrating status, such as displays of wealth (conspicuous consumption), fashionability, membership in the "right" clubs and churches, identification with the leisure classes or with royalty, provide obvious avenues for status compensation among the inferiorized as well as for everyone else.[101]

Scrupulous adherence to middle-class norms aims toward avoidance of the composite portrait in the struggle for respectability. In Sartre's words, "They have allowed themselves to be poisoned by the stereotype that others have of them, and they live in fear that their acts will correspond to this stereotype."[102]

Guilt-Expiation Rituals

Sacrifice is an ancient institution which, as a public practice, has fallen into disfavor. Yet ritual sacrifices continue to be performed in the everyday lives of inferiorized peoples as the final act to the primordial guilt drama. Sacrifice has been classically conceived as "the destruction of a victim for the purpose of maintaining or restoring a right relationship of man to the sacred order. It may effect a bond of union with the divinity to whom it is offered, or constitute a peculiar expiation and propitiation to 'cover,' 'wipe out,' neutralize or carry away evil and guilt contracted wittingly or unwittingly."[103] Sacrifice remains rooted in the masochistic "permanent exchange" fantasy. The sacrifier inflicts deprivations upon himself or herself in a magical contract with the transcendent, reified Dominator.[104] The dominating social order is postulated as given. "But since this reality is taken to be the form and shape of the unchangeable, consciousness is unable of itself to cancel that reality." The reified consciousness believes happiness to be "an external gift, which the unchangeable here hands over for the consciousness to make use of."[105] The guilt which arises in the confrontation with the omnipotent other levies a final toll in the form of self-inflicted humiliation.[106] The primitive social function endures in the modern rites; in the words of the anthropologists, Henri Hubert and Marcel Mauss, "By expiation they redeem themselves from social obloquy, the consequence of error, and re-enter the community. . . . The social norm is thus maintained without danger to themselves, without diminution for the group."[107]

The guilt-based response to domination becomes habituated as a ceremonial. Its reenactment functions as "an *action for defense* or *insurance, a protective measure*."[108] Chinese thought-reform culminated in ritual "confession" as atonement for imputed crimes.[109] Modern social masochism reveals itself in widespread practices of everyday life: psychosomatic illnesses, hypochondria, self-abasement, depression, failure- or accident-proneness, obsessive cleanliness.[110]

Guilt-expiation rituals are incipient in the compensatory conservatism of inferiorized peoples (as above). They become most clearly evident in certain self-mutilating alterations. Plastic surgery upon the "Jewish" physiognomy performs a sacrificial ritual for Gentile society.[111] The arduous process of straightening hair and lightening skin in black people suggests something more than a method of escaping from identity.[112] Baldwin reflects autobiographically,

One's hair was always being attacked with hard brushes and combs and Vaseline: it was shameful to have "nappy" hair. One's legs and arms and face were always being greased, so that one would not look "ashy" in the wintertime. One was always being mercilessly scrubbed and polished, as though in the hope that a stain could thus be washed away—I hazard that the Negro children of my generation, anyway, had an earlier and more painful acquaintance with soap than any other children anywhere.[113]

Herbert Hendin's (wholly inadequate) analysis of black suicide turned up, with remarkable frequency, a double guilt syndrome centering around the subjects' blackness and homosexuality. Suicide, the ultimate self-sacrifice, terminated lives (in several instances) of guilt-ridden, unaccepted (homo)sexuality directed toward whites among young black men.[114]

The masochistic orientation of gay people appearing before psychiatrists has been noted.[115] Michael Riordan typifies the sense of self-annihilation experienced during aversion "therapy" in an autobiographical article entitled "Capital Punishment."[116] "Voluntary" acquiescence to extended electroshock constitutes a punishing ritual exacted by heterosexual society in which the gay person "atones" for his imputed transgression. Sacrificial mutilation is epitomized in "transsexual" surgery. Castration "fits" the gay man back into the reified moral order by reasserting the primacy of heterosexual norms. As Thomas Kando remarks:

Unlike normal females, transsexuals have a deviant past while subscribing to conservative middle-class values, the exact reverse of an increasing number of women. Ironically, transsexuals wish to be women but end up approximating men's sexual conservatism. While some militancy among them has been reported (. . .) most can still be typified as the Uncle Toms of the sexual liberation movement, in sharp contrast with other sexual minorities.[117]

Magical Ideologies

The guilt-based response to domination assumes or postulates an immutable order whose logic the subject struggles to divine.[118] The contradiction between the dominated subjects' set of life possibilities, and rules and expectations presented as adequate by bourgeois society, produces failure and frustration. The heightened insecurity of the inferiorized situation demands new knowledge congruent with the real life situation. In the "tension" or "gap" of this social contradiction which preconditions the lives of the subordinated, arise speculative systems rooted in the interest of ameliorating life. Ideological reconciliations of this life contradiction produce a range of nonpracticable systems affirming the reification of power in the dominating order. The masochistic attitude externalizes the subjectivity of the subject in the oppressive other, then seeks to recover it by means of a "secret" contract.[119] Lukács' sociology of knowledge provides the cue to the understanding of ideologies:

> Mythologies are always born where two terminal points, or at least two stages in a movement, have to be regarded as terminal points without its being possible to discover any concrete mediation between them and the movement. . . . But mythology inevitably adopts the structure of the problem whose opacity had been the cause of its own birth.[120]

Magical ideologies dissolve as people are able to effectively master their own life situation. Dissolution of oppressive contradictions eliminates the ground for mythological divinations of the workings of domination. The collapse of taken-for-granted methods of coping with the world, however, reintroduces the possibility of mythologization. Disaster, for example, provides the conditions for the development of millenarian ideologies: "The disaster victim, for whom the ordinary cues and landmarks of living have been removed, is left passive, receptive to suggestion, and in need of a substitute environment. He requires a new configuration of social relationships and values to explain his new predicament."[121] Millenarianism among peasants similarly develops out of crop failures and famine.[122] Alfred Schutz and Thomas Luckmann describe the universality of the phenomenon:

> the "suspicion" of a fundamental inadequacy of the life worldly stock of knowledge . . . if it affects the various moments of the relative opacity of the lifeworld in general (mostly through the shock of "crises" not easily mastered), can motivate a "leap" into non-everyday provinces of reality. From these provinces the lifeworldly stock of knowledge can appear as completely insufficient. The world can become a mystery that becomes transparent only by means of knowledge, superordinated to everyday reality.[123]

This "disaster" and "suspicion" are inescapable moments in the ontogenesis of every inferiorized person. His or her discovery of self as inferiorized, i.e., awareness of the contradiction of his or her life situation,[124] constitutes a crisis which is endemic. The inferiorized person, as we have seen, falls back on a variety of strategies for coping with domination in abandoning the inadequate socially given stock of knowledge. The dominated are phenomenologically disaster victims in extenuation, thereby rendered susceptible to magical ideologies as first attempts to deal adequately with a hostile environment.

Magical ideologies, then, represent a form of "understanding" social reality in "bad faith." They remain trapped in the masochistic attitude, "ceding to someone else full power and authority to fix and prescribe what actions are to be done."[125] Internal blinders shield the subject from confrontation with the real menace to himself or herself posed by the inferiorized situation. In his celebrated analysis of Lola Voss, Ludwig Binswanger describes her compulsive superstitiousness as "clinging to an alleged, blindly operating power, and evasion of the opportunity to retrieve oneself from thrownness and return to being one's real self. . . . Through superstition the existence [Dasein] salvages whatever remainders of 'world,' and thus of the self, that can be salvaged from existential anxiety. Without the foothold of superstition, the existence [Dasein] would sink into the night of naked horror or lose itself 'head over heels' to the world."[126] The superstitious seek to induce order into a highly uncertain and threatening environment to gain at least the illusion of mastery and thus security. Wartime bombing in Britain, for example, created the condition for popular rituals and personal self-denials practiced magically to "ward off" the terror from the skies.[127]

These magical attempts to make sense of the world manifest themselves as neurosis or schizophrenia,[128] popular fantasies,[129] astrology and superstition, messianism and chiliasm. Psychoanalysis of black people frequently reveals redemption fantasies of rescue from persecution by whites, or change of color in self or one's children.[130] Astrology, which provides another popular avenue of escape from anxiety, flourishes during times of uncertainty or crisis. Alvin Poussaint, a black psychiatrist, notes: "Longing to impose an order on man's life, which otherwise seemed ruled by chance and caprice, men began to study the stars hoping to discover a link between their course and that of human events. . . . The belief that each man's destiny is ruled by the planets has helped give blacks feelings of self-importance, fate control and security."[131]

Messianism stems from the masochistic attitude which hopes for divine or magical release from oppression. Passive waiting for *mana* characterizes the faith embodied in Judaic doctrine, an aspiration developed by an enslaved people and retained through centuries of persecution.[132] Black religion maintains the same passive attendance to divine bounty[133] (an orientation traceable to the Jewish inheritance in Christianity). Salvation in an afterlife figured prominently in the religion of American slaves[134] and continues in modern religious fatalism and submission.[135] "They [blacks] are urged to confine their ambition to affairs of the soul and forget earthly power and position."[136] The black church counsels renunciation of "material things" and of hostility and violence, in favor of divine protection. Oppression is rationalized as one of the mysterious workings and ways of God.[137] The prevalence of chiliastic cults among blacks[138] is paralleled by the rise of a popularly based fundamentalist church among gay people, called the Metropolitan Community Church. The participation of gay people in established religion has become increasingly visible with development of "gay caucuses" among almost all Jewish, Roman Catholic, and Protestant denominations. The pervasiveness of astrology merits further attention.

The holders of magical ideologies are wont to petition the "they" for signs of approval. Cosmic dispensations are read by "signs" drawn from the ideological lexicon. "Luck" plays an especially important role in the world-views of miners and sailors, individuals particularly vulnerable to their environment.[139] Gambling offers another idea system of this genre.

Myrdal notes, that among blacks, "some Spiritualist churches actually give out lucky numbers to be played"[140] Lotteries have frequently been sponsored by churches[141]; the state has increasingly displaced the church in this function as it has grown more omnipresent and powerful. The psychology of gambling, in any case, displays many of the characteristics of the other magical ideologies. Gambling requires extreme submissiveness before fate (a reification of the dominating other). The masochistic contract is fulfilled as the gambler offers a sacrifice (money) to "bribe" the "they" for signs of favor. The search for "grace" in gambling is clear in Zola's study of the working class:

One regular revealed the meaning of being a winner when amid the talk and praise of his selection, he yelled, "What do you think I am, a nobody?" It was a statement so appealing that it was taken up as a byword and used over and over again by the group.[142]

Gambling further provides the function of a guilt-expiation ritual, punishing the gambler through frequent losses.[143]

> Consciously or unconsciously he believes in his right to ask Fate for special privileges and protection. He hopes that Fate will give proof that he is favored over all the others and he will be permitted to win. Winning is the proof that he is lucky. It is pleasurable not only for the money (some gamblers play for little or no money), but it is a token of special privilege and power. The neurotic gambler seeks a sign from Fate that he is omnipotent.[144]

Magical ideologies manifest yet another mode of existence *within* the logic of domination. Magical ideologies bridge the contradictory poles of the oppressive relation reconciling the subordinated to the inferiorization dynamic. This "ideal" solution covers over the inequality which remains intact. "All mythology overcomes and dominates and shapes the forces of nature in the imagination and by imagination; it therefore vanishes with the advent of real mastery over them."[145]

The circuitry of masochism becomes reified in a series of ideological moments which recall the original sociological functions. The "offer" of divine or other-worldly rewards maintains the attitude of waiting among the inferiorized. The dominated "discover" an interest in the dominating system becoming attached to a universe of meanings which provides a semiadequate orientation to the world and solace for suffering. "The continuance, even the eternal duration of the system gives meaning to their whole existence. If it were to be dismantled in the future, just when they had the prospect of enjoying its advantages, all their merits and sacrifices would have been in vain."[146]

Christianity has long sanctioned the guilt-based response; in the early stages of the growth of capitalism, "the religion of the age assigned one virtue to the working classes, the virtue of bearing with Christian patience the inconveniences of a lower station."[147] The inferiorized groups examined here have also understood their life situation in these terms, as we have seen. It is on this point that Marxian and Freudian analyses coincide.

The gods retain their threefold task: they must exorcize the terrors of nature, they must reconcile men to the cruelty of Fate, particularly as it is shown in death, and they must compensate them for the sufferings and privations which a civilized life in common has imposed on them.[148]

Religion is the sigh of the oppressed creature, the feeling of a heartless world and the soul of soulless circumstances. It is the *opium* of the people.[149]

In-Group Hostility

> The whole complex of anti-Semitism among minority groups, and among Jews themselves, offers serious problems and deserves a study of its own. Even the casual observations provided by our sample suffice to corroborate the suspicion that those who suffer from social pressure may frequently tend to transfer this pressure onto others rather than to join hands with their fellow victims.
>
> —ADORNO et al.[150]

Hierarchy, as we have seen, provides a self-perpetuating dynamic.[151] The unequal distribution of status allows the dominated to "console" themselves through comparison with yet more degraded people. Domination constructs its own underpinnings with this "poor man's snobbery."

The solidification of inequality in this way occurs not only in the relation of superior and inferiorized groups. The inferiorization dynamic permeates the range of intergroup, in-group, and microsocial relations. Geographical or generational differences may be exploited to pass the composite portrait onto other inferiorized people in an attempt to "exonerate" oneself. Even within families, trait hierarchies may function to confer greater privileges upon one sibling over another. At the most fundamental level, intimate dyadic relationships display the dominant value hierarchy. Sexual aesthetics conditioning the most personal one-to-one relationships partake in the logic of domination.

Child psychologists have most thoroughly documented the internalization of dominant trait hierarchies in studies of black kindergartners and schoolchildren. In a series of studies developed after the Second World War, the tendency among blacks to devalue blacks has been repeatedly confirmed. The voluminous literature captures the predominant response of blacks who have found themselves in the ontogenetic crisis of discovering the self as inferiorized. The socially presented pseudochoice[152] is at this age less likely to be transcended.

The response is elicited through several different experimental techniques. The Clarks confirmed the widespread association of white with beauty and black with ugliness in a coloring exercise administered to primary schoolchildren, where the subjects were asked to color drawings of themselves.[153] H. Stevenson and E. Stewart, who presented hypothetical situations to 225 three—to—seven-year-olds, state: "A greater frequency of own-race rejection on the part of the Negro Ss compared to the white Ss is seen in the lower proportion of Negro Ss making own-race choices in selecting playmates, companions to go home with, and guests for a birthday party, and in selecting own-race dolls as looking more like themselves. The Negro Ss placed the Negro children in negative positions in the Incomplete stories more frequently than the white Ss placed white children in such positions. The Negro Ss chose Negroes more frequently as being an aggressor . . . , as being less likely to give aid . . . , as losing in a tug of war . . . , and as being a badman."[154] A 1967 replication of Clarks' classic 1939 experiment which requires three—to—eight-year-olds to express preference for white or black puppets, found "some evidence of an increase in white color preference among Negro children."[155] Porter invited kindergarten children to insert black or white dolls into a playhouse at periodic intervals to dramatize a presented storyline. The most rigorous and comprehensive of such studies of the self-perception of black children, published in 1971, concludes:

> Blacks have significantly lower preference for dolls of their own race than whites do, and both black and white children tend to prefer the white dolls. Since white preference is high and correct self-classification is low for black children, it seems that the black child's self-identification may be strongly affected by his feelings about race.[156]

Similar conclusions are drawn from psychoanalytic interpretations of children's drawings. Coles characterizes the drawings of a six-year-old black girl caught in the school desegregation turmoil:

> She drew white people larger and more lifelike. Negroes were smaller, their bodies less intact. A white girl we both knew to be her own size appeared several times taller. While Ruby's own face . . . lacked an eye in one drawing, an ear in another, the white girl never lacked any features. . . . Moreover, Ruby drew the white girl's hands and legs carefully, always making sure that they had the proper number of fingers and toes. Not so with her own limbs, or those of any other Negro children she chose (or was asked) to picture. A thumb or forefinger might be missing, or a whole set of toes. The arms were shorter, even absent or truncated.[157]

This very concrete indicator of the menaced subject represents a reflection of the self opposed to the hostile, dominant other. The distortion and absence of limbs and diminution of own physical size suggest the essence of the inferiorized experience: a sense of narrowness, crampedness, enclosedness—confinement to a "closet"; a sense of impotence, ineffectiveness, desubjectivization. Porter discovered the same tendency in "the lower-class Negro boy who drew himself as a small, grey blob in the corner of the page, asking that it be labeled with his name (. . .), or by the lower-class Negro girl who carefully drew a person and then picked up a blue crayon and obliterated the figure completely with systematic strokes. When asked what she had drawn, the child said sadly that she had produced a picture of herself."[158]

The research literature confirming these findings extends well beyond these few examples.[159] The most recent research presents (conflicting) evidence that greater self-acceptance is appearing among black children of the 1970s.[160] The statistical generalizations here, however, bear the defects enumerated above (see section entitled "Caveat").

Acceptance of the color hierarchy imposed by whites appears among black adolescents. Social rejection of dark-skinned peers and preference for the light, is evident in Johnson's study of 2,250 black youths.[161] Self-devaluation appears especially salient among black youths as compared to their white peers. Hauser states in his examination of lower-class, black, male adolescents: "Interwoven throughout the [preceding] narratives—and through the years of interviews—were the Negroes' degraded self-estimates, their unremitting belittlement of themselves. . . . The themes of worthlessness, undesirability, and uselessness recurred in many contexts. There were no Negroes for whom these themes were subtle. For the whites such topics when present seemed minor: worthlessness did not assume the same unmistakable prominence."[162]

The most frequent answer to complete the sentence "When I look in the mirror I . . .," among both black and white youths was: "I see myself," in a study by Deutsch. "But 20 percent of the Negro boys give such dysphoric responses as 'I cry,' 'am sad,' 'look ugly,' and the like, while such responses occur in only 9 percent of the white boys."[163] The struggle to come to grips with inferiorized identity "reverberates" throughout the adolescent's being-in-the-world. His efforts to assert himself—to gain mastery over the means for survival and action, cannot evade the restrictions which precondition his existence. Remarks one young man: "There is not too much for being a Negro. I would rather be called anything but that, but since I'm one I have to take it."[164]

Black college students (at a black university) appear willing to believe that whites have better personality adjustment in terms of general activity, restraint, ascendance, emotional stability, objectivity, and personal relations.[165] Blacks rate whites superior in intelligence, mechanical ability, trustworthiness, and willingness to work, granting themselves only conversation ability and sex appeal.[166] The seduction of inferiorized people into adoption of the composite portrait in their own self-perception persists.[167] Some themes, such as hypersexuality, may be taken up with some pride.

Increasing consolidation in the black community strengthens the black counterreality, which asserts itself in black pride and black power. The media visibility of the black liberation movement tends to obscure the entrenched coping strategies examined here. Sloganeering has not swept away the socialization of generations, though it represents a move toward rejection of guilt-based and ghettoized responses to domination. Frazier delineates the liberalization which rests as a veneer over the more deeply ingrained habits of oppression:

> While pretending to be proud of being a Negro, they ridicule Negroid physical characteristics and seek to modfy or efface them as much as

possible. Within their own groups they constantly proclaim that "niggers" make them sick. . . . They are insulted if they are identified with Africans.[168]

Poussaint observes the same phenomenon:

It is surprising how many blacks are still embarrassed by and opposed to "au naturel" hair. Teenage girls complain that their parents won't let them wear their hair in a natural. Otherwise militant parents will protest that a natural doesn't look wholesome or decent, when it's on *their daughter!* Some conditioned blacks argue that only girls with "bad hair" should wear their hair in a natural. . . . Despite the black power movement, many blacks have a long way to go psychologically before they will accept their blackness.[169]

The adoption and practice of inferiorization among the inferiorized themselves is evident in numerous contexts. The distribution of power, privilege, and freedom according to a trait-hierarchy tends to be duplicated among relations of the inferiorized with each other. The lower castes in India affirm the caste system in their rivalry for minor comparative advantages in prestige. Many Untouchable groups, for example, practice degrees of Untouchability with each other, refusing commensualism or intermarriage with other inferiorized people.[170] A 1960 sociological survey of lower castes found 86 percent willing to describe those who object to caste conventions as a traitor, compared to 48 percent among the upper castes.[171] The contempt of the working class for those in low-status occupations or unemployed has been noted.[172]

The modern history of European Jews illustrates the dynamic. Nineteenth-century nationalism prompted many Jews to "assimilate" through patriotic identification. National Jews frequently passed the anti-Semitic stereotype onto foreign Jews asserting national loyalties over the common oppression of Jewishness. French Jews in the Dreyfus period, chose the honorific term *israélites* for themselves protesting along with French anti-Semites against immigration of German and East European *juifs*.[173] Dutch Jews expressed some resentment toward German Jews fleeing Nazism.[174] German Jews habitually distinguished themselves from " 'culturally alien' and 'intellectually inferior' " East European Jews.[175] Kurt Lewin recounts an incident from his experience:

"The most striking [incident] for me, was the behavior of a well-educated Jewish refugee from Austria on the occasion of his meeting a couple of other Jewish refugees. In a tone of violent hatred, he burst out into a defense of Hitler on the ground of the undesirable characteristics of the German Jew."[176] Rivalries and suspicion have been traditional between the Ashkenazic, Sephardic, and Hassidic.[177] Generational divisions permit an Oedipal displacement of the composite portrait, where the assimilating second generation stigmatizes the first for its "Jewish" defects.[178]

The composite portrait poisons even face-to-face interaction, alienating individual from individual. A *Privatdozent* recalls traveling with Jewish friends on a train in Germany in 1937. The appearance of colleagues from the university prompts the *Dozent* to explain his association with his traveling companions as a "chance" encounter. The Jewish friends later apologize for their presence embarrassing the *Dozent* before his colleagues.[179] The inferiorized person may attempt to abstract himself from the group, stigmatizing all other group members as "inferior." Here we return to "bad faith," conversion, and cooptation. Bernstein remarks:

> The individual . . . assumes the inferiority of all or nearly all Jews, except himself. For the individual always lives under the illusion, so senseless to any impartial observer, that he himself has reached the heights of the non-Jewish qualities.[180]

A defensive attitude seizes the atomized individual; guilt infuses perception of compatriots. Writes Simon Herman:

> Always I had to fight that feeling within me of being ashamed of them. I hated the way they ate, the way they spoke loudly in tramcars, the way they overdressed, and the more I hated them the more I defended them.[181]

Status differences existed among black slaves: house slaves believed themselves superior to field slaves;[182] church officials to laymen;[183] freed blacks to contemporary slaves; mulattoes to pure blacks.[184] The color hierarchy distances light-skinned from dark-skinned blacks.[185] Rivalries flourish in the distinctions.[186] Even privileges within families may accord to the color hierarchy.[187] The dark-skinned black who attempts familiarity with the light, before a white audience, risks rejection by and discreditation of the light-skinned black.

> In the eyes of the whites he is caught red-handed in a debasing revelation; he thus stands accused until he can clear himself. If he can make it obvious to the whites that he has put a supercilious distance between himself and the darker person, very little or no explanation may be necessary. But if the darker person be a relative, say his mother, he . . . may . . . proceed to estrange himself from her for the occasion. He may decide to recognize her and thus reveal the true extent of his pollution.[188]

Members of inferiorized groups become the target not only of aggression from the superordinate,[189] but from fellow members. Resentment against the dominant other can be vented only at a suicidal risk; the racist dynamic deflects hostility back toward the already dominated. The black rate for crimes against persons exceeds the white rate by ten times.[190] The black death rate from homicide is also ten times the white rate.[191] Blacks then are more often the victims of crimes committed by blacks.[192]

Intermarriage statistics reflect the trait hierarchy in valuation of others as a marriage partner. Exogamous marriage among blacks and Jews is primarily a male prerogative. The statistics suggest a status trade-off: the upwardly mobile, white-collar male more frequently marries a lighter-skinned or Gentile wife.[193] Freeman et al., found that upwardly mobile wives are more likely than downwardly mobile wives to be lighter than husbands; blue-collar men are more likely to be lighter than their wives if the woman is from a white-collar family.[194] The status exchange is potentially destructive to a relationship where imbalance can arise over time. Grier and Cobbs report a case of a woman who appeared before them for psychiatric treatment, having become pathologically alarmed with her husband's upward mobility subsequent to their marriage. With his success, she feared abandonment for a lighter wife.[195]

The inferiorized person whose sense of value, aesthetics, or status remains informed by the trait hierarchy cannot but perceive himself or herself as unworthy of admiration or affection. Long-term, intimate relationships with like-situated others are sabotaged by an inability to recognize worth, beauty, or admirability in the other. The other confronts the subject as a persistent reminder of his or her own identity. Guilt-based or ghettoized responses to inferiorization require repression or privatization of own identity and contempt for others who embody it. Conflict is often rooted in the white ideal which stands over black relations,[196] the Gentile ideal over Jewish relations,[197] the heterosexual sex-role ideal which stands over gay relations.[198]

The logic of domination underlies the valuation of (perceived-as) masculine traits among gay men. The contempt held by gay men for effeminate men is well documented.[199] Again, displacement of the composite portrait onto a selected portion of the inferiorized group allows the ghettoized to "save" themselves for "respectability" through compensatory conformity. Devaluation of other gay people casts a pall over successful long-term erotic relationships. As Altman remarks: "I know in reflecting on my own experiences how far popular beliefs about homosexuality, and the guilts that I felt, prevented me from accepting that I had fallen in love. Indeed, with memories of those myths that deny the homosexual the experience of love, I fled the first man who might have become my lover and sought an (unsuccessful) affair with a woman."[200] The same sentiment is expressed by a guilt-ridden lesbian interviewed by David H. Rosen: "Both are closed to me: the male because I *cannot* establish such a relationship, and the female because I must not establish such a relationship."[201] The contaminated aesthetic appears in the frequency in which the German gay male specifies his preferred sexual type as "a completely normal looking type, that couldn't possibly appear homosexual to anyone."[202]

The heterosexual ideal negates gay sexuality ultimately in the attraction to heterosexuals *per se*. Attachment to "straight," bisexual, and married individuals reinforces the masochistic orientation from which it springs, with assured failure to establish a continuing relationship.[203] Transsexualism among males[204] is associated with preference for only heterosexual male partners.[205] Reciprocated affection here delegitimizes the "masculinity" or heterosexuality of the other, terminating the attraction.

Escape from gay identity may be attempted by rigid adherence to heterosexual role requirements. This strategy requires genitalization of homosexuality (as strictly sexual) with avoidance of affection or defined-as feminine (insertee) sexual acts. The ideology of the "hustler" requires repression of emotional involvement and acceptance of money for escape from gay identity. John Rechy's novel *City of Night*, on the hustlers' world, specifies the bad-faith orientation: "Whatever a guy does with other guys, if he does it for money, that dont make him queer. Youre still straight. It's when you start doing it for free, with other guys, that you start growing wings."[206] Rechy adds, "Sex for me became the mechanical reaction of This on one side, that on the other. And the boundary must not be crossed."[207]

Laud Humphreys' study of washroom sex confirms the prevalence of married men, "closet queens" (approximately: those relying most upon withdrawal and escape from identity), and bisexuals.[208] The vitiation of interpersonal relationships among the inferiorized arises in the guilt-based and ghettoized strategies to domination. Subsequent interviews with the participants in rapid, impersonal sex reveal psychological isolation of homosexuality into a mental compartment encased by compensatory conservatism. Humphreys remarks, "they share highly conservative social and political views, surrounding themselves with an aura of respectability that I call the breastplate of righteousness."[209] The sexual fetishization of anatomy recurs as a syndrome among the guilt-ridden gay people who appear before psychiatrists.[210] These findings are congruent with the association by Adorno et al. of the authoritarian personality with emotionless, instrumentalized sexuality.[211] Gay men living with other gay men conversely show more self-acceptance and less guilt. The rejection of guilt-based or avoidance responses to gay identification accompanies exploration of the affectional-emotional possibilities of homosexuality. Weinberg and Williams concretize the relation in correlating less depression, interpersonal awkwardness, loneliness, guilt, shame, or anxiety, with "dancing 'slow' dances and necking with other males" and development of long-term relationships.[212]

The prevalence of these same sexual syndromes among superordinate groups demonstrates the complexity of the issues. The logic of domination contributes one element to the more general rationalization of the erotic sphere and the emotional inhibitions demanded by the male sex role.

The Arts of Contraversion

The man of *ressentiment* is neither upright
nor naïve nor honest and straightforward
with himself. His soul *squints*; his spirit
loves hiding places, secret paths, and back
doors, everything covert entices him as *his*
world, *his* security, *his* refreshment; he
understands how to keep silent, how not
to forget, how to wait, how to be provi-
sionally self-deprecating and humble.

—NIETZSCHE[213]

As the subordinated develop their own society, the possibility
of casting away accommodating facades becomes increasingly realized. The social construction of counterinterpretations of reality
through new communicative networks, literary and artistic traditions, nurture new expectations and a willingness to subvert the
delimiting rationality. Passive resistance, apathy, and withdrawal
become superseded by contraversive tactics, both ideological and
practical. A prideful sensibility begins to come to grips with the
thought-systems which underpin the oppressive system. "Crimes
of omission," which refuse to contribute to the reconstruction of
dominating institutions, lay the groundwork for public manifestations of discontent. The subordinated come to challenge everyday relations to challenge standards of deference, the privatization
of "disrespectable" behaviors, ridicule presented as "humor."

We have surveyed the range of life strategies by which people
cope with but do not overcome inferiorization. The guilt-based
responses, escape, and withdrawal continue to fall under the sign
of compliance insofar as the socially received order stands stead-
fast. When hegemonic oppression gives way to liberal toleration,
the bounds of permissible behavior remain to protect the established distribution of freedoms and privileges. "Toleration" allows
a "private" sphere; an atomized, personal zone; at best, a bounded
social space for "difference." These ghettos require renunciation
by the inferiorized of the life possibilities reserved for the
superordinate.

Nietzsche's portrayal of the slave morality captures the frustration and pain of the oppressed condition. He mistakenly bifurcates humanity into slaves and noblemen, failing to recognize the universality of the slave's actions, i.e., the will to power negotiating the confines of socially structured limitations solidified over many generations. *Ressentiment* is the impotent rage of the subject reacting to confinement who is forced to repress himself or herself in the interests of survival. *Ressentiment* is opposition cathected into socially "safe" channels (in Marcuse's terms, "repressive desublimation"), which thereby preserves the system of inequality. "Guilt-engendered activity is at best *restitution* (sacrifice, propitiation, atonement) which rarely frees, but brings with it resentment and frustration rage which in turn feed new guilt into the [psychological] system."[214]

Yet *ressentiment* is clearly the sign of discontent and opposition; its impulse remains ultimately contraversive and noncompliant. Even the masochist reveals his subjectivity. Intentionality, which characterizes human consciousness itself, cannot but move outward, act, and thereby constitute the demand for freedom. The behavior reviewed here reveals *in every instance* the intention of improved understanding or mastery of surrounding obstacles despite its contribution to a social system which reproduced the obstacles. Kafka's protagonist in *The Trial* is essentially ambivalent: the oppression which encompasses him demands submission—even a religious attitude toward it; at the same time, revolt simmers within.[215] Bettelheim tells a simple story of how to follow concentration camp rules in order to obtain adequate medical treatment.[216] The paradox is epitomized by Grier and Cobbs, "Sambo may well have been our first black militant."[217] Memmi, in reflecting upon his personal odyssey from mimesis to self-affirmation, remarks, "I sought not so much to reject myself as to conquer the world. I rejected myself as a Jew because I was rejecting the place assigned to me, and in which my people were content to remain."[218]

With the first stages of community formation flourish the arts of contravention. Slaves knew how to mitigate their condition with "stubbornness" or "mischief." "Carelessness" and abuse of property demonstrated the slaves' contempt, sabotaged the functioning of the oppressive system, and exposed them to the least possible retribution. Feigned illnesses and pregnancies, brief conspiracies, and escape into the bush run continuously through slave chronicals.[219] The inferiorized develop a cleverness for "beating the system" and compensating for inequalities, plus a "stupidity" for facilitating the workings of a system which acts against them. Jaroslav Hašek's novel, *The Good Soldier Schweik*, exemplifies the latter strategy of neutralizing control, by, in this case, army superiors. Every dominated group knows the power of derisive collusion. Overenthusiastic responses to pious statements of control ideologies embarrass their propagators and signal the group's solidary resistance to its implementation. Schoolboys are masters at this. Jewish, black, and gay people are adept at special intonations and nuanced vocabularies annihilating hallowed presentations of reality. Superordinate members may be unaware or somewhat uneasy of the subversive trend readily appreciated by inferiorized audiences.[220] The art of verbal aggression becomes highly refined in the black practice of the "dozens."[221] Yiddish is renowned for its "Why not?" challenge to questions which demand a simple "Yes."[222] The camp wit aims unerringly at pretention and hypocrisy.

Humor is an art of contraversion which reflects the condition of the subject. Humor allows an aggressive impulse which remains repressed in other circumstances.[223] As with other forms of hostility, inferiorized fellows present the first target. A recurring anti-Semitism marks traditional Jewish humor.[224] The humor of black people displays a similar tendency to ridicule blacks, to even a greater extent than white ridicule of blacks.[225] At the same time, cultural difference is reaffirmed; inferiorization itself may enter into the ridicule. "There is seldom a serious promise to change the offending situation or to meet the demands of the enemy. All contain a kind of melancholy resignation and occasionally a stubborn pledge: This is the way we are and will be as long as we are Jewish"[226] or black or gay.

Humor sponsored by social solidarity aims toward social satire and annihilation of superordinate ideologies. This humor participates in the sensibilities peculiar to the community: chutzpah, soul, camp. These extremely rich artful practices defy categorization. They belong to the progressive movement of community, culture, and enrichment of meanings. Each is inextricably rooted in the historical particularity of the group; comparison can only pass over the essential feature of each sensibility: its uniquenesss as an expression of cultural individuality.

A few comments on social function are in order. Each arises profoundly from the "we-feeling" of the group and indicates its solidarity. Each accomplishes ongoingly the transvaluation of values necessary for the development of a counterreality adequate to the group's existential situation. Each tends to remold the group as an "elect." A phrase, a motion, or manner of dress draws the cloak of togetherness about actor and audience. It conspires against the unitiated, the conventional, the bourgeois, against "decency" and propriety.

Soul springs from black pride, from perseverance before adversity, from sensuality and black music, from pain and the religious heritage. "Soul is the *graceful* survival under impossible circumstances."[227] Soul is aesthetic and practice.

Camp dramatizes the absurdity and arbitrariness of social convention. It parodies everyday expectations, naturality, normality, and whatever else is taken for granted. Camp toys with and mauls a tasteless and sometimes cruel order. It is a deadly serious frivolity, "a rendition of the straight world as impotent, laughable, harmless, and ultimately an aspect of the gay world."[228] Camp is aesthetic and practice.

These are sensibilities grown out of *suffering*, viz., "that tension of the soul in unhappiness which cultivates its [the soul's] strength, its shudders face to face with great ruin, its inventiveness and courage in enduring, persevering, interpreting, and exploiting suffering, and whatever has been granted to it of profundity, secret, mask, spirit, cunning, greatness."[229] Inferiorization ironically *liberates* creative, innovative potential among artists and intellectuals whose conflictual social situation explodes conventionality. Barred from the frictionless social roles reserved for members of groups that set their rules, they develop a genius for multiple identities, for puncturing the taken-for-granted world, and for revealing its inner workings.

The themes of this study could be reexplored in the language and literature of each group. The movement from masochism to affirmation manifests itself in novels and poetry—an analysis beyond the scope of this work.

V NOTES ON CONSOLIDATION

Assimilationism

> The subjects for whose sake the subjection,
> reification and demythization of nature
> were begun, are themselves so repressed,
> reified and disenchanted in self regard,
> that even their emancipatory efforts be-
> come the contrary: the confirmation of the
> context of delusion in which they are
> imprisoned.
>
> WELLMER[1]

The medieval intolerance of refugees from its closed and rigid order of social positions metamorphoses into "assimilationism" in liberal, bourgeois societies. Integration or "assimilation" into the opportunity structure open to dominant groups requires aban-donment of the inferiorized identity, world-view, and social net-works. This demanding total transformation of the self, then, is to introduce the individual to *candidacy* for the life possibilities of the superordinate. Statistical analysis reveals that the assimi-lationist route benefits a very few, while reaffirming the general inequality of the group.

Liberalist toleration transforms the inferiorized from criminals, heretics, and slaves to minorities, deviants, and the "sick." Purges and pogroms give way to the treatment of "social problems." Here arises the "Jewish question," the "Negro problem," the "homosexual problem." The threat to social order posed by restive, inferiorized peoples can be met by another ideology. The formidable task of extermination can be laid aside, for preservation of the established distribution of freedom can be accomplished under the shield of "assimilation." Assimilationism promises a "deal." The identity, culture, and values of the inferiorized are to be negated (or at least concealed) for the *promise* or opportunity of improved life chances. Submission to the social rules which preserve the superordinance of the white, Gentile, heterosexual group(s) supposedly mitigates the barriers confining inferiorized existence. Goffmanesque "face-work" or "impression-management" are the requirements for concealing "faux pas" which might deprivatize "stigma."

Empirical research delineates a consistent portrait. Superordinate groups recruit a token sample for certain privileges, offering symbolic benefits to the larger group, e.g., cosmetic law reform or radical chic.[2] Like the wage-earner who works hard to benefit from the demands of the capitalist order and who may, in fact, attain amelioration of status and income, the assimilationist occasionally succeeds, at great cost, in improving his or her life chances, but fails to alter the overall social scheme allocating resources and privilege. The palliative to the Jewish or Negro or homosexual problem is presented as "education." "Good will" and tolerance are liberal prescriptions to smooth away discomfiting disorder. An ideological fog shrouds the fundamental distribution of power and privilege. Bernstein remarks, "the liberal will not be overly inclined to make a close investigation of enmity relations, as he is *a priori* convinced that they ought to fade away before his ethical postulates."[3]

We examined the responses of the subordinated in the last section of the preceding chapter. The assimilationist promise evokes an *angstful* struggle for the symbols of respectability and for closeted invisibility. The first community organizations seek "image"-improvement through "public relations" and concealment of "embarrassing" nonconformists. Liberals in both dominant and dominated groups conspire to suppress the disrespectable identity and its cultural heritage. Characterizing Jewish assimilationism, Memmi writes:

Their highest ambition was that no one might find anything to say about them at all; nor, moreover, about any Jew in the world. The Jews? What Jews? What are you talking about? They didn't see a thing. They spent their whole lives laboriously trying to make everyone believe in their non-existence. . . . But no one is deceived by the trick, and Jewish fate continues to stare the spectators in the face. . . . In the concentration camps, in front of the crematory furnaces, the Franco-Israelites repeated, like Saint Paul: "I am French. I am a French citizen!"[4]

Assimilationist blacks mirror the approach. Black businesses and organizations, evangelical churches, and jazz are abandoned for white institutions and cultural norms.

They have arranged a little isolated world for themselves and want to hear as little as possible about their being Negroes or the existence of a Negro problem. They make it a point not to read Negro papers or Negro books; they keep themselves and their children apart from "common Negroes."[5]

Closetry exists at a public level as well, when gay people set out to demonstrate their "normality." Tolerance is earned by making difference unspeakable.

The "good" homosexual does not mention the affairs he has from time to time or the men he is seeing. If he falls in love, he does not make others uncomfortable by trying to share his joy with them. If an affair comes to a sudden end, he does not embarrass his straight friends by telling them of his unhappiness. He should not mention having sex with other men, because most straight people find the whole idea distasteful. If he has a lover, the two of them should behave like gentlemen—straight gentlemen—in front of other people. This is particularly noticeable when it comes to displays of affection.[6]

The bourgeois gay press—for example, the widely circulated *Advocate*—conspires with assimilationism to demand of gay men that they "clean up their acts" by observing the strictures of conventional morality as a prerequisite for civil rights. When sex between consenting adults *in private* becomes legal, any affection expressed *in public* remains subject to prosecution for "indecent acts."

The assimilated Jew, the whitewashed black, and the closeted gay person hopes to reemerge in an uncontaminated guise. French and German Jews attempted to abandon the *juif* or *Jude* for the *israélite* or *Israelit*; American blacks tried out *colored people*, then *Negro*; homosexuals adopted *homophile*. Redesignation failed to create assimilation. Self-affirmation is signaled by a vocabulary turning back toward identity: *Jew, black, gay, or lesbian.*

Collective Resistance

Certain objective, historical conditions facilitate the impetus toward contraversive, self-affirmative modalities of coping with domination, and concomitant abandonment of guilt-based and withdrawal modes.

Community arises out of the collection of atomized individuals defined by an other retaining greater freedom and privilege for itself. Communication among like-situated people over time engenders social networks and language which nurture a new aggregation and understanding adequate to their peculiar situation. Everyday life together allows the development of a "lore" or common stock of knowledge. Shared experiences identify effective strategies for coping with social limitations, methods of survival and self-betterment, sources of freedom and joy. Brotherhood or sisterhood is not the simple correlate of, for example, physical resemblances; it is the mutual creation (socialization or understanding) of each member by the other. Says Sartre, "We are brothers insofar as . . . we are *our own sons,* our common invention."[7] Self-esteem studies have had difficulty in accounting for the *either* low *or* high self-esteem found among inferiorized people, failing to recognize the qualitative gap differentiating the experiences of isolated individuals governed by the superordinate reality paradigm and community-integrated members participating in the ongoing production of a particularly strong self-identity. The "leap" across the dialectical tension dividing these states is frequently experienced in the personal trauma of "coming out of the closet" for gay people, of encounter and immersion in blackness for black people,[8] of perhaps religious commitment or Zionism for Jews. Solidarization tends to mark increasing abandonment of guilt-based responses for self-affirmation. Sense of self, understanding, and effectiveness may indeed be enhanced through this process, as compared to the inherited identity taken for granted and passively assimilated by superordinate members. Warren observes: "gay time spent within gay spaces gains a highly exclusive, trusting, and valuable character by its very secrecy"; it provides "the sense of membership in an elect group, the warmth of belonging, and the security of a clear self-definition."[9]

We have observed how early community formations remain subordinated to the rationality of domination and reduplicate the oppressive order. We have seen how contraversive trends strengthen resistance simultaneously incipient in the community. There is, as Memmi remarks, a Jewishness, which is "completely positive."[10] Consolidation culminates in the movement to overcome the oppressive system and reorder social relations. The sociological conditions conducive to rebellion and revolution are inadequately understood and beyond the scope of this work. A compendium of behavior which helps reproduce the oppressive order inversely delineates the mechanisms to its transcendence. That concatenation of conditions (or, to recall Louis Althusser, "overdetermination") which brings about the push to transcendence requires clarification. Study of the three groups suggests an incomplete sketch of directions for research.

Acceleration of militancy of "class consciousness" requires: (1) a sense of class or group membership, a recognition of identity between self and like-situated others (in our terms, transcendence of the socially presented pseudochoice); (2) recognition of the divergence of own and other-group interests, i.e., the fundamental political foundation of the groups' relation; (3) a totalistic polarization governed by an idea or by several ideas of social alternatives.[11]

Movement through these stages appears to be enhanced by the following:

1. The existence of large numbers in the same class situations (i.e., an absence of internal social cleavages).[12]
2. Geographical concentration. The ghetto itself tends to fulfill this condition. Urban riots among black people in the United States occurred frequently in the summer, when large numbers of people congregated together in the streets.[13] The so-called "Stonewall Rebellion" that marked the birth of gay liberation flared up in midsummer in the largest gay ghetto in the United States, Greenwich Village.[14]

3. Identifiable targets. Black urban rioters attacked ghetto merchants and their property, police and their property.[15]
4. Sudden "events" or rapid changes in social position. War, natural catastrophes, and economic dislocations have precipitated millenarian movements.[16] Radicalization of workers occurs frequently in the first, proletarianized generation impressed into industry from agriculture.[17] Slave revolts followed economic depression.[18] Black urban riots were most frequently sparked by "the killing of, arrest of, or interference with black men and women by policemen."[19] Police harassment figures prominently in the development of gay militancy.[20]
5. An intellectual leadership with readily understood goals. Chiliastic fervor among Italian peasants produced appeals to God for rescue and "prophets who, though not unarmed, did not know what to do with their arms, and were defeated for ever."[21]

The perception of alternative remains central to the dynamic. The frequency of foreign-born leaders of black movements in the United States (from Nat Turner, to Marcus Garvey, to Stokely Carmichael) suggests different expectations or a heightened awareness of possibilities among those who can make cross-cultural comparisons. Even the first feeble gestures of assimilationist and apologist groups nurture liberatory aspirations. Even symbolic or token concessions can concretize socially available alternatives for inferiorized members and raise expectations. The impetus is toward resubjectivization of the reified subject; reformism may set the stage for militancy by generating greater confidence in own powers. The mere existence of organized cells identified with the inferiorized group as such, facilitates consolidation. "The institutional group, as an abstract skeleton of the united class, is a permanent invitation to unify; it is already a class sovereignty when the class is still entirely atomized."[22]

Alienation and Class

Freedom presents two aspects: the one
concerns its substance and purport—its
objectivity—the thing [in] itself; the other
relates to the form of freedom, involving
the consciousness of his activity on the
part of the individual; for freedom demands that the individual recognize himself in such acts, that they should be virtually his, it being his interest that the
results in question should be attained.

—HEGEL[23]

A phenomenology of oppression recognizing suffering where
it exists, must found any adequate liberatory analysis. The des-
ignation of oppressed classes solely by means of formal criteria
fails to remain historically flexible or dialectically embedded in
social reality. Understanding the concepts of "labor," "production," and "alienation" as fundamental sociological categories
(as Marx does in his early writings in embarking on the analysis
of oppression), permits a conceptual system adequate to recognizing oppression in the manifold places it is found.

Resubjectivization begins with being-for-itself. The revolutionary trend is immanent in everyday life which contravenes, if only
minimally, the rationality of oppression. "Being-for-itself
[Fürsichsein] is not a state but a process, for every external condition must continuously be transformed into a phase of self-realization, and each new external condition that arises must be
subjected to this treatment."[24] The progressive countertrend to socially structured limitations develops as the subject recognizes
himself or herself as an object of history and then acts, understanding his or her own unique historical situation.[25] Gramsci
strikes at the essence of "praxis":

the real philosopher is, and cannot be other than, the politician, the
active man who modifies the environment, understanding by environment the *ensemble* of relations which each of us enters to take part in.
. . . To create one's personality means to acquire consciousness of them

and to modify one's own personality means to modify the *ensemble* of these relations.[26]

For the inferiorized person, this process leads through the discovery of identity with like-situated fellows. The socially presented (pseudo)identity alienates the inferiorized person from his or her own actions. As we have seen, that person's social production is appropriated to reproduce a universe of practices and meanings which negates his or her own freedom. This denial of self is sanctified ideologically; the rhetoric of sin, sickness, and deviance congeals this self-estrangement as appropriate, legitimate, or natural. Wilhelm Reich declared in "What is Class Consciousness?":

> The reactionaries take advantage of the guilt feelings of mass individuals, of their ingrained modesty, their tendency to suffer privation silently and willingly, sometimes even happily. . . . To develop their class-consciousness, to bring them to the point of revolt, then, one must recognize the principle of self-denial as harmful, lifeless, stupid, and reactionary.[27]

The centrality of ostensibly psychological categories like black pride or gay pride or the *Jasagen zum Judentum*[28] policy among militants, arises from the movement of resubjectivization. In this context, Nietzsche's criterion for freedom becomes comprehensible. In recognizing the social production of guilt and its function in the preservation of social order, he questioned in *La Gaia Scienza*: "What is the seal of attained liberty? To be no longer ashamed of oneself."[29]

In his early, seminal meditations upon the nature of oppression and alienation, Marx reveals the phenomenological roots of the analysis which led out of Hegelian idealism to dialectical materialism. *Toward a Critique of Hegel's Philosophy of Law* indicates the touchstone which betrays the inadequacy of Hegel's system. Because suffering remains, free self-conscious society cannot have been attained. That Hegel's system could expel existing suffering from its purview convinced Marx of its "barrenness." Marx's criticism "ends with the doctrine that *man is the highest being for man*, hence with the *categorical imperative to overthrow all conditions* in which man is a degraded, enslaved, neglected, contemptible being.[30]

The proletariat suffers limitation of its life chances. It is locked in a system of domination which appropriates its labor to reproduce that dominating system. The proletarian's actions are not ' his" (or "hers"); he does not recognize himself in his practice; his work fulfills interests that negate him.

> My labor, therefore, is manifested as the objective, sensuous, perceptible, and indubitable expression of my *self-loss* and my *powerlessness*.[31]

> What constitutes the externalization of labor? First is the fact that labor is external to the laborer—that is, it is not part of his nature—and that the worker does not affirm himself in his work but denies himself, feels miserable and unhappy, develops no free physical and mental energy but mortifies the flesh and ruins his mind. . . . His work, therefore, is not voluntary, but coerced, *forced labor*. . . . Finally, the external nature of work for the worker appears in the fact that it is not his own but another person's, that in work he does not belong to himself but to someone else. . . . It is the loss of his own self.[32]

> The class of the proletariat feels annihilated in estrangement; it sees in it its own powerlessness and reality of an inhuman existence.[33]

But somewhere along the way, we have become the victim of a sleight of hand. The proletariat has been selected by a set of general criteria for recognizing oppression, as the dominated group. Alienation from the means of (self-)production has become the exclusive preserve of a so-called "universal" class.[34]

To avoid the literalization of the concept of production or labor as the practice of the industrial proletariat, let us recall Marx's own definition offered in the *Economic and Philosophical Manuscripts of 1844*: "Labor is man's coming-to-be for himself within externalization or as externalized man."[35] Yet the particularization of "labor" as the labor of, specifically, the industrial working class has tended to blind socialist analysis to the larger compass of the alienation of labor and alienation from the means of production. The general analysis, of which the analysis of the nineteenth-century working class is but an instance, has far greater application and implications. Fixation upon Marx's own later examination of this class has created a brittle orthodoxy immune to the manifest permutations of domination. Reification of the Marxist system has reintroduced the analytical "barrenness" Marx sought to avoid in the Hegelian system: ignorance of suffering. The orientation characterizes not only the Leninist and Trotskyist developments, but writers in the so-called Hegelian Marxist tradition.[36] "Domination and exploitation, however, are not mere juridical relations but, first and foremost, something felt and lived in the first person, independently of whatever ideological mystification may be used to theorize it away."[37]

The fundamental critique of Marx's theory of alienation focuses upon the inability of people to realize themselves in the objects of their own creation.

> Production is not merely the making of products: the term signifies on the one hand "spiritual" production, that is to say creations (including social time and space), and on the other, material production or the making of things; it also signifies the self-production of a "human being" in the process of historical self-development which involves the production of social relations.[38]

The products of the labor of the working class are appropriated and used in the perpetuation of capital. Exclusion from control over the means of mental and physical production characterizes the inferiorization of Jewish, black, and gay people. Exclusion from economic control entails economic dependence; blocked access to the means of communications necessitates the failure of these groups to recognize themselves in their "own" culture, and reproduces atomization (alienation of man from man). They are alienated from the means of production, from the fruits of their own labor, and from each other, by a social order which acquires their labor for itself, affixing their name(s) only to devalued and degraded objects.

The experiences of the groups examined here demands a phenomenology of class, i.e., recognition of social differentiation of life chances *where it exists*. Sartre remarks, "If they have a common bond, if all of them deserve the name of Jew, it is because they have in common the situation of a Jew, that is, they live in a community which takes them for Jews."[39] The structure of domination in its polymorphous manifestations creates a *rationality* in which all must participate. The distributive code requires conformity to its precepts for survival. "Segregated, discriminated against, satellized—they [the dominated] are gradually relegated *to a position of non-marked terms* by the structuration of the system as a code. Their revolt thus aims at the abolition of this code."[40]

If radical theory is not to ossify into yet another ideal straight-jacket contorting the material world, the historically changing political relationship founding suffering and alienation cannot be ignored. Particularization of the politics of oppression to the ideal type of the nineteenth-century English working class fails to recognize the universality of capitalism as a system of domination. This narrowness has contributed to notorious neglect by the "Left" of oppressed classes such as these examined here. Without a phenomenology of unfreedom, the contemporary historical stage remains unknown; social reordering cannot but recreate disenfranchised groups. Gramsci's vision is then rendered ideal, that "Structure ceases to be an external force which crushes man, assimilates him to itself and makes him passive; and is transformed into a means of freedom, and instrument to create a new ethico-political form and a source of new initiatives."[41]

NOTES

I INTRODUCTION

Project

1. Albert Memmi, *Portrait of a Jew*, pp. 321–322.
2. Analogy drawn from Theodor Adorno, *Negative Dialectics*, p. 180.
3. See Section entitled "Caveat: 'Self-Esteem' as a Psychological Construct" in Chapter III.
4. Alfred Schutz, "Interpretive Sociology," p. 269.
5. Ibid.
6. See Section entitled "Naturalism and Therapeutic Ideologies" in Chapter II.
7. Stanford Lyman, *The Black American in Sociological Thought: A Failure of Perspective*, p. 171.
8. See Bruno Bettelheim, "The Dynamism of Anti-Semitism in Gentile and Jew," p. 153.
9. Albert Memmi, *Dominated Man*, p. 88.
10. See Section: "In-Group Hostility" in Chapter IV.
11. Albert Memmi, *The Liberation of the Jew*, p. 13.

Dialectics of Freedom and Domination

12. André Gorz, *Socialism and Revolution*, p. 101.
13. Jean Paul Sartre, *Search for a Method*, p. 95.
14. My translation; cf. Jean Paul Sartre: "Elle est simplement le rapport d'intériorité univoque de l'individu comme *praxis* au champ objectif qu'il organise et dépasse vers sa propre fin. . . . la souveraineté c'est l'homme lui-même en tant qu'acte, en tant que travail unificateur, en tant qu'il a prise sur le monde et qu'il le change" (*Critique de la raison dialectique* [précédé de Question de méthode], p. 588).

15. *Cf.* Max Weber: "the situation in which the manifested will (command) of the *ruler* or rulers is meant to influence the conduct of one or more others (*the ruled*) and actually does influence it in such a way that their conduct to a socially relevant degree occurs as if the ruled had made the content of the command the maxim of their conduct for its very own sake" (*Economy and Society*, p. 946).

16. Bernd Baldus, "The Study of Power," p. 179.

17. The synonymity of *possibility* and *power* is a linguistic unity in French, where *pouvoir* means both *to be able* and *power*.

18. See section "Alienation and Class" in Chapter V.

19. See Erving Goffman: "a place of residence and work where a large number of like-situated individuals, cut off from the wider society for an appreciable period of time, together lead an enclosed formally administered round of life" (*Asylums*, p. xiii).

20. Judith Kramer, *The American Minority Community*, p. 254.

21. Gorz, *Socialism and Revolution*, p. 13n.

22. The fraudulence of the *deviance–minority* distinction for blacks is affirmed by Joyce Ladner, ed., *The Death of White Sociology*, p. 418, and Ethel Sawyer, "Methodological Problems in Studying So-Called 'Deviant' Communities," p. 361.

Social Construction of Identity

23. Friedrich Nietzsche, *Beyond Good and Evil*, p. 210 (#262).

24. Kramer, *American Minority Community*, p. 4.

25. The dialectical movement of ethnogenesis is described succinctly by L. Singer: "1) A portion of a population becomes distinguished, on some basis or bases, in the context of a power relationship.... 2) The members of this distinguished population segment are 'assigned' to a particular social role and fate; ... 3) As these people react to the situation in which they find themselves, they become aware of their commonality of fate.... 5) The further development of the emerging ethnic group will then depend, in part, on the nature of the structures that develop, the content of the group's 'self-image,' and the shared conception of its destiny" ("Ethnogenesis and Negro-Americans Today," 424).

26. My translation; cf. Sartre: "Le collectif se définit par son être, c'est-à-dire en tant que toute *praxis* se constitue par lui comme simple *exis*; c'est un object matériel et inorganique du champ pratico-inerte en tant qu'une multiplicité discrète d'individus agissants se produit en *lui* sous le signe de l'Autre comme unité réelle dans l'Etre, c'est-à-dire comme synthèse passive et en tant que l'objet constitué se pose comme essentiel et que son inertie pénètre *chaque praxis* individuelle comme sa détermination fondamentale par l'unité passive, c'est-à-dire par l'interpénétration *préalable* et *donnée* de tous en tant qu'Autres" (*Critique de la raison dialectique*, pp. 307–308).

27. Some of the conditions inhibiting and promoting this recognition are explored in the section entitled "Cultural Transmission" in Chapter II and in Chapter V.

28. The statement is, however, "extreme" in that self–other dialectics *within* the inferiorized group determine identity as well as the interaction between dominated and dominant groups.

29. Robert Blauner, *Racial Oppression in America*, pp. 140–141.
30. Barry Wellman, "Social Identities in Black and White," p. 57.
31. Memmi, *The Liberation of the Jew*, p. 29.
32. Isaac Deutscher, *The Non-Jewish Jew and Other Essays*, p. 51.
33. Dennis Altman, *Homosexual*, p. 219.
34. Irving Horowitz, *Israeli Ecstasies/Jewish Agonies*, p. 192.
35. See Daniel Bell, "Reflections on Jewish Identity," p. 473. Derived from Emil Fackenheim.
36. This process is explored less ideal-typically in Chapter V.
37. Erving Goffman, *Stigma*, p. 144n.
38. Carol Warren, *Identity and Community in the Gay World*, pp. 150–151.
39. Louis Wirth and Herbert Goldhamer, "The Hybrid and the Problem of Miscegenation," p. 303.
40. This distinction has arisen at times in Jewish history. See Section entitled "Assimilationism" in Chapter V.
41. Warren, p. 122; see Barry Dank, "Coming Out in the Gay World; p. 182; see Donn Teal, *The Gay Militants*, p. 44f. On the nuances of *Negro* and *black*, see, e.g., William Cross, "The Negro-to-Black Conversion Experience."
42. Marvin Wolfgang and Bernard Cohen, *Crime and Race*, p. 7.
43. Gunnar Myrdal, *An American Dilemma*, p. 115.
44. Raul Hilberg, *The Destruction of the European Jews*, p. 48.
45. Ibid, p. 53.
46. Ibid., p. 52.
47. See, e.g., A. P. MacDonald, "The Importance of Sex-Role to Gay Liberation," 169, on the willingness to accept homosexuality when it is accompanied by conformity to other aspects of sex-role norms.
48. H. Edward Ransford, "Skin Color, Life-Chances, and Anti-White Attitudes," p. 177; see Section entitled "In-Group Hostility" in Chapter IV.
49. Colin Williams and Martin Weinberg, *Homosexuals and the Military*, pp. 115–128; see also Laud Humphreys, *Out of the Closets*, p. 37n.
50. Poul Borchsenius, *History of the Jews*, p. 21.
51. Hilberg, p. 49.

Ontogenesis

52. See Goffman, *Asylums*, p. 147, on the comparable experience of the person labeled *insane*; Herbert Aptheker, *American Negro Slave Revolts*, p. 54, on the discovery of self as slave; Harold Isaacs, *India's Ex-Untouchables*, p. 42, on the discovery of self as lowest-caste in India.
53. Judith Porter, *Black Child, White Child*, pp. 76, 79.
54. Kenneth Clark and Mamie Clark, "Emotional Factors in Racial Identification and Preference in Negro Children," p. 62.
55. See idem, "Development of Consciousness of Self and the Emergence of Racial Identification in Negro Preschool Children," p. 591; Edward Weaver, "How Do Children Discover They Are Negroes?" p. 108; W. E. B. DuBois, *The Souls of Black Folk*, p. 16; E. Franklin Frazier, *Negro Youth at the Crossways*, p. 84f.
56. Elie Cohen, *Human Behavior in the Concentration Camp*, p. 192; Kurt Lewin, *Resolving Social Conflicts*, p. 170; Memmi, *Portrait of a Jew*, p. 58; Everett Stonequist, *The Marginal Man*, p. 124.

57. Memmi, *Portrait of a Jew*, p. 26; see also Jean Paul Sartre, *Anti-Semite and Jew*, pp. 75–76.
58. Kramer, p. 215.
59. Dank, "Coming Out," p. 182. See Denise Cronin, "Coming Out among Lesbians." Dank reports an instance of a sixty-five-year-old man whose coming-out period encompassed fifty-three years (p. 192).
60. I.e., Family structures which are not necessarily cross-generational, but often peer-oriented.
61. See, e.g., J. Scott Francher and Janet Henkin, "The Menopausal Queen," p. 670, and Warren. See, e.g., Anne Koedt, "Loving Another Woman" and Jill Johnston, *Lesbian Nation*, for personal accounts of coming out.
62. See Dank, p. 187; Philip Blumstein and Pepper Schwartz, "Lesbianism and Bisexuality." The feeling of being "at home" strikes at the root of the idea of *"Jemeinigkeit"* which founds Heidegger's concept of "authenticity."
63. Altman, p. 14.

II SYSTEMATIC RESTRICTION OF LIFE CHANCES

Historical Outline: Jewish

1. Bibliography: Hannah Arendt, *The Origins of Totalitarianism*; Sidney Bolkosky, *The Distorted Image*; Poul Borchsenius, *Behind the Wall*; idem, *The History of the Jews*; Simon Dubnov, *History of the Jews*; Raul Hilberg, *The Destruction of the European Jews*; Jacob Katz, *Out of the Ghetto*; Michael Marrus, *The Politics of Assimilation*; Michael Meyer, *The Origins of the Modern Jew*; P. G. J. Pulzer, *The Rise of Political Anti-Semitism in Germany and Austria*; Howard Sachar, *The Course of Modern Jewish History*; Ismar Schorsch, *Jewish Reactions to German Anti-Semitism, 1870–1914*.

Historical Outline: Black

2. Herbert Aptheker, *American Negro Slave Revolts*, p. 53.
3. Idus Newby, *Jim Crow's Defense*, pp. 89–90.
4. Robert Brisbane, *The Black Vanguard*, p. 124.
5. Gunnar Myrdal, *An American Dilemma*, p. 559.
6. Irving Kovarsky and William Albrecht, *Black Employment*, pp. 77–78; Raymond Franklin and Solomon Resnik, *The Political Economy of Racism*, p. 38; Gabriel Kolko, *Wealth and Power in America*, p. 93.
7. Franklin and Resnik, p. 46.
8. Kovarsky and Albrecht, p. 77.
9. Leonard Savitz, "Black Crime," pp. 468–469.
10. Ibid., pp. 499–500.
11. Marvin Wolfgang and Marc Riedel, "Race, Judicial Discretion, and the Death Penalty," p. 119.
12. Bibliography: Peter Bergman, *The Chronological History of the Negro in America*; Mary Berry, *Black Resistance/White Law*; Robert Brisbane, *Black Activism*; Joe Feagin and Harlan Hahn, *Ghetto Revolts*; E. Franklin Frazier, *The Negro in the United States*; George Fredrickson, *The Black Image in the*

White Mind; Joyce Ladner, ed., The Death of White Sociology; Barrington Moore, Social Origins of Dictatorship and Democracy; Alphonso Pinkney, Black Americans; Alexander Thomas and Samuel Sillen, Racism and Psychiatry; Robin Winks, The Blacks in Canada; C. Vann Woodward, The Strange Career of Jim Crow.

Historical Outline: Gay

13. H. Montgomery Hyde, ed., The Three Trials of Oscar Wilde, p. 12.
14. See Martin Weinberg and Alan Bell, eds., Homosexuality.
15. Walter Barnett, Sexual Freedom and the Constitution, pp. 20, 299–303.
16. Marcel Saghir and Eli Robins, Male and Female Homosexuality, pp. 165–167; Martin Weinberg and Colin Williams report that 25 percent of their homophile sample had been arrested on a charge related to homosexuality (Male Homosexuals, p. 108); see Martin Dannecker and Reimut Reiche, Der gewöhnliche Homosexuelle, p. 368.
17. See Laud Humphreys, Out of the Closets, pp. 22, 35; Michael Schofield, Sociological Aspects of Homosexuality, p. 73f.
18. See Colin Williams and Martin Weinberg, Homosexuals and the Military; John Chiles, "Homosexuality in the United States Air Force", p. 529.
19. Saghir and Robins, p. 128.
20. Weinberg and Williams, p. 98.
21. Bibliography: Derrick Bailey, Homosexuality and the Western Christian Tradition; John Gerassi, The Boys of Boise; Heinz Heger, Die Männer mit dem rosa Winkel; A Homosexual Emancipation Miscellany c. 1835–1952; H. Montgomery Hyde, The Other Love; Hendrik Ruitenbeek, The New Sexuality; Brian Reade, Sexual Heretics; Donn Teal, The Gay Militants; John Lauritsen and David Thorstad, The Early Homosexual Rights Movement (1864–1935); James Steakley, The Homosexual Emancipation Movement in Germany.

Cultural Transmission

22. Albert Memmi, Portrait of a Jew, p. 83f.
23. Howard Ehrlich, The Social Psychology of Prejudice, p. 33; see Winks, p. 363.
24. Jonathan Kozol, Death at an Early Age, p. 69f.
25. Gerald Hannon, "School Is a Drag?" p. 12; see Kenneth Plummer, p. 144.
26. Rictor Norton, "The Homosexual Literary Tradition," p. 674.
27. See Ephraim Rosen and Ian Gregory, Abnormal Psychology, p. 395; Curtis Barrett et al., Abnormal Psychology, p. 436; Leonard Ullman and Leonard Krasner, A Psychological Approach to Abnormal Behavior, p. 484f; Abraham Maslow and Béla Mittelmann, Principles of Abnormal Psychology, p. 197; Paul Stern, The Abnormal Person and His World.
28. Roy Dorcus and G. Wilson Shaffer, Textbook of Abnormal Psychology, p. 260; Richard Suinn, Fundamentals of Behavior Pathology, p. 317; Jack Strange, Abnormal Psychology, p. 188.
29. Dorcus and Shaffer, p. 260; Rosen and Gregory pp. 121, 377, 382; Strange, p. 187; Barney Katz and Robert Lewis, The Psychology of Abnormal Behavior; Suinn, p. 316.

30. Robert White, *The Abnormal Personality*, p. 379; Suinn, p. 317; Maslow and Mittelmann, p. 197; Katz and Lewis.
31. White, p. 379; Dorcus and Shaffer, p. 261.
32. Suinn, p. 316; Rosen and Gregory, p. 390; Maslow and Mittelmann, pp. 450, 452.
33. Dorcus and Shaffer, p. 260.
34. Suinn, p. 316; Ullmann and Krasner, p. 267.
35. See Suinn, p. 317; Rosen and Gregory, p. 371.
36. Peretz Bernstein, *Jew-Hate as a Sociological Problem*, p. 71.
37. Ibid., p. 54.
38. See later section entitled "Composite Portrait of the Inferiorized Person."
39. Z. Diesendruck, "Antisemitism and Ourselves," p. 46.
40. E. Franklin Frazier, *Black Bourgeoisie*, p. 123.
41. Dennis Altman, *Homosexual*, p. 39.
42. Ian Young, "Pigs & Fishes," p. 16.
43. John Murphy, "Queer Books."
44. "Who Could They Possibly Mean?" p. 10.
45. Herbert Marcuse, "Repressive Tolerance," p. 96.

Naturalism and Therapeutic Ideologies

46. Hilberg, pp. 10–12; Alex Bein, "The Jewish Parasite", p. 3; Morton Seiden, *The Paradox of Hate*, p. 163.
47. Thomas Szasz, *The Manufacture of Madness*, p. 154.
48. Idem, "The Sane Slave", pp. 228–231.
49. Idem., *The Manufacture of Madness*, p. 214.
50. I.e., "fléau social." Legal stigmatization is automatic. "Le casier judiciare d'un homosexuel qui s'est fait 'pincer' porte la mention: 'a commis un outrage public à la pudeur avec une personne de son sexe'" (Front Homosexuel d'Action Révolutionnaire, *Rapport contre la normalité*, p. 39).
51. On therapeutic ideologies, see Peter Berger and Thomas Luckmann, *The Social Construction of Reality*, pp. 112–113; Murray Edelman, "The Political Language of the Helping Professions," p. 295.
52. Andrew Billingsley, "Black Families in White Social Science," p. 436. On the black matriarchy theory, see also Jacqueline Jackson, "Black Women in a Racist Society," p. 185f; William Ryan, *Blaming the Victim*, pp. 5, 61–85; E. Earl Baughman, *Black Americans*; Thomas and Sillen, p. 90f; William Grier and Price Cobbs, *Black Rage*, p. 84; Marvin Wyne, Kinnard White, and Richard Coop, *The Black Self*, pp. 19–28.
53. Lawrence Hatterer, *Changing Homosexuality in the Male*, pp. 18, 38, 276f.
54. Charles Socarides, *The Overt Homosexual*, p. 49.
55. See Evelyn Hooker, "The Adjustment of the Male Overt Homosexual," p. 18; Judy Chang and Jack Block, "A Study of Identification in Male Homosexuals," p. 307; Robert Dean and Harold Richardson, "Analysis of MMPI Profiles of 40 College-Educated Overt Male Homosexuals," p. 483; Norman Thompson, Boyd McCandless, and Bonnie Strickland, "Personal Adjustment of Male and Female Homosexuals and Heterosexuals," p. 240; Martin Hoffman, *The Gay World*, p. 154f; Saghir and Robins, especially pp. 113, 117, 276; D. H. Barlow, G. G. Abel, E. B. Blanchard, and M. Mavissakalian, "Plasma Testosterone Levels and Male Homosexuals," p. 571; K. Brodie, N. Gartrell, C. Doering,

and T. Rhue, "Plasma Testosterone Levels in Heterosexual and Homosexual Men," p. 82.

56. Maurice Feldman and M. J. MacCulloch, Homosexual Behavior, p. 34.
57. Irving Bieber et al., Homosexuality, p. 319. This is a particularly fruitful source of psychiatric ideology, being a survey of psychiatrists, not a survey of homosexuals.
58. Lionel Ovesey, Homosexuality and Pseudohomosexuality, p. 119.
59. Stanley Lesse, "Oh God! Who Created Heaven and Earth and Even Psychiatrists and Psychologists, Please Protect Us from Well-Meaning but Confused 'Experts' " p. 151.
60. Socarides, pp. 217–218.
61. Ibid., p. 46.
62. Ibid., p. 216; see section entitled "Politics of Guilt" in Chapter III.
63. Feldman and MacCulloch, p. 135.
64. Socarides, p. 80.
65. Drawn from a list of problems in gay relationships compiled by Hatterer, p. 128.
66. Socarides, p. 82; my emphasis.
67. Hatterer, p. 128.
68. Feldman and MacCulloch, p. 3; Teal, pp. 297–301.
69. Gerald Davison and G. Terence Wilson, "Attitudes of Behavior Therapists toward Homosexuality," p. 686.
70. Feldman and MacCulloch, especially p. 21f.
71. Ibid., p. 164.
72. Weinberg and Bell, especially pp. 35, 287.
73. No "cure" criterion is offered by Bieber et al.
74. Laurence Ince, "Behavior Modification of Sexual Disorders," p. 446.
75. David Barlow, Harold Leitenberg, and W. Stewart Agras, "Experimental Control of Sexual Deviation through Manipulation of the Noxious Scene in Covert Sensitization," p. 600.
76. W. G. Lamberd, "The Treatment of Homosexuality as a Monosymptomatic Phobia," p. 512.
77. Charles Moan and Robert Heath, "Septal Stimulation for the Initiation of Heterosexual Behavior in a Homosexual Male," p. 23.
78. Saghir and Robins, pp. 92–104, 246; Ralph Gundlach and Bernard Riess, "Self and Sexual Identity in the Female," p. 228.
79. Saghir and Robins, p. 214.
80. Hatterer, p. 137. In a rare flash of insight, Hatterer confesses: "Many confirmed homosexuals who are highly active sexually and totally uninhibited can often mechanically perform very effectively on their first impersonal heterosexual encounter—that is, they are able to achieve orgastic satisfaction and give it to the woman. However, the emotional component of the total relationship in the sexual encounter is absent, and the experience usually is highly masturbatory in nature" (p. 337).
81. K. Freund, "Male Homosexuality," p. 32.

Composite Portrait of the Inferiorized Person

82. Memmi, Portrait of a Jew, p. 179.
83. Originally applied to Jews by Theodor Adorno, Else Frenkel-Brunswik, Daniel Levinson, and R. Nevitt Sanford in The Authoritarian Personality, p. 619.

84. Max Horkheimer and Theodor Adorno, *The Dialectic of Enlightenment*, p. 184.
85. Borchsenius, *Behind the Wall*, p. 122.
86. Theodor Adorno, et al. pp. 63, 610; Memmi, *Portrait of a Jew*, p. 99.
87. Adolf Hitler, *Mein Kampf*, p. 75.
88. Guy Johnson, "The Stereotype of the American Negro," *Characteristics of the American Negro*, p. 3; Adorno et al., p. 610; Myrdal, p. 107; Newby, p. 44; Bruno Bettelheim and Morris Janowitz, *Social Change and Prejudice*, p. 143; Winks, p. 293.
89. G. Johnson, p. 11; Fredrickson, p. 276.
90. Michael Biddiss, "Gobineau and the Origins of European Racism," p. 262; Fredrickson, p. 57.
91. Fredrickson, p. 58; Newby, p. 122; Frazier, p. 123.
92. Andrew Hodges, and David Hutter, *With Downcast Gays*, p. 7; see Altman, p. 53; Szasz, *The Manufacture of Madness*, p. 160.
93. Charles Stember, ed., *Jews in the Mind of America*, p. 55; see Joel Kovel, *White Racism*, p. 51.
94. Jews: Gertrude Selznick and Stephen Steinberg, *The Tenacity of Prejudice*, p. 10; Stember, p. 55; Bernstein, p. 61; blacks: Bettelheim and Janowitz, p. 143; colonials: Dominique Mannoni, *Prospero and Caliban*, p. 127n; gay people: Carol Warren, *Identity and Community in the Gay World*, p. 65.
95. Robert Coles, *Children of Crisis*, p. 68.
96. Sigmund Freud, "A General Introduction to Psychoanalysis," p. 452.
97. Bernstein, p. 100.
98. Horkheimer and Adorno, p. 86.
99. Seiden, pp. 162, 217.
100. Hitler, pp. 78, 448.
101. Adorno et al., p. 833.
102. Rhett Jones, "Proving Blacks Inferior," p. 125.
103. Fredrickson, p. 276; Brisbane, p. 73; Frazier, p. 624.
104. Thomas and Sillen, p. 102f.
105. Myrdal, p. 108; Alvin Poussaint, *Why Blacks Kill Blacks*, p. 92; G. Johnson, p. 19; Russell Middleton and John Moland, "Humor in Negro and White Subcultures," p. 65; Frantz Fanon, *Black Skin, White Masks*, p. 157; Winks, p. 296.
106. Mannoni, p. 110.
107. Frederickson, p. 273, Berry.
108. Marvin Wolfgang and Bernard Cohen, *Crime and Race*, p. 81.
109. Brisbane, p. 28.
110. Raymond de Becker, *The Other Face of Love*, p. 7.
111. Roger Mitchell, *The Homosexual and the Law*, p. 56.
112. Eugene Levitt and Albert Klassen, "Public Attitudes toward Homosexuality," pp. 36, 32.
113. See Humphreys, p. 29f.
114. Herbert Marcuse, *Eros and Civilization*, p. 45.
115. See James Bayton and Tressie Muldrow, "Interacting Variables in the Perception of Racial Personality Traits."
116. Jean Paul Sartre, *Anti-Semite and Jew*, p. 46; Grier and Cobbs, pp. 90–94.; Marcuse, p. 45.
117. Arendt, p. 85.
118. See Kovel, p. 231f.
119. See Bernstein, p. 238.

120. Stember, p. 273.
121. Marrus, pp. 206–208.
122. Stember, p. 165.
123. Bailey, p. 145.
124. Ibid., p. 135f.; Vern Bullough, "Heresy, Witchcraft, and Sexuality," p. 183.
125. Barnett, p. 90.
126. Levitt and Klassen, p. 34.
127. "Who Could They Possibly Mean?" p. 10.
128. Hilberg, p. 10.
129. Marrus, p. 206.
130. Kenneth Stampp, "Rebels and Sambos," 370, argues that Aptheker confuses white rumors about slave conspiracies with actual rebellions, which were, in fact, very few.
131. Hitler, p. 77; Bernstein, p. 272; see Adorno et al., pp. 63, 96f, 612f; Bettelheim and Janowitz, p. 142; Stember, p. 55; Selznick and Steinberg, p. 9.
132. Mitchell, p. 59; Benjamin DeMott, " 'But he is a homosexual. . . .' " p. 37f.
133. Peter Fisher, The Gay Mystique, p. 186; Ruitenbeek, pp. 18–21.
134. Bettelheim and Janowitz, p. 143.
135. Maurice Merleau-Ponty, Sense and Non-Sense, p. 143.
136. Abram Kardiner and Lionel Ovesey, The Mark of Oppression, p. 89; Bettelheim and Janowitz, p. 231; Adorno et al., p. 63; Fanon, p. 26; Johnson, p. 18.
137. Selznick and Steinberg, p. 15; Stember, p. 55; Johnson, p. 19.
138. Robert Johnson, "Negro Reactions to Minority Group Status," p. 197.
139. Albert Memmi, The Liberation of the Jew, p. 113.
140. Stember, p. 77.
141. Harold Isaacs, India's Ex-Untouchables, p. 28.
142. Jerry Hirsch, "Behavior-Genetic Analysis and Its Biosocial Consequences," p. 38.
143. See earlier section entitled "Historical Outline: Black."
144. Ovesey, p. 57.
145. Theodore Weissbach and Gary Zagon, "The Effect of Deviant Group Membership upon Impressions of Personality," p. 265.
146. Bernstein, p. 52; Bettelheim and Janowitz, p. 143; Adorno et al., p. 64; Newby, p. 121; Mannoni, p. 127n; Albert Memmi, The Colonizer and the Colonized, p. 79f.
147. G. Johnson, p. 10; Thomas and Sillen, p. 129; Fredrickson, p. 54f; Myrdal, p. 107.
148. G. W. F. Hegel, The Phenomenology of Mind, p. 236.
149. Erik Erikson, Childhood and Society, p. 24.
150. Memmi, The Liberation of the Jew, p. 67.
151. Mannoni, p. 200.
152. James Baldwin and Nikki Giovanni, A Dialogue, pp 88–89.
153. Altman, p. 57.

Popular Ideologies

155. See J. L. Simmons, "Public Stereotypes of Deviants," p. 228; Elizabeth Rooney and Don Gibbons, "Societal Reactions to 'Crimes Without Victims,' " pp. 108–109 on the consistency of traits assigned to gay people.
156. Bettelheim and Janowitz, pp. 153–161.

157. Joan Joesting, Alan Ogus, and Robert Joesting, "Consistencies in Views of Deviants by College Students," p. 138; Stember, p. 107, outlines the decline of anti-Semitism in the post-World War II period.
158. Levitt and Klassen, p. 41.
159. Ibid., p. 35; see Rooney and Gibbons.
160. Yehudi Cohen, "Some Aspects of Ritualized Behavior in Interpersonal Relationships," p. 205f; Myrdal, p. 611f; Fanon, p. 31; Bertram Doyle, The Etiquette of Race Relations in the South.
161. Warren, pp. 53, 96.
162. Oliver Cox, Caste, Class, and Race, p. 367.
163.   It is self-evident that a belief that God ordained a caste system, that it is the burden of the white man to reshape the culture of nonwhites to conform to his own, that it is the destiny of a political leader to lead the forces of righteousness in an inevitably successful war against the forces of darkness, or that a silent majority supports a course of action that is widely and bitterly attacked, are cognitions that cannot be proven false by the everyday experience of those who hold them. Performing as they do the basic function for the anxious human being of giving meaning to his life and to the confusing events around him, assuring him of divinely willed or inevitable status and of close attachment to a movement that is just and destined to succeed in exterminating evil, such myths create valued self-conceptions and political roles that are highly resistant to incompatible or complicating reformation.

(Murray Edelman, Politics as Symbolic Action, p. 42).

    For the formation of the authority-oriented character it is especially decisive that the children should learn, under pressure from the father not to trace every failure back to its social causes but to remain at the level of the individual and to hypostatize the failure in religious terms as sin or in naturalistic terms as deficient natural endowment.

(Max Horkheimer, Critical Theory, p. 109).
164. Robert Lane, "Fear of Equality," p. 35.
165. Albert Memmi, Dominated Man, p. 201.
166. Sartre, p. 26.
167. Memmi, Dominated Man, p. 200; see section entitled "In-Group Hostility" in Chapter IV.
168. The romantic liberalism of those who would defend dominated groups by stigmatizing others partakes of this same subtle racism. See Section entitled "Psychological Withdrawal" in Chapter IV.
169. Memmi, Dominated Man, p. 193.
170. Sartre, p. 34.

III   OPPRESSION AND CONSCIOUSNESS

Atomization and Insecurity

1. Theodor Adorno, Negative Dialectics, p. 313.
2. Albert Memmi, The Liberation of the Jew, pp. 113–115, 267; idem, The Portrait of a Jew, pp. 15–36.
3. G. W. F. Hegel, The Phenomenology of Mind, p. 229.
4. See also Huey Newton, To Die for the People, pp. 79–81, on black invisibility.
5. James Baldwin, Nobody Knows My Name, p. 73; see Jean Paul Sartre, Anti-Semite and Jew; James Baldwin and Nikki Giovanni, A Dialogue, p. 17.
6. Peter Berger and Thomas Luckmann, The Social Construction of Reality, p. 165.

7. Bruno Bettelheim, "Individual and Mass Behavior in Extreme Situations," p. 426.
8. Socarides, *The Overt Homosexual*, p. 228.
9. Judith Kramer, *The American Minority Community*, p. 11.
10. E. Earl Baughman, *Black Americans*, p. 64; see Marian Radke, Helen Trager, and Hadassah Davis, "Social Perceptions and Attitudes of Children," p. 439; Newton, p. 81.
11. Martin Hoffman, *The Gay World*, p. 191; Kenneth Plummer, *Sexual Stigma*, p. 145.
12. Martin Weinberg and Colin Williams, *Male Homosexuals*, p. 26.

Distribution of Restricted Life-Chances

13. See Bernd Baldus, "Social Structure and Ideology."
14. Michael Mann, *Consciousness and Action among the Western Working Class*, p. 31; see Maurice Pinard, *The Rise of a Third Party*, p. 151.
15. Gary Marx, *Protest and Prejudice*, p. 69; see Judith Porter, *Black Child, White Child*, p. 127.
16. Joe Feagin and Harlan Hahn, *Ghetto Revolts*, p. 118.
17. Gloria Powell, "Self-Concept in White and Black Children," pp. 310–311.

Ambiguous Identity

18. Dominique Mannoni, *Prospero and Caliban*, p. 119.
19. Everett Stonequist, *The Marginal Man*, p. 13.
20. See Chapter IV.
21. Albert Memmi, *The Colonizer and the Colonized*, p. 15.
22. Judith Porter, *Black Child, White Child*, p. 175.
23. See James Bayton and Tressie Muldrow, "Perception of Racial Personality Traits," p. 392; H. Edward Ransford, "Skin Color, Life Chances, and Anti-White Attitudes," p. 177.
24. Michael Schofield, *Sociological Aspects of Homosexuality*, pp. 174–175; Hoffman, pp. 17f, 48f; Jerrold Greenberg, "A Study of the Self-Esteem and Alienation of Male Homosexuals," p. 137; David H. Rosen, *Lesbianism*, p. 36.
25. Weinberg and Williams, p. 215; see Laud Humphreys, "New Styles in Homosexual Manliness," p. 76.
26. Jill Johnston, *Lesbian Nation*, p. 179; see Philip Blumstein and Pepper Schwartz, "Lesbianism and Bisexuality," pp. 283, 291.
27. Ismar Schorsch, *Jewish Reactions to German Anti-Semitism*, p. 67.
28. Donn Teal, *The Gay Militants*.
29. For a recent example, see Laud Humphreys, *Out of the Closets*, p. x *passim*.

Minority Salience, Class, and Mobility

30. Morris Rosenberg, *Society and the Adolescent Self-Image*, p. 67.
31. Barry Wellman, "Social Identities in Black and White," p. 65.
32. E. Franklin Frazier, *Black Bourgeoisie*; Robert Johnson, "Negro Reactions to Minority Group Status," pp. 208–209.
33. Seymour Parker and Robert Kleiner, "Status Position, Mobility, and Ethnic Identification of the Negro," p. 66.

34. Steven Asher and Vernon Allen, "Racial Preference and Social Comparison Processes," p. 93.
35. Sidney Goldstein and Calvin Goldscheider, *Jewish Americans*, pp. 7–9; Judith Kramer and Seymour Leventman, *Children of the Gilded Ghetto*, p. 9f.
36. Weinberg and Williams, p. 232.

Parental Authoritarianism

37. Sigmund Freud, "Dostoevsky and Parricide," p. 73.
38. Stanley Coopersmith, *The Antecedents of Self-Esteem*, p. 100.
39. Howard Cameron, "A Review of Research and an Investigation of Emotional Dependency among Negro Youth," pp. 345, 353–354.
40. Rosenberg, pp. 49, 144.
41. Theodor Adorno, Else Frenkel-Brunswik, Daniel Levinson, and R. Nevitt Sanford, *The Authoritarian Personality*, p. 385, see p. 342; Bruno Bettelheim and Morris Janowitz, *Social Change and Prejudice*, p. 209.
42. Emanuel Berger, "The Relation between Expressed Acceptance of Self and Expressed Acceptance of Others," p. 782.
43. Irving Sarnoff, "Identification with the Aggressor," p. 214.
44. Bruce Maliver, "Anti-Negro Bias among Negro College Students," pp. 51–53.
45. Ralph Epstein and S. S. Komorita, "Prejudice among Negro Children as Related to Parental Ethnocentrism and Punitiveness," p. 36.
46. Richard Trent, "The Relation between Expressed Self-Acceptance and Expressed Attitudes toward Negroes and Whites among Negro Children," p. 30.
47. Lawrence Hatterer, *Changing Homosexuality in the Male*, p. 38.
48. Irving Bieber et al., *Homosexuality*, pp. 63–117; see Charles Socarides, *The Overt Homosexual*, p. 76.
49. Hatterer, p. 38.
50. Bieber et al., p. 85.
51. See Weinberg and Williams, p. 160; Marcel Saghir and Eli Robins, *Male and Female Homosexuality*, p. 117.

Caveat: Self-Esteem as a Psychological Construct

52. John McCarthy and William Yancey, "Uncle Tom and Mr. Charlie," p. 648; William Yancey, Leo Rigsby, and John McCarthy, "Social Position and Self-Evaluation," p. 338; Jerold Heiss and Susan Owens, "Self-Evaluations of Blacks and Whites," p. 360.
53. See earlier section entitled "Distribution of Restricted Life-Chances."
54. Robert Crain and Carol Weisman, *Discrimination, Personality, and Achievement*, p. 74.
55. The quality of Gary Marx, *Protest and Prejudice*, must be acknowledged in this context.
56. Heiss and Owens, p. 364.
57. Crain and Weisman, p. 72.
58. Rosenberg, pp. 305–307.
59. Weinberg and Williams.
60. Dwight Dean, "Alienation," p. 756.

61. Thomas Langner, "A Twenty-two Item Screening Score of Psychiatric Symptoms Indicating Impairment," p. 269f.
62. Morris Rosenberg and Roberta Simmons, *Black and White Self-Esteem*, p. 10.
63. See first section in this chapter, entitled "Atomization and Insecurity."
64. Baughman, p. 48; see Rosenberg and Simmons, p. 8.
65. See sections on withdrawal in Chapter IV.
66. McCarthy and Yancey; Rosenberg and Simmons, p. 131.
67. Porter, p. 160.
68. Alfred Schutz and Thomas Luckmann, *The Structures of the Life-World*, p. 14.
69. Ibid., p. 154.
70. See section entitled "Escape from Identity" in Chapter IV.

Politics of Guilt

71. Alexis de Tocqueville, *Democracy in America*, p. 148.
72. Mircea Eliade, *The Myth of the Eternal Return*, pp. 97–98.
73. Hegel, p. 491.
74. Sigmund Freud, "Civilization and Its Discontents," p. 793; see Z. Diesendruck, "Antisemitism and Ourselves," p. 45.
75. Maurice Merleau-Ponty, *Sense and Non-Sense*, p. 38.
76. Frantz Fanon, *Black Skin, White Masks*, p. 139.
77. Newton, p. 79.
78. William Grier and Price Cobbs, *Black Rage*, p. 8; see Janet Kennedy, "Problems Posed in the Analysis of Negro Patients," p. 204.
79. Grier and Cobbs, p. 13.
80. See Saghir and Robins, who find that gay people are more likely to attribute their depressions to the gay experience, and more likely to enter psychotherapy at this point, even though the rate of depression is no higher than among a heterosexual comparison group (pp. 117, 276).
81. Mark Zborowski, *People in Pain*, p. 235.
82. Irving Janis, *Psychological Stress* p. 45.
83. Ruth Jaffe, "Sense of Guilt within Holocaust Survivors," p. 308; see William Niederland, "Psychiatric Disorders among Persecution Victims," p. 458.
84. Stanley Rosenman, "The Paradox of Guilt in Disaster Victim Populations," p. 220.
85. Gertrude Selznick and Stephen Steinberg, *The Tenacity of Prejudice*, p. 61.
86. Friedrich Nietzsche, *On the Genealogy of Morals*, p. 87.
87. Robert Lifton, " 'Thought Reform' of Western Civilians in Chinese Communist Prisons," p. 189.
88. Robert Lifton, *Thought Reform and the Psychology of Totalism*.
89. Idem, " 'Thought Reform' of Western Civilians in Chinese Communist Prisons," p. 179.
90. Ibid., p. 189.
91. Ibid., p. 190; see Section entitled "Guilt-Expiation Rituals" in Chapter IV.
92. See Section entitled "Mimesis" in Chapter IV.
93. Freud, "Civilization and Its Discontents," p. 792.
94. Ibid., p. 793.
95. Theodore Reik, *Masochism in Sex and Society*, p. 315.
96. See Gustav Bychowski, "Some Aspects of Masochistic Involvement," p. 248.
97. Reik, p. 161.

98. *Gilles Deleuze, Sacher-Masoch*, p. 77.
99. Jean Paul Sartre, *Being and Nothingness*, p. 379.
100. See Section entitled "Magical Ideologies" in Chapter IV.
101. Deleuze, p. 63.
102. Shirley Panken, *The Joy of Suffering*, p. 125.
103. Bruno Bettelheim, "Individual and Mass Behavior in Extreme Situations," p. 450.
104. E. O. James, *Sacrifice and Sacrament*, p. 116.
105. Memmi, *The Liberation of the Jew*, p. 119.
106. Hortense Powdermaker, "The Channeling of Negro Aggression by the Cultural Process," p. 757.
107. See Socarides, pp. 216–217; see section entitled "Naturalism and Therapeutic Ideologies" in Chapter II.

Phenomenology of Life-Limitations

108. Karl Marx, *Grundrisse*, p. 96.
109. John and Barbara Hammond, *The Town Labourer, 1760–1832*, p. 192.
110. Baldus, p. 369.
111. See Adorno et al., p. 671; Max Horkheimer and Theodor Adorno, *The Dialectic of Enlightenment*, p. 38; Herbert Marcuse, *One-Dimensional Man*.
112. Adorno, p. 358.
113. Georg Lukács, *History and Class Consciousness*, pp. 165, 193.
114. Fanon, p. 154.
115. Ludwig Binswanger, *Being-in-the-world*, p. 212.
116. Martin Heidegger, *Being and Time*, p. 167.
117. Ibid., p. 188.
118. Ibid., p. 222.
119. Ibid., pp. 165–166.
120. Horkheimer, p. 199.
121. Hegel, p. 261; see earlier section entitled "Parental Authoritarianism."
122. Panken, p. 139. See Harold Kelman, "Masochism and Self-Realization," p. 27. Baughman, on the other hand, claims that *"for some individuals, being black actually is advantageous as far as self-esteem is concerned.* This is true because the discrimination that blacks have endured enables a black man to point 'out there' to explain his frustrations, failures, and so on, rather than to deficiencies in his own self" (p. 46). Without group consolidation, this illusory "advantage" underlies the defeatism and dependency of the desubjectivized subject conforming to the rationale of the oppressive system. In community, it may indeed come to function dialectically as a lever toward consolidation and effective opposition. The inadequacy of the "self-esteem" construct is further demonstrated in this example.
123. See section entitled "Magical Ideologies" in Chapter IV.
124. Hegel, pp. 265–266.
125. See David Herman and Marie Nelson, who write: "the masochist is a person conditioned to perceive himself not as an *I-subject*, but as an *it-object*, a 'thing' that has use-value rather than relational value in the human scheme of things" ("The Treatment of Psychosocial Masochism," pp. 353–354). Leon Salzman, "Masochism," p. 20.

126. Adorno et al., pp. 248–250; see Wilhelm Reich, *The Mass Psychology of Fascism*. pp. xiii–xv.
127. Ray Canning and James Baker, "Effect of the Group on Authoritarian and Non-Authoritarian Persons," p. 580; Helen Lewis, *Shame and Guilt in Neurosis*, p. 165f; Irving Janis, "Personality as a Factor in Susceptibility to Persuasion," p. 61.
128. Marion Radke-Yarrow and Bernard Lande, "Personality Variables and Reactions to Minority Group Belonging," p. 270; see Joseph Adelson, "A Study of Minority Group Authoritarianism," p. 478.
129. D. L. Noel, "Group Identification among Negroes," p. 76.
130. Gary Marx, "*Protest and Prejudice*, p. 81.
131. Martin Grossack, "Group Belongingness and Authoritarianism in Southern Negroes—a Research Note," p. 266.
132. See Adorno et al., pp. 800, 857–863; Reich, "What is Class-Consciousness?" p. 25.
133. Adorno et al., p. 800.

IV STRATEGIES COPING WITH DOMINATION

Mimesis

1. G. W. F. Hegel, *The Phenomenology of Mind*, p. 237.
2. Robert Lifton, *Thought Reform and the Psychology of Totalism*, p. 131.
3. Theodor Adorno, *Negative Dialectics*, p. 167.
4. Georg Lukács, *History and Class Consciousness*, p. 49.
5. Stanley Elkins, *Slavery*.
6. Kenneth Stampp, "Rebels and Sambos," p. 389.
7. William White, *The Meaning of Disease*, p. 171.
8. Roy Waldman, *Humanistic Psychiatry*, p. 61.
9. William Grier and Price Cobbs, *Black Rage*, p. 179. Earlier typologies of responses to stigmatizing labels are proposed by Robert A. Scott, *The Making of Blind Men*, pp. 22–23, and Joseph Gusfield, *Symbolic Crusade*, pp. 66–68.
10. Anna Freud, *The Ego and the Mechanisms of Defense*, p. 110.
11. Elie Cohen, *Human Behavior in the Concentration Camp*, p. 179.
12. See ibid., p. 176.
13. Bruno Bettelheim, "Individual and Mass Behavior in Extreme Situations," p. 449.
14. Erving Goffman, *Asylums*, p. 63.
15. Santokh Anant, "Inter-Caste Differences in Personality Pattern as a Function of Socialization," p. 145.
16. Hortense Powdermaker, "The Channeling of Negro Aggression by the Cultural Process," p. 751; see Alvin Poussaint, *Why Blacks Kill Blacks*, pp. 61, 78; Cohen, p. 197.
17. Robert McKenzie, "The Shelby Iron Company," p. 348; Dominique Mannoni, *Prospero and Caliban*.
18. Bettelheim, p. 450.
19. Everyday nimetic behavior is analyzed below; see section entitled "Psychological V ithdrawal" later in this chapter.

20. Albert Memmi, *The Colonizer and the Colonized*, p. 16; see Peretz Bernstein, *Jew-Hate as a Sociological Problem*, p. 180; Eleonore Sterling, "Jewish Reactions to Jew-Hatred in the First Half of the Nineteenth Century," p. 408.
21. Cohen, p. 200; see Bettelheim, p. 448.
22. Poul Borchsenius, *Behind the Wall*, p. 113f.
23. Edward Flannery, *The Anguish of the Jews*, p. 172.
24. James Parkes, *Antisemitism*, p. 42.
25. Poul Borchsenius, *The History of the Jews*, p. 150.
26. George Mosse, *Nazi Culture*, p. 76.
27. F. Oliver Brachfeld, *Inferiority Feelings in the Individual and the Group*, p. 128; see Sidney Bolkosky, *The Distorted Image*.
28. Francis Broderick and August Meier, eds., *Negro Protest Thought in the Twentieth Century*, p. 6; see Idus Newby, *Jim Crow's Defense*, p. 128.
29. Gunnar Myrdal, *An American Dilemma*, p. 32.
30. Poussaint, p. 19.
31. Florence Halpern, "Self-Perception of Black Children and the Civil Rights Movement," p. 523.
32. Martin Weinberg and Colin Williams, *Male Homosexuals*, p. 177; see Barry Dank, "The Homosexual"; C. A. Tripp, *The Homosexual Matrix*, p. 211.
33. Andrew Hodges and David Hutter, *With Downcast Gays*, p. 13.
34. See, e. g., Edward Sagarin, "The Good Guys, the Bad Guys, and the Gay Guys," p. 3, a paeon to self-hatred, or Edward Sagarin, *Odd Man In*, pp. 78–110, for *ex cathedra* derogatory pronouncements upon gay people made in the name of sociology.

Escape from Identity

35. See section entitled "Ontogenesis" in Chapter I.
36. See "Composite Portrait of the Inferiorized Person" in Chapter II.
37. See Chapter II.
38. See "Politics of Guilt" in Chapter III.
39. Sigmund Freud, "Dostoevsky and Parricide," p. 66.
40. Albert Memmi, *The Liberation of the Jew*, p. 263.
41. Jean Paul Sartre, *Being and Nothingness*, p. 70; see section below entitled "Guilt-Expiation Rituals."
42. Ismar Schorsch, *Jewish Reactions to German Anti-Semitism*, p. 4f.
43. Sidney Hook, "Reflections on the Jewish Question," p. 479.
44. N. A. Pelcovits, "What about Jewish Anti-Semitism?" p. 118.
45. Leonard Broom, Helen Beem, and Virginia Harris, "Characteristics of the 1,107 Petitioners for Change of Name," p. 33; see E. Maass, "Integration and Name Changing among Jewish Refugees from Central Europe in the United States," p. 163f; Memmi, *The Liberation of the Jew*, pp. 31–42.
46. Jean Paul Sartre, *Anti-Semite and Jew*, especially p. 93.
47. Pelcovits, p. 121.
48. E. Franklin Frazier, *Negro Youth at the Crossways*, p. 180.
49. Morton Chethik, Elizabeth Fleming, Morris Mayer, and John McCoy, "Quest for Identity," p. 74.
50. Henry Myers and Leon Yochelson, "Color Denial in the Negro," p. 44.
51. Carol Warren, *Identity and Community in the Gay World*, pp. 155–156; see Thomas Fitzgerald, "A Theoretical Typology of Homosexuality in the United States," p. 31.

52. Jill Johnston, *Lesbian Nation*, p. 68.
53. Marcel Saghir and Eli Robins, *Male and Female Homosexuality*, pp. 61, 231.
54. Weinberg and Williams, pp. 100, 118.
55. Colin Williams and Martin Weinberg, *Homosexuals and the Military*, pp. 134, 174; Saghir and Robins, pp. 126, 285; Jan Loney, "Background Factors, Sexual Experiences, and Attitudes toward Treatment in Two 'Normal' Homosexual Samples," p. 61; Jerrold Greenberg, "A Study of the Self-Esteem and Alienation of Male Homosexuals," p. 141; see Martin Dannecker and Reimut Reiche, *Der gewöhnliche Homosexuelle*, p. 357; where 13 percent agree and 22 percent respond "perhaps."
56. See section below entitled "In-Group Hostility."
57. Saghir and Robins, pp. 95, 255; H. Laurence Ross, "Modes of Adjustment of Married Homosexuals," p. 388.
58. Williams and Weinberg, p. 119.
59. Seymour Parker and Robert Kleiner, *Mental Illness in the Urban Negro Community*, p. 51.
60. Friedrich Nietzsche, "Thus Spoke Zarathustra" p. 305.
61. Alfred Schutz and Thomas Luckmann, *The Structures of the Life-World*, p. 60.

Social Withdrawal

62. Sartre, *Anti-Semite and Jew*, p. 109.
63. See section entitled "Ontogenesis" in Chapter I; see William Cross, "Discovering the Black Referent."
64. Judith Kramer, *The American Minority Community*, p. 68.
65. Louis Wirth, *The Ghetto*, p. 27.
66. Stanford Lyman and Marvin Scott, *A Sociology of the Absurd*, p. 92; see Nancy Achilles, "Development of the Homosexual Bar as an Institution," p. 99.
67. Calvin Larson and Richard Hill, "Segregation, Community Consciousness, and Black Power," p. 271.
68. See section entitled "Atomization and Insecurity" in Chapter III.
69. Raul Hilberg, *The Destruction of the European Jews*, pp. 666, 16; see G. W. Allport, J. S. Bruner, and E. M. Jandorf, "Personality under Social Catastrophe," p. 15.
70. Regina Goff, *Problems and Emotional Difficulties of Negro Children*, p. 46.
71. W. E. B. DuBois, *Black Reconstruction in America*, p. 702; see Powdermaker, p. 756.
72. Goffman, p. 62.
73. See Kurt Lewin, *Resolving Social Conflicts*, p. 198; Albert Memmi, *Portrait of a Jew*, p. 253; Allport, Bruner, and Jandorf, p. 15; E. Franklin Frazier, *Black Bourgeoisie*, p. 112; John Dollard, *Caste and Class in a Southern Town*, p. 253.
74. Bernstein, p. 229; see Seymour Sarason, "Jewishness, Blackness, and the Nature-Nurture Controversy," p. 965.
75. Louis Wirth and Herbert Goldhamer, "The Hybrid and the Problem of Miscegenation," pp. 302, 307; Myers and Yochelson, p. 42f.
76. See Myrdal, p. 129; Oliver Cox, *Caste, Class, and Race*, p. 430.
77. Kramer, p. 29; Grier and Cobbs, p. 68; Powdermaker, p. 756; W. R. Chivers, "Race Discrimination and Negro Personality," p. 264.
78. Donn Teal, *The Gay Militants*, p. 44.

79. See Warren, p. 93f; John Gerassi, *The Boys of Boise*, p. 105.
80. Cf. the passing strategies of India's ex-Untouchables, Harold Isaacs, *India's Ex-Untouchables*, p. 143.
81. See Chivers, p. 266; Bernstein, p. 61.
82. Memmi, *Liberation of the Jew*, p. 119.
83. Myrdal, p. 640; see the suit of Oliver Sipple (the man who saved United States President Gerald Ford from assassination), charging the press with defamation for revealing his homosexuality.
84. See Hannah Arendt, *The Origins of Totalitarianism*, pp. 64–67, 84; Schorsch, p. 63; Howard Sachar, *The Course of Modern Jewish History*, p. 140.
85. The apparent growing acceptance of gay people willing to conform to sex-role norms and continued rejection of sex-role violators, must be noted in this context.

Psychological Withdrawal

86. See section entitled "Composite Portrait of the Inferiorized Person" in Chapter II.
87. Harvey Strassman, Margaret Thaler, and Edgar Schein, "A Prisoner of War Syndrome," p. 1,001.
88. Stampp, p. 386.
89. David Ausubel, "Ego Development among Segregated Negro Children," p. 37; see DuBois, pp. 701–702; William McCord, John Howard, Bernhard Friedberg, and Edwin Harwood, *Life Styles in the Black Ghetto*, p. 131f; Eugene Brody, "Cultural Exclusion, Character and Illness," p. 856.
90. Gordon Allport, *The Nature of Prejudice*, p. 140.
91. Jewish: Pelcovits, p. 121; black: Abram Kardiner and Lionel Ovesey, *The Mark of Oppression*, p. 343; Alexander Thomas and Samuel Sillen, *Racism and Psychiatry*, p. 58; Grier and Cobbs p. 178; Myrdal, p. 761f; gay: Lyman and Scott, 87; Evelyn Hooker, "Male Homosexuals and Their 'Worlds'," p. 104; Martin Hoffman, *The Gay World*, p. 182; Lionel Ovesey, *Homosexuality and Pseudohomosexuality*, p. 54; Charles Socarides, *The Overt Homosexual*, pp. 73, 94.
92. Oliver Brachfeld, p. 251.
93. Irving Bieber, et al., *Homosexuality*, p. 188.
94. Memmi, *Portrait of a Jew*, p. 234; Bolkosky, pp. 62–66; see "Assimilationism" in Chapter V.
95. Joseph Adelson, "A Study of Minority Group Authoritarianism," p. 479; see section below: "In-Group Hostility."
96. Aaron Antonovsky, "Like Everyone Else, Only More So," p. 428.
97. David Riesman, "A Philosophy for 'Minority' Living," p. 98; see Lewin, p. 196.
98. Huey Newton, *To Die for the People*, p. 80.
99. Frazier, p. 160.
100. Dennis Altman, *Homosexual*, p. 19; see Laud Humphreys, "New Styles of Homosexual Manliness," p. 76; Dank, p. 183; Karla Jay and Allen Young, *Out of the Closets*, p. 165f.
101. On Jewish conspicuous consumption, see Judith Kramer and Seymour Leventman, *Children of the Gilded Ghetto*, p. 115.
102. Sartre, *Anti-Semite and Jew*, p. 95; recall James Baldwin, "One had the choice of either 'acting just like a nigger' or of not acting just like a nigger—and

only those who have tried it know how impossible it is to tell the difference"
(*Nobody Knows My Name*, p. 73).

Guilt-Expiation Rituals

103. E. O. James, *Sacrifice and Sacrament*, p. 13.
104. See section entitled "Politics of Guilt" in Chapter III.
105. Hegel, p. 260.
106. See Gerhart Piers and Milton Singer, *Shame and Guilt*, especially pp. 35, 40; Theodor Reik, *Masochism in Sex and Society*, especially p. 319; Henri Hubert and Marcel Mauss, *Sacrifice: Its Nature and Function*; Sigmund Freud, "Civilization and Its Discontents."
107. Hubert and Mauss, p. 103.
108. Sigmund Freud, "Obsessive Actions and Religious Practices," p. 123.
109. Robert Lifton, " 'Thought Reform' of Western Civilians in Chinese Communist Prisons," p. 190.
110. See James Knight, *Conscience and Guilt*, p. 88f.
111. Riesman, p. 418.
112. See Grier and Cobbs, p. 42f; Frazier, p. 158.
113. Baldwin, p. 73.
114. Herbert Hendin, *Black Suicide*.
115. See also Michael Schofield, *Sociological Aspects of Homosexuality*, p. 127.
116. Michael Riordan, "Capital Punishment," p. 15.
117. Thomas Kando, "Males, Females, and Transsexuals," p. 64; see Johnston, p. 137; Laud Humphreys, *Out of the Closets*, p. 138; Ira Pauly, "Adult Manifestations of Male Transsexualism."

Magical Ideologies

118. See section entitled "Politics of Guilt" in Chapter III, and preceding section.
119. See "Politics of Guilt."
120. Lukács, p. 194.
121. Michael Barkun, *Disaster and the Millenium*, p. 56.
122. E. J. Hobsbawm, *Primitive Rebels*, p. 57f; see Mannoni, p. 148.
123. Schutz and Luckmann, p. 171.
124. See section entitled "Ontogenesis" in Chapter I.
125. G. W. F. Hegel, *The Philosophy of History*, p. 29.
126. Ludwig Binswanger, *Being-in-the-world*, pp. 298, 318.
127. Janis, p. 57.
128. See Roger Bastide, *The Sociology of Mental Disorder*, p. 205.
129. See Murray Edelman, *The Symbolic Uses of Politics*, p. 76.
130. See Kardiner and Ovesey; Frantz Fanon, *Black Skin, White Masks*, p. 44.
131. Poussaint, p. 53; see Theodor Adorno, *Minima Moralia*, pp. 238–244; Marvin Wyne, Kinnard White, and Richard Coop, *The Black Self*, p. 50.
132. See Borchsenius, *Behind the Wall*, pp. 180f, 196f; Memmi, *Liberation of the Jew*, p. 150.
133. William Grier and Price Cobbs, *The Jesus Bag*, p. 162.
134. Herbert Aptheker, *American Negro Slave Revolts*, p. 80f; Frazier, p. 115.
135. Gary Marx, *Protest and Prejudice*, p. 103; Grier and Cobbs, pp. 196–197.
136. Grier and Cobbs, p. 160.

137. Ibid., p. 160–161.
138. E. Franklin Frazier, *The Negro Church in America*, p. 64f.
139. P. Blumberg, "Magic in the Modern World," p. 151; Robert Crain and Carol Weisman, *Discrimination, Personality, and Achievement*, p. 53; Wyne, White and Coop, p. 49.
140. Myrdal, p. 940.
141. Ralph Greenson, "On Gambling," p. 62.
142. Irving Zola, "Observations on Gambling in a Lower-Class Setting," pp. 451–452.
143. Freud, *Doestoevsky and Parricide*, p. 79.
144. Greenson, p. 67.
145. Karl Marx, *Grundrisse*, p. 110.
146. Max Horkheimer, *Critical Theory*, p. 63.
147. John and Barbara Hammond, *The Town Labourer 1760–1832*, p. 310.
148. Sigmund Freud, *The Future of an Illusion*, p. 24.
149. Karl Marx, *Early Texts*, p. 116.

In-Group Hostility

150. Theodor Adorno, Else Frenkel-Brunswik, Daniel Levinson, and R. Nevitt Sanford, *The Authoritarian Personality*, p. 612.
151. See section entitled "Popular Ideologies" in Chapter II.
152. See section entitled "Escape from Identity" earlier in this chapter.
153. Kenneth Clark and Mamie Clark, "Emotional Factors in Racial Identification and Preference in Negro Children," p. 53; see Morris Rosenberg and Roberta Simmons, *Black and White Self-Esteem*, p. 43.
154. Harold Stevenson and Edward Stewart, "A Developmental Study of Race Awareness in Young Children," p. 408.
155. Steven Asher and Vernon Allen, "Racial Preference and Social Comparison Processes," p. 163; see Hugh Butts, "Skin-Color Perception and Self-Esteem," p. 122.
156. Judith Porter, *Black Child, White Child*, p. 119.
157. Robert Coles, *Children of Crisis*, p. 47.
158. Porter, p. 150.
159. See Marian Radke, Helen Trager, and Hadassah Davis, "Social Perceptions and Attitudes of Children," p. 374; Mary Goodman, *Race Awareness in Young Children*, pp. 169–173; C. Landreth and B. C. Johnson, "Young Children's Responses to a Picture and Inset Test Designed to Reveal Reactions to Persons of Different Skin Colour," p. 63; J. Kenneth Morland, "Racial Acceptance and Preference of Nursery School Children in a Southern City," p. 279; Porter, p. 67f.
160. Joseph Hraba and Geoffrey Grant, "Black is Beautiful," p. 400; Jeanne Fish and Charlotte Larr, "A Decade of Change in Drawings by Black Children," p. 421; Susan Ward and John Braun, "Self-Esteem and Racial Preference in Black Children," p. 646; John Brigham, "Views of Black and White Children Concerning the Distribution of Personality Characteristics," p. 144; Richard Lerner and Christie Buehrig, "The Development of Racial Attitudes in Young Black and White Children," p. 45.
161. Charles Johnson, "The Guidance Problems of Negro Youth," p. 42.

162. Stuart Hauser, *Black and White Identity Formation*, p. 191; see Robert Williams and Harry Byars, "Negro Self-Esteem in a Transitional Society," p. 123.
163. Martin Deutsch, "Minority Group and Class Status as Related to Social and Personality Factors in Scholastic Achievement," p. 65.
164. Martin Grossack, "Group Belongingness among Negroes," p. 28.
165. James Bayton, Lettie Austin, and Kay Burke, "Negro Perception of Negro and White Personality Traits," p. 382.
166. Crain and Weisman, p. 73.
167. Max Meenes, "A Comparison of Racial Stereotypes of 1930 and 1942," p. 332; see Richard Waite, "The Negro Patient and Clinical Theory," p. 429f; Poussaint, p. 78; Kardiner and Ovesey.
168. Frazier, *Black Bourgeoisie*, p. 186.
169. Poussaint, p. 21; see Robert Brisbane, *Black Activism: Racial Revolution in the United States, 1954–1970*, p. 180.
170. Isaacs, p. 29.
171. R. Rath and R. G. Sircar, "Inter Caste Relationship as Reflected in the Study of Attitudes and Opinions of Six Hindu Caste Groups," p. 8.
172. Robert Lane, *Political Ideology*, p. 79.
173. Michael Marrus, *The Politics of Assimilation*, p. 170.
174. Cohen, p. 190.
175. Bolkosky, p. 6.
176. Lewin, p. 187.
177. Simon Herman, *The Reaction of Jews to Anti-Semitism*, p. 72.
178. Schorsch, pp. 47, 227n.
179. Allport, Bruner, and Jandorf, p. 11.
180. Bernstein, p. 284.
181. Herman, p. 72; see Z. Diesendruck, "Anti-Semitism and Ourselves," p. 45.
182. John Blassingame, *The Slave Community*, p. 192.
183. Poussaint, p. 62.
184. Frazier, *Black Bourgeoisie*, p. 116.
185. Idem, *Negro Youth at the Crossways*, pp. 52, 99; Myrdal, pp. xcvi, 697; Kramer, p. 248; Grier and Cobbs, p. 79.
186. Hauser, p. 66; Kardiner and Ovesey, p. 348f.
187. Frazier, *Negro Youth at the Crossways*, p. 52; Myers and Yochelson, p. 42; Bingham Dai, "Some Problems of Personality Development in Negro Children," p. 562; Cox, p. 361; Hauser, p. 106; Poussaint, p. 104.
188. Cox, p. 361n.
189. See "Structural Constraints" in Chapter II.
190. Marvin Wolfgang and Bernard Cohen, *Crime and Race*, p. 31; John Davis, "Blacks, Crime, and American Culture," p. 95.
191. Leonard Savitz, "Black Crime," p. 479.
192. See Mydral, p. 764; Powdermaker, p. 753; Poussaint, p. 79; Grier and Cobbs, p. 30f.
193. Sidney Goldstein and Calvin Goldscheider, *Jewish Americans*, p. 155; Gilbert Bovell, "Psychological Considerations of Color Conflicts among Negroes," p. 448; Wirth and Goldhamer, p. 291; Brisbane, p. 180.
194. Howard Freeman, David Armor, J. Michael Ross, and Thomas Pettigrew, "Color Gradation and Attitudes among Middle-Income Negroes," p. 370; see J. Richard Udry, Karl Bauman, and Charles Chase, "Skin Color, Status, and Mate Selection," p. 732.
195. Grier and Cobbs, p. 800.

196. Ibid., pp. 87–89; Fanon; Goodman, p. 75.
197. Sartre, *Anti-Semite and Jew*, p. 104.
198. Schofield, p. 160; Johnston, p. 126.
199. Williams and Weinberg, p. 152; Dank, p. 191; Brenda Dickey, "Attitudes towards Sex Roles and Feelings of Adequacy in Homosexual Males," p. 121; Martin Dannecker and Reimut Reiche, *Der gewöhnliche Homosexuelle*, pp. 351–356.
200. Altman, p. 53.
201. David H. Rosen, *Lesbianism*, p. 24.
202. My translation; cf. Dannecker and Reiche, "Von einem ganz normal aussehenden Typ, dem man möglichst, nicht ansieht, dass er homosexuell ist" (p. 356).
203. Hoffman, p. 15; James Coleman, "My Homosexuality and My Psychotherapy," p. 191; Fitzgerald, p. 31; Saghir and Robins, p. 329.
204. See section entitled "Guilt-Expiation Rituals" earlier in this chapter.
205. K. Freund, "Male Homosexuality," p. 55; Pauly.
206. John Rechy, *City of Night*, p. 40; see Altman, p. 15.
207. Rechy, p. 54; see Albert Reiss, "The Social Integration of Queers and Peers," p. 268; Simon Raven, "Boys Will Be Boys," p. 281; Altman, pp. 14, 20. "New Styles in Homosexual Manliness," p. 76;
208. Humphreys, see Richard Troiden, "Homosexual Encounters in a Highway Rest Stop," p. 219; Hoffman, p. 48; Fitzgerald, p. 31.
209. Humphreys, "New Styles in Homosexual Manliness," p. 76.
210. See Hoffman, p. 19.
211. Adorno et al., pp. 398, 416, 848, 862, 866–869.
212. Weinberg and Williams, pp. 160, 157, 236; see Warren, p. 160.

The Arts of Contraversion

213. Friedrich Nietzsche, *On the Genealogy of Morals*, p. 38.
214. Piers and Singer, p. 45.
215. See Joseph Gabel, *Sociologie de l'aliénation*, p. 46.
216. Bruno Bettelheim, "The Dynamism of Anti-Semitism in Gentile and Jew," p. 156.
217. Grier and Cobbs, p. 25.
218. Memmi *The Liberation of the Jew*, p. 22.
219. See Darold Wax, "Negro Resistance to the Early American Slave Trade," p. 1; Eugene Genovese, *Roll, Jordan, Roll*.
220. See Ethel Sawyer, "Methodological Problems in Studying So-Called 'Deviant' Communities," p. 369; Goffman, p. 316; Warren.
221. Grier and Cobbs, pp. 3–11.
222. Anton Lourié, "The Jew as a Psychological Type," p. 126f.
223. Sigmund Freud, "Jokes and Their Relation to the Unconscious," p. 142; Martin Grotjahn, *Beyond Laughter*, p. 14.
224. Grotjahn, pp. 22, 25; Memmi, *The Liberation of the Jew*, pp. 43–54; Theodor Reik, *Jewish Wit*, pp. 162, 220–222.
225. Russell Middleton and John Moland, "Humor in Negro and White Subcultures," p. 66.
226. Grotjahn, p. 25; see Memmi, *The Liberation of the Jew*, p. 53; Reik, p. 236.
227. Grier and Cobbs, p. 167; see Charles Keil, *Urban Blues*, pp. 164–193; Ulf

Hannerz, *Soulside*, pp. 44–57; Ulf Hannerz, "The Significance of Soul"; Charles Pinderhughes, "Racism and Psychotherapy."

228. Warren, p. 129; see Altman, p. 18; Tripp, pp. 184–190; Susan Sontag, "Notes on Camp."

229. Friedrich Nietzsche, *Beyond Good and Evil*, p. 154.

V NOTES ON CONSOLIDATION

Assimilationism

1. Albrecht Wellmer, *Critical Theory of Society*, p. 131.
2. Recall the role of Jews and homosexuals as "pets" or fascinating oddities in French salons (See section entitled "Composite Portrait of the Inferiorized Person" in Chapter II) or the fashionability of inviting Black Panthers to "sophisticated" parties in the United States.
3. Peretz Bernstein, *Jew-Hate as a Sociological Problem*, p. 29.
4. Albert Memmi, *The Liberation of the Jew*, pp. 23–25, 59; see idem., *Portrait of a Jew*, p. 75.
5. Gunnar Myrdal, *An American Dilemma*, p. 764; see William Cross, "Discovering the Black Referent" and Charles Hamilton, *Black Power*, p. 54; Alvin Poussaint, *Why Blacks Kill Blacks*, p. 66.
6. Peter Fisher, *The Gay Mystique*, p. 122; see Jill Johnston, *Lesbian Nation*, pp. 186, 189; Laud Humphreys, *Out of the Closets*, p. 139.

Collective Resistance

7. My translation; cf. Jean Paul Sartre, "Nous sommes frères en tant qu'après l'acte créateur du serment nous sommes *nos propres fils*, notre invention commune" (*Critique de la raison dialectique* (précédé de Question de méthode*), p. 453).
8. See Cross.
9. Carol Warren, *Identity and Community in the Gay World*, pp. 18, 164. Despite popular myths to the contrary, the "horizontal" family networks of the gay community are likely to provide its members a support through the aging process lacking in heterosexual society, where a "menopausal identity-crisis" is built in to the life careers of men and especially women. See J. Scott Francher and Janet Henkin, "The Menopausal Queen," pp. 673–674; Martin Weinberg, "The Male Homosexual," p. 536.
10. Memmi, *Portrait of a Jew*, pp. 265, 275.
11. See Michael Mann, *Consciousness and Action among the Western Working Class*, p. 13; W. S. Landecker, "Status Congruence, Class Crystallization, and Social Cleavage," p. 228.
12. See Max Weber, *Economy and Society*, p. 305; Herbert Aptheker, *American Negro Slave Revolts*, p. 114; Albert Memmi, *Dominated Man*, p. 131.
13. Joe Feagin and Harlan Hahn, *Ghetto Revolts*, p. 162; B. McKelvey, "Cities as Nurseries of Self-Conscious Minorities," p. 367f; Louis Wirth, *The Ghetto*, p. 36; Weber, p. 305.
14. Donn Teal, *The Gay Militants*.

15. Feagin and Hahn, p. 46; Leonard Berkowitz, "The Study of Urban Violence," p. 14f.
16. Michael Barkun, *Disaster and the Millenium*, p. 45.
17. Mann, p. 40f.
18. Aptheker, p. 114f.
19. Feagin and Hahn, p. 144; Robert Fogelson, "From Resentment to Confrontation: the Police, the Negroes, and the Outbreak of the Nineteen-Sixties Riots," p. 247; see Sartre, p. 384.
20. Dennis Altman, *Homosexual*, p. 97f; Teal, pp. 17f, 191; see Weber, p. 305.
21. E. J. Hobsbawm, *Primitive Rebels*, p. 92; see Weber, p. 305.
22. My translation; cf. Sartre "Le groupe institutionnel, comme squelette abstrait de la classe unie, est invite permanente à s'unir, il est déjà souveraineté de la classe quand celle-ci est tout entière sérialité" (p. 647).

Alienation and Class

23. G. W. F. Hegel, *The Philosophy of History*, p. 364.
24. Herbert Marcuse, *Reason and Revolution*, p. 139.
25. Marcuse, p. 10f.
26. Gramsci, *Selections from the Prison Notebooks of Antonio Gramsci*.
27. Wilhelm Reich, "What is Class-Consciousness?" p. 23.
28. See Kurt Lewin, *Resolving Social Conflicts*, p. 198.
29. Friedrich Nietzsche, *Joyful Wisdom*, p. 209 (#275).
30. Karl Marx, "Economic and Philosophic Manuscripts (1844)" pp. 257–258.
31. Ibid., p. 282.
32. Ibid., p. 292.
33. Karl Marx and Friedrich Engels, *The Holy Family, or Critique of Critical Criticism*, p. 43.
34. See Marx, pp. 262–263.
35. Ibid., p. 322.
36. See Georg Lukács, *History and Class Consciousness*, p. 205; Wellmer, p. 11.
37. Paul Piccone, "Reading the Grundrisse," p. 239.
38. Henri Lefèbvre, *Everyday Life in the Modern World*, pp. 30–31.
39. Jean Paul Sartre, *Anti-Semite and Jew*, p. 67; see Leo Kuper, "Race, Class and Power," p. 400.
40. Jean Baudrillard, *The Mirror of Production*, p. 134.
41. Gramsci, p. 367.

BIBLIOGRAPHY

Achilles, Nancy. 1967 [1964]. "Development of the Homosexual Bar as an Institution." In *Sexual Deviance*, edited by John Gagnon and William Simon. New York: Harper & Row.

Adelson, Joseph. 1953. "A Study of Minority Group Authoritarianism." *Journal of Abnormal and Social Psychology* 48:479.

Adorno, Theodor. 1973 [1966]. *Negative Dialectics*, Translated from the German by E. B. Ashton. New York: Seabury.

——, Else Frenkel-Brunswik, Daniel Levinson, and R. Nevitt Sanford. 1950. *The Authoritarian Personality*. New York: Harper.

Allport, Gordon. 1958 [1954]. *The Nature of Prejudice*. Garden City, N. Y.: Doubleday, Anchor Books.

Allport, G. W., J. S. Bruner, and E. M. Jandorf. 1941. "Personality under Social Catastrophe: Ninety Life-Histories of the Nazi Revolution." *Character and Personality* 10 (Sept.): 15.

Altman, Dennis. 1971. *Homosexual: Oppression and Liberation*. New York: Outerbridge & Dienstfrey.

Anant, Santokh. 1966. "Inter-Caste Difference in Personality Pattern as a Function of Socialization." *Phylon* 27 (Summer): 145.

Antonovsky, Aaron. 1960. "Like Everyone Else, Only More So: Identity, Anxiety, and the Jew." In *Identity and Anxiety: Survival of the Person in Mass Society*, edited by Maurice Stein, Arthur Vidich, and David White, New York: Free Press.

Aptheker, Herbert. 1945 [1943]. *American Negro Slave Revolts*. New York: International Publishers.

Arendt, Hannah. 1966 [1951]. *The Origins of Totalitarianism*. New York: Harcourt, Brace and World.

Asher, Steven and Vernon Allen. 1969. "Racial Preference and Social Comparison Processes." *Journal of Social Issues* 25: 161.

Ausubel, David. 1963 [1956]. "Ego Development among Segregated Negro Children." In *Mental Health and Segregation*, edited by Martin Grossack. New York: Springer.

Bailey, Derrick. 1955. *Homosexuality and the Western Christian Tradition*. London: Longmans, Green.

Baldus, Bernd. 1974. "Social Structure and Ideology: Cognitive and Behavioral Responses to Servitude among the Machube of Northern Dahomey." *Canadian Journal of African Studies* 8: 2.

———. 1975. "The Study of Power: Suggestions for an Alternative." *Canadian Journal of Sociology* 1 (Summer): 179.

Baldwin, James. 1968 [1961]. *Nobody Knows My Name: More Notes of a Native Son*. New York: Dell.

——— and Nikki Giovanni. 1973. *A Dialogue*. Philadelphia: Lippincott.

Barkun, Michael. 1974. *Disaster and the Millenium*. New Haven, Conn.: Yale University Press.

Barlow, D. H., G. G. Abel, E. B. Blanchard, and M. Mavissakalian. 1974. "Plasma Testosterone Levels and Male Homosexuals: a Failure to Replicate." *Archives of Sexual Behavior* 3(6): 571.

Barlow, David, Harold Leitenberg, and W. Stewart Agras. 1969. "Experimental Control of Sexual Deviation through Manipulation of the Noxious Scene in Covert Sensitization." *Journal of Abnormal Psychology* 74 (Oct.): 600.

Barnett, Walter. 1973. *Sexual Freedom and the Constitution: An Inquiry into the Constitutionality of Repressive Sex Laws*. Albuquerque: Univ. of New Mexico Press.

Barrett, Curtis et al. 1972. *Abnormal Psychology: Current Perspectives* Del Mar, Cal.: CRM Books.

Bastide, Roger. 1972 [1965]. *The Sociology of Mental Disorder*. Translated from the French by Jean McNeil. London: Routledge & Kegan Paul.

Baudrillard, Jean. 1975. *The Mirror of Production*. Translated from the French by Mark Poster. St. Louis, Mo.: Telos.

Baughman, E. Earl. 1971. *Black Americans: A Psychological Analysis*. New York: Academic Press.

Bayton, James, Lettie Austin, and Kay Burke. 1971 [1965]. "Negro Perception of Negro and White Personality Traits." In *The Psychological Consequences of Being a Black American: A Sourcebook of Research by Black Psychologists*, edited by Roger Wilcox. New York: Wiley.

Bayton, James and Tressie Muldrow. 1971 [1968]. "Interacting Variables in the Perception of Racial Personality Traits." In *The Psychological Consequences of Being a Black American: A Sourcebook of Research by Black Psychologists*, edited by Roger Wilcox. New York: Wiley.

Becker, Raymond de. 1969 [1964]. *The Other Face of Love*. Translated from the French by Margaret Crosland and Alan Daventry. New York: Grove Press.

Bein, Alex. 1964. "The Jewish Parasite: Notes on the Semantics of the Jewish Problem, with Special Reference to Germany." *Leo Baeck Institute Year Book* 9: 3.

Bell, Daniel. 1961. "Reflections on Jewish Identity." *Commentary* 31 (June): 473.

Berger, Emanuel. 1952. "The Relation between Expressed Acceptance of Self and Expressed Acceptance of Others." *Journal of Abnormal and Social Psychology* 47 (Oct.): 782.

Berger, Peter and Thomas Luckmann. 1967 [1966]. *The Social Construction of Reality: A Treatise in the Sociology of Knowledge*. Garden City, N. Y.: Doubleday, Anchor Books.

Bergman, Peter. 1969. *The Chronological History of the Negro in America*. New York: New American Library.

Berkowitz, Leonard. 1968. "The Study of Urban Violence: Some Implications of Laboratory Studies of Frustration and Aggression." *American Behavioral Scientist* 11 (March–April): 14.

Bernstein, Peretz. 1951 [1926]. *Jew-Hate as a Sociological Problem*. Translated from the German by David Seraph. New York: Philosophical Library.

Berry, Mary. 1971. *Black Resistance/White Law: A History of Constitutional Racism in America*. New York: Appleton-Century-Crofts.

Bettelheim, Bruno. 1943. "Individual and Mass Behavior in Extreme Situations." *Journal of Abnormal and Social Psychology* 38: 426.

———. 1947. "The Dynamism of Anti-Semitism in Gentile and Jew." *Journal of Abnormal and Social Psychology* 42: 153.

———, and Morris Janowitz. 1967 [1950]. *Social Change and Prejudice: Including Dynamics of Prejudice*. New York: Free Press.

Biddiss, Michael. 1966. "Gobineau and the Origins of European Racism." *Race* 7 (Jan.): 262.

Bieber, Irving et al. 1962. *Homosexuality: A Psychoanalytic Study*. New York: Basic Books.

Billingsley, Andrew. 1973 [1970]. "Black Families in White Social Science." In *The Death of White Sociology*, edited by Joyce Ladner. New York: Random House.

Binswanger, Ludwig. 1968. *Being-in-the-world: Selected Papers of Ludwig Binswanger*. Translated from the German by Jacob Needleman. New York: Harper & Row.

Blassingame, John. 1972. *The Slave Community: Plantation Life in the Antebellum South*. New York: Oxford University Press.

Blauner, Robert. 1972. *Racial Oppression in America*. New York: Harper & Row.

Blumberg, P. 1963. "Magic in the Modern World." *Sociology and Social Research* 47 (Jan.): 151.

Blumstein, Philip and Pepper Schwartz. 1974. "Lesbianism and Bisexuality." In *Sexual Deviance and Sexual Deviants*, edited by Erich Goode and Richard Troiden. New York: Morrow.

Bolkosky, Sidney. 1975. *The Distorted Image: German Jewish Perceptions of Germans and Germany, 1918–1935*. New York: American Elsevier.

Borchsenius, Poul. 1964 [1957]. *History of the Jews: Behind the Wall: The Story of the Ghetto*. Vol. 3. Translated from the Danish by Reginald Spink. London: Allen & Unwin.

———. 1965 [1958]. *The History of the Jews: The Chains Are Broken: The Story of Jewish Emancipation*. Vol. 4. Translated from the Danish by Michael Heron. New York: Simon and Schuster.

Bovell, Gilbert. 1943. "Psychological Considerations of Color Conflicts among Negroes." *Psychoanalytic Review* 30: 448.

Brigham, John. 1974. "Views of Black and White Children Concerning the Distribution of Personality Characteristics." *Journal of Personality* 42 (March): 144.

Brisbane, Robert. 1970. *The Black Vanguard: Origins of the Negro Social Revolution, 1900–1960*. Valley Forge, Pa.: Judson.

———. 1974. *Black Activism: Racial Revolution in the United States, 1954–1970*. Valley Forge, Pa.: Judson.

Broderick, Francis and August Meier, eds. 1965. *Negro Protest Thought in the Twentieth Century*. Indianapolis, Ind.: Bobbs-Merrill.

Brodie, K., N. Gartrell, C. Doering, and T. Rhue. 1974. "Plasma Testosterone Levels in Heterosexual and Homosexual Men." *American Journal of Psychiatry* 131 (1): 82.

Brody, Eugene. 1966. "Cultural Exclusion, Character and Illness." *American Journal of Psychiatry* 122 (Feb.): 856.

Broom, Leonard, Helen Beem, and Virginia Harria. 1955. "Characteristics of the 1,107 Petitioners for Change of Name." *American Sociological Review* 20 (Feb.): 33.

Bullough, Vern. 1974. "Heresy, Witchcraft, and Sexuality." *Journal of Homosexuality* 1 (Winter): 183.

Butts, Hugh. 1963. "Skin-Color Perception and Self-Esteem." *Journal of Negro Education* 32 (Spring): 122.

Bychowski, Gustav. 1959. "Some Aspects of Masochistic Involvement." *Journal of the American Psychoanalytic Association* 7: 248.

Cameron, Howard. 1971 [1967]. "A Review of Research and an Investigation of Emotional Dependency among Negro Youth." In *The Psychological Consequences of Being a Black American: A Sourcebook of Research by Black Psychologists*, edited by Roger Wilcox. New York: Wiley.

Canning, Ray and James Baker. 1959. "Effect of the Group on Authoritarian and Non-Authoritarian Persons." *American Journal of Sociology* 64 (May): 580.

Carmichael, Stokely and Charles Hamilton. 1967. *Black Power: The Politics of Liberation in America*. New York: Random House.

Chang, Judy and Jack Block. 1960. "A Study of Identification in Male Homosexuals." *Journal of Consulting Psychology* 24 (4): 307.

Chethik, Morton, Elizabeth Fleming, Morris Mayer, and John McCoy. 1967. "Quest for Identity: Treatment of Disturbed Negro Children in a Predominantly White Treatment Center." *American Journal of Orthopsychiatry* 37 (Jan.): 74.

Chiles, John. 1972. "Homosexuality in the United States Air Force." *Comprehensive Psychiatry* 13 (Nov.–Dec.): 529.

Chivers, W. R. 1934. "Race Discrimination and Negro Personality." *Social Forces* 13 (Dec.): 264.

Clark, Kenneth and Mamie Clark. 1939. "Development of Consciousness of Self and the Emergence of Racial Identification in Negro Preschool Children." *Journal of Social Psychology* 10: 591.

————. 1963 [1950]. "Emotional Factors in Racial Identification and Preference in Negro Children." In *Mental Health and Segregation*, edited by Martin Grossack. New York: Springer.

Cohen, Elie. 1954. *Human Behavior in the Concentration Camp*. Translated from the Dutch by M. H. Braaksma. London: Jonathan Cape.

Cohen, Yehudi. 1958. "Some Aspects of Ritualized Behavior in Interpersonal Relationships." *Human Relations* 11 (3): 205.

Coleman, James. 1973. "My Homosexuality and My Psychotherapy." In *Homosexuality: A Changing Picture*, edited by Hendrik Ruitenbeck. London: Souvenir.

Coles, Robert. 1967 [1964]. *Children of Crisis: A Study of Courage and Fear*. Boston: Little, Brown.

Coopersmith, Stanley. 1967. *The Antecedents of Self-Esteem*. San Francisco: Freeman.

Cox, Oliver. 1959 [1948]. *Caste, Class, and Race: A Study in Social Dynamics*. Garden City, N. Y.: Doubleday.

Crain, Robert and Carol Weisman. 1972. *Discrimination, Personality, and Achievement: A Survey of Northern Blacks*. New York: Seminar.

Cronin, Denise. 1974. "Coming Out Among Lesbians." In *Sexual Deviance and Sexual Deviants*, edited by Erich Goode and Richard Troiden. New York: Morrow.

Cross, William. 1971. "Discovering the Black Referent: The Psychology of Black Liberation." In *Beyond Black or White: An Alternate America*, edited by Vernon Dixon and Badi Foster. Boston: Little, Brown.

———. 1973 [1971]. "The Negro-to-Black Conversion Experience." In *The Death of White Sociology*, edited by Joyce Ladner. New York: Random House.

Dai, Bingham. 1953 [1946] "Some Problems of Personality Development in Negro Children." In *Personality in Nature, Society, and Culture*, edited by Clyde Kluckhohn and Henry Murray. New York: Knopf.

Dank, Barry. 1971. "Coming Out in the Gay World." *Psychiatry* 34 (May): 182.

———. 1974 [1973]. "The Homosexual." In *Sexual Deviance and Sexual Deviants*, edited by Erich Goode and Richard Troiden. New York: Morrow.

Dannecker, Martin and Reimut Reiche. 1974. *Der gewöhnliche Homosexuelle: eine soziologische Untersuchung über männliche Homosexuelle in der Bundesrepublik*. Frankfurt: Fischer.

Davis, John. 1976. "Blacks, Crime, and American Culture." *The Annals of the American Academy of Political and Social Science*. 423 (Jan.): 95.

Davison, Gerald and G. Terence Wilson. 1973. "Attitudes of Behavior Therapists toward Homosexuality." *Behavior Therapy* 4 (Oct.): 686.

Dean, Dwight. 1961. "Alienation: Its Meaning and Measurement." *American Sociological Review* 26 (Oct.) 756.

Dean, Robert and Harold Richardson. 1964. "Analysis of MMPI Profiles of 40 College-Educated Overt Male Homosexuals." *Journal of Consulting Psychology* 28 (6): 483.

Deleuze, Gilles. 1971. *Sacher-Masoch: An Interpretation*. Translated from the French by Jean McNeil. London: Faber.

DeMott, Benjamin. 1973. "'But he is a homosexual . . .'." In *Homosexuality: A Changing Picture*, edited by Hendrik Ruitenbeek. London: Souvenir.

Deutsch, Martin. 1963 [1960]. "Minority Group and Class Status as Related to Social and Personality Factors in Scholastic Achievement." In *Mental Health and Segregation*, edited by Martin Grossack. New York: Springer.

Deutscher, Isaac. 1968. *The Non-Jewish Jew and Other Essays*. New York: Oxford University Press.

Dickey, Brenda. 1961. "Attitudes towards Sex Roles and Feelings of Adequacy in Homosexual Males." *Journal of Consulting Psychology* 25 (2): 121.

Diesendruck, Z. 1946. "Antisemitism and Ourselves." In *Essays on Antisemitism*, edited by Keppel Pinson. New York: Conference on Jewish Relations.

Dollard, John. 1957 [1937]. *Caste and Class in a Southern Town*. Garden City, N. Y.: Doubleday, Anchor Books.

Dorcus, Roy and G. Wilson Shaffer. 1950 [1934]. *Textbook of Abnormal Psychology*. Baltimore: Williams & Wilkins.

Doyle, Bertram. 1971 [1937]. *The Etiquette of Race Relations in the South: A Study in Social Control*. New York: Schocken.

Dubnov, Simon. 1973. *History of the Jews: From the Congress of Vienna to the Emergence of Hitler*. Vol. 5. Translated from the Russian by Moshe Spiegel. South Brunswick, N. J.: Yoseloff.

DuBois, W. E. B. 1961 [1903]. *The Souls of Black Folk: Essays and Sketches*.

———. 1962 [1935]. *Black Reconstruction in America: An Essay toward a History of the Part Which Black Folk Played in the Attempt to Reconstruct Democracy in America, 1860–1880*. New York: Russell & Russell.

Edelman, Murray. 1964. *The Symbolic Uses of Politics.* Urbana: Univ. of Illinois Press.

———. 1971. *Politics as Symbolic Action: Mass Arousal and Quiescence.* Chicago: Markham.

———. 1974. "The Political Language of the Helping Professions." *Politics and Society* 4 (3): 295.

Ehrlich, Howard. 1973. *The Social Psychology of Prejudice: A Systematic Theoretical Review and Propositional Inventory of the American Social Psychological Study of Prejudice.* New York: Wiley.

Eliade, Mircea. 1954 [1949]. *The Myth of the Eternal Return or, Cosmos and History.* Translated from the French by Willard Trask. New York: Pantheon.

Elkins, Stanley. 1968 [1959]. *Slavery: A Problem in American Institutional and Intellectual Life.* Chicago: Univ. of Chicago Press.

Epstein, Ralph and S. S. Komorita. 1970 [1966]. "Prejudice among Negro Children as Related to Parental Ethnocentrism and Punitiveness." In *Black Americans and White Racism: Theory and Research,* edited by Marcel Goldschmid. New York: Holt, Rinehart and Winston.

Erikson, Erik. 1963. *Childhood and Society.* New York: Norton.

Fanon, Frantz. 1967 [1952]. *Black Skins, White Masks.* Translated from the French by Charles Markmann. New York: Grove Press.

Feagin, Joe and Harlan Hahn. 1973. *Ghetto Revolts: The Politics of Violence in American Cities.* New York: Macmillan.

Feldman, Maurice and M. J. MacCulloch. 1971. *Homosexual Behavior: Therapy and Assessment.* Oxford: Pergamon.

Fenichel, Otto. 1940. "Psycho-Analysis of Antisemitism." *American Imago* 1: 24.

Fish, Jeanne and Charlotte Larr. 1972. "A Decade of Change in Drawings by Black Children." *American Journal of Psychiatry* 129 (Oct.): 421.

Fisher, Peter. 1972. *The Gay Mystique: The Myth and Reality of Male Homosexuality.* New York: Stein and Day.

Fitzgerald, Thomas. 1963. "A Theoretical Typology of Homosexuality in the United States." *Corrective Psychiatry and Journal of Social Therapy* 9 (1): 31.

Flannery, Edward. 1965. *The Anguish of the Jews: Twenty-three Centuries of Anti-Semitism.* New York: Macmillan.

Fogelson, Robert. 1968. "From Resentment to Confrontation: The Police, the Negroes, and the Outbreak of the Nineteen-Sixties Riots." *Political Science Quarterly* 83 (June): 247.

Francher, J. Scott and Janet Henkin. 1973. "The Menopausal Queen: Adjustment to Aging and the Male Homosexual" *American Journal of Orthopsychiatry* 43 (July): 670.

Franklin, Raymond and Solomon Resnik. 1973. *The Political Economy of Racism.* New York: Holt, Rinehart and Winston.

Frazier, E. Franklin. 1957 [1949]. *The Negro in the United States.* New York: Macmillan.

———. 1962. *Black Bourgeoisie: The Rise of a New Middle Class in the United States.* New York: Collier.

———. 1964. *The Negro Church in America.* Liverpool, England: Liverpool University.

———. 1967 [1940]. *Negro Youth at the Crossways: Their Personality Development in the Middle States.* New York: Schocken.

Fredrickson, George. 1971. *The Black Image in the White Mind: The Debate on Afro-American Character and Destiny, 1817–1914.* New York: Harper & Row.

Freeman, Howard, David Armor, J. Michael Ross, and Thomas Pettigrew. 1966.

"Color Gradation and Attitudes among Middle-Income Negroes." *American Sociological Review* 31 (June): 370.

Freud, Anna. 1973 [1937]. *The Ego and the Mechanisms of Defense*. Translated from the German by Cecil Baines. New York: International Universities.

Freud, Sigmund. 1952 [1917]. "A General Introduction to Psycho-Analysis." Translated from the German by Joan Riviere. In *The Major Works of Sigmund Freud*. Great Books of the Western World. Vol. 54. Chicago: Encyclopaedia Britannica.

———. 1952 [1929]. "Civilization and Its Discontents." Translated from the German by Joan Riviere. In *The Major Works of Sigmund Freud*. Great Books of the Western World. Vol. 54. Chicago: Encyclopaedia Britannica.

———. 1960 [1905]. "Jokes and Their Relation to the Unconscious." In *The Standard Edition of the Complete Psychological Works of Sigmund Freud*, Vol. 8, edited by James Strachey. London: Hogarth.

———. 1964 [1927] *The Future of an Illusion*. Translated from the German by W. D. Robson-Scott. Garden City, N. Y.: Doubleday, Anchor Books.

———. 1964 [1907]. "Obsessive Actions and Religious Practices." In *The Standard Edition of the Complete Psychological Works of Sigmund Freud*, Vol. 9, edited by James Strachey. London: Hogarth.

———. 1971. "Dostoevsky and Parricide." In *Guilt: Man and Society*, edited by Roger Smith. Garden City, N. Y.: Doubleday, Anchor Books.

Freund, K. 1974. "Male Homosexuality: An Analysis of the Pattern." *Understanding Homosexuality: Its Biological and Psychological Bases*, edited by J. A. Loraine. Lancaster, England: MTP.

Front Homosexuel d'Action Révolutionnaire. 1971. *Rapport contre la normalité*. Paris: Editions Champ Libre.

Gabel, Joseph. 1970. *Sociologie de l'aliénation*. Paris: Presses universitaires de France.

Genovese, Eugene. 1974. *Roll, Jordan, Roll: The World the Slaves Made*. New York: Pantheon.

Gerassi, John. 1968 [1966]. *The Boys of Boise: Furor, Vice, and Folly in an American City*. New York: Collier.

Goff, Regina. 1949. *Problems and Emotional Difficulties of Negro Children*. New York: Columbia University Press.

Goffman, Erving. 1961. *Asylums: Essays on the Social Situation of Mental Patients and Other Inmates*. Garden City, N. Y.: Doubleday, Anchor Books.

———. 1963. *Stigma: Notes on the Management of Spoiled Identity*. Englewood Cliffs, N. J.: Prentice-Hall.

Goldstein, Sidney and Calvin Goldscheider. 1968. *Jewish Americans: Three Generations in a Jewish Community*. Englewood Cliffs, N. J.: Prentice-Hall.

Goodman, Mary. 1952. *Race Awareness in Young Children*. Cambridge, Mass.: Addison-Wesley.

Gorz, André. 1973 [1967]. *Socialism and Revolution*. Translated from the French by Norman Denny. Garden City, N. Y.: Doubleday, Anchor Books.

Gramsci, Antonio. 1973 [1935]. *Selections from the Prison Notebooks of Antonio Gramsci*. Translated from the Italian by Quinton Hoare and Geoffrey Nowell Smith. London: Lawrence and Wishart.

Greenberg, Jerrold. 1973. "A Study of the Self-Esteem and Alienation of Male Homosexuals." *Journal of Psychology* 83 (Jan.): 137.

Greenson, Ralph. 1947. "On Gambling." *American Imago* 4 (April): 62.

Grier, William and Price Cobbs. 1968. *Black Rage*. New York: Basic Books.

———. 1971. *The Jesus Bag*. New York: McGraw-Hill.

Grossack, Martin. 1963 [1956]. "Group Belongingness among Negroes." In *Mental Health and Segregation*, edited by Martin Grossack. New York: Springer.

———. 1957. "Group Belongingness and Authoritarianism in Southern Negroes— a Research Note." *Phylon* 18 (3): 266.

Grotjahn, Martin. 1957. *Beyond Laughter*. New York: Blakeston.

Gundlach, Ralph and Bernard Riess. 1968. "Self and Sexual Identity in the Female: A Study of Female Homosexuals." In *New Directions in Mental Health*. Vol. 1, edited by Bernard Reiss. New York: Grune & Stratton.

Gusfield, Joseph. 1972 [1963]. *Symbolic Crusade: Status, Politics and the American Temperance Movement*. Urbana: Univ. of Illinois Press.

Halpern, Florence. 1970. "Self-Perception of Black Children and the Civil Rights Movement." *American Journal of Orthopsychiatry* 40 (April): 523.

Hammond, John and Barbara. 1966. *The Town Labourer, 1760–1832: The New Civilization*. London: Longmans.

Hannerz, Ulf. 1969. *Soulside: Inquiries into Ghetto Culture and Community*. New York: Columbia University Press.

———. 1973. "The Significance of Soul." In *Black Experience: Soul*, edited by Lee Rainwater. New Brunswick, N. J.: Transaction.

Hannon, Gerald. 1972. "School Is a Drag?" *Body Politic* 3 (March–April): 12

Hatterer, Lawrence. 1970. *Changing Homosexuality in the Male: Treatment for Men Troubled by Homosexuality*. New York: McGraw-Hill.

Hauser, Stuart. 1971. *Black and White Identity Formation: Studies in the Psychosocial Development of Lower Socioeconomic Class Adolescent Boys*. New York: Wiley.

Hegel, G. W. F. 1952. *The Philosophy of History*. Translated from the German by J. Sibree. Great Books of the Western World. Vol. 46. Chicago: Encyclopaedia Britannica.

———. 1967 [1931]. *The Phenomenology of Mind*. Translated from the German by J. B. Baillie: Harper & Row.

Heger, Heinz. 1972. *Die Männer mit dem rosa Winkel: der Bericht eines Homosexuellen über seine KZ-Haft von 1939–1945*. Hamburg: Merlin.

Heidegger, Martin. 1962 [1931] *Being and Time*. Translated from the German by John MacQuarrie and Edward Robinson. New York: Harper & Row.

Heiss, Jerold and Susan Owens. 1972. "Self-Evaluations of Blacks and Whites." *American Journal of Sociology* 78 (Sept.): 260.

Hendin, Herbert. 1969. *Black Suicide*. New York: Basic Books.

Herman, David and Marie Nelson. 1973. "The Treatment of Psychosocial Masochism." *Psychoanalytic Review* 60 (Fall): 353.

Herman, Simon. 1945. *The Reaction of Jews to Anti-Semitism: A Social Psychological Study Based Upon the Attitudes of a Group of South African Jewish Students*. Johannesburg: Witwatersrand University.

Hilberg, Raul. 1961. *The Destruction of the European Jews*. Chicago: Quadrangle.

Hirsch, Jerry. 1973 [1969]. "Behavior-Genetic Analysis and Its Biosocial Consequences." In *Comparative Studies of Blacks and Whites in the United States* edited by Kent Miller and Ralph Dreger. New York: Seminar.

Hitler, Adolf. 1940 [1925] *Mein Kampf*. Translated from the German by John Chamberlain et al. New York: Reynal & Hitchcock.

Hobsbawm, E. J. 1963 [1959]. *Primitive Rebels: Studies in Archaic Forms of Social Movement in the 19th and 20th Centuries*. Manchester, England: Manchester University.

Hodges, Andrew and David Hutter. 1974. *With Downcast Gays: Aspects of Homosexual Self-Oppression.* London: Pomegranate.

Hoffman, Martin. 1973 [1968]. *The Gay World: Male Homosexuality and the Social Creation of Evil.* New York: Bantam.

———. 1975. *A Homosexual Emancipation Miscellany, c. 1835–1952.* New York: Arno.

Hook, Sidney. 1949. "Reflections on the Jewish Question." *Partisan Review* 16 (May): 479.

Hooker, Evelyn. 1957. "The Adjustment of the Male Overt Homosexual." *Journal of Projective Techniques* 21: 18.

———. 1965. "Male Homosexuals and their 'Worlds'." In *Sexual Inversion: The Multiple Roots of Homosexuality,* edited by Judd Marmor. New York: Basic Books.

Horkheimer, Max. 1972 [1968]. *Critical Theory: Selected Essays.* Translated from the German by Matthew O'Connell et al. New York: Herder and Herder.

——— and Theodor Adorno. 1972 [1944]. *The Dialectic of Enlightenment.* Translated from the German by John Cumming. New York: Herder and Herder.

Horowitz, Irving. 1974. *Israeli Ecstasies/Jewish Agonies.* New York: Oxford University Press.

Hraba, Joseph and Geoffrey Grant. 1970. "Black is Beautiful: A Reexamination of Racial Preference and Identification." *Journal of Personality and Social Psychology* 16 (3): 400.

Hubert, Henri and Marcel Mauss. 1968 [1898]. *Sacrifice: Its Nature and Function.* Translated from the French by W. D. Halls. Chicago: Univ. of Chicago Press.

Humphreys, Laud. 1971. "New Styles in Homosexual Manliness." In *The Homosexual Dialectic,* edited by Joseph McCaffrey. Englewood Cliffs, N. J.: Prentice-Hall.

———. 1972. *Out of the Closets: The Sociology of Homosexual Liberation.* Englewood Cliffs, N. J.: Prentice-Hall.

Hyde, H. Montgomery. 1970. *The Other Love: A Historical and Contemporary Survey of Homosexuality in Britain.* London: Heinemann.

———. ed. 1956 [1948]. *The Three Trials of Oscar Wilde.* New York: New York University Press.

Ince, Laurence. 1973. "Behavior Modification of Sexual Disorders." *American Journal of Psychotherapy* 27 (July): 446.

Isaacs, Harold. 1965 [1964]. *India's Ex-Untouchables.* New York: John Day.

Jackson, Jacqueline. 1973. "Black Women in a Racist Society." In *Racism and Mental Health: Essays,* edited by Charles Willie, Bernard Kramer, and Bertram Brown. Pittsburgh, Pa.: Univ. of Pittsburgh Press.

Jaffe, Ruth. 1970. "Sense of Guilt within Holocaust Survivors." *Jewish Social Studies* 32 (Oct.): 308.

James, E. O. 1962. *Sacrifice and Sacrament.* London: Thames and Hudson.

Janis, Irving. 1963. "Personality as a Factor in Susceptibility to Persuasion." In *The Science of Human Communication: New Directions and New Findings in Communication Research,* edited by Wilbur Schramm. New York: Basic Books.

———. 1974 [1958]. *Psychological Stress: Psychoanalytic and Behavioral Studies of Surgical Patients.* New York: Academic Press.

Joesting, Joan, Alan Ogus, and Robert Joesting. 1973. "Consistencies in Views of Deviants by College Students." *Psychological Reports* 33 (Aug.): 138.

Johnson, Charles. 1963 [1947]. "The Guidance Problems of Negro Youth." In *Mental Health and Segregation,* edited by Martin Grossack. New York: Springer.

Johnson, Guy. 1944. "The Stereotype of the American Negro." In *Characteristics of the American Negro*, edited by Otto Klineberg. New York: Harper.

Johnson, Robert. 1962 [1957]. "Negro Reactions to Minority Group Status." In *American Minorities: A Textbook of Readings in Intergroup Relations*, edited by Milton Barron. New York: Knopf.

Johnston, Jill. 1973 [1970]. *Lesbian Nation: The Feminist Solution*. New York: Simon and Schuster.

Jones, Rhett. 1973 [1965]. "Proving Blacks Inferior: The Sociology of Knowledge." In *The Death of White Sociology*, edited by Joyce Ladner. New York: Random House.

Kando, Thomas. 1974. "Males, Females, and Transsexuals: A Comparative Study of Sexual Conservatism." *Journal of Homosexuality* 1: 64.

Kardiner, Abram and Lionel Ovesey. 1972 [1951]. *The Mark of Oppression: Explorations in the Personality of the American Negro*. New York: Meridian.

Katz, Barney and Robert Lewis. 1961 [1948]. *The Psychology of Abnormal Behavior: A Dynamic Approach*. New York: Ronald.

Katz, Jacob. 1973. *Out of the Ghetto: The Social Background of Jewish Emancipation, 1770–1870*. Cambridge, Mass.: Harvard University Press

Keil, Charles. 1966. *Urban Blues*. Chicago: Univ. of Chicago Press.

Kelman, Harold. 1959. "Masochism and Self-Realization." In *Individual and Family Dynamics* edited by Jules Masserman. New York: Grune & Stratton.

Kennedy, Janet. 1963 [1952]. "Problems Posed in the Analysis of Negro Patients." In *Mental Health and Segregation*, edited by Martin Grossack. New York: Springer.

Knight, James. 1969. *Conscience and Guilt*. New York: Appleton-Century-Crofts.

Koedt, Anne. 1974 [1971]. "Loving Another Woman." In *Sexual Deviance and Sexual Deviants*, edited by Erich Goode and Richard Troiden. New York: Morrow.

Kolko, Gabriel. 1969 [1962]. *Wealth and Power in America: An Analysis of Social Class and Income Distribution*. New York: Praeger.

Kovarsky, Irving and William Albrecht. 1970. *Black Employment: The Impact of Religion, Economic Theory, Politics, and Law*. Ames: Iowa State University Press.

Kovel, Joel. 1970. *White Racism: A Psychohistory*. New York: Pantheon.

Kozol, Jonathan. 1967. *Death at an Early Age: The Destruction of the Hearts and Minds of Negro Children in the Boston Public Schools*. Boston: Houghton Mifflin.

Kramer, Judith. 1970. *The American Minority Community*. New York: Crowell.

―― and Seymour Leventman. 1961. *Children of the Gilded Ghetto: Conflict Resolution of Three Generations of American Jews*. New Haven, Conn.: Yale University Press.

Kuper, Leo. 1972. "Race, Class and Power: Some Comments on Revolutionary Change." *Comparative Studies in Society and History* 14 (Summer): 400.

Ladner, Joyce, ed. 1973. *The Death of White Sociology*. New York: Random House.

Lamberd, W. G. 1969. "The Treatment of Homosexuality as a Monosymptomatic Phobia." *American Journal of Psychiatry* 126 (Oct.): 512.

Landecker, W. S. 1970. "Status Congruence, Class Crystallization, and Social Cleavage." *Sociology and Social Research* 54 (July): 228.

Landreth, C. and B. C. Johnson. 1953. "Young Children's Responses to a Picture and Inset Test Designed to Reveal Reactions to Persons of Different Skin Colour." *Child Development* 24: 63.

Lane, Robert. 1959. "Fear of Equality." *American Political Science Review* 53 (March): 35.

———. 1968. *Political Ideology: Why the American Common Man Believes What He Does.* New York: Free Press.

Langner, Thomas. 1962. "A Twenty-two Item Screening Score of Psychiatric Symptoms Indicating Impairment." *Journal of Health and Human Behavior* 3 (Winter): 30

Larson, Calvin and Richard Hill. 1972. "Segregation, Community Consciousness, and Black Power." *Journal of Black Studies* 2 (March): 271.

Lauritsen, John and David Thorstad. 1974. *The Early Homosexual Rights Movement (1864–1935)* New York: Times Change.

Lefèbvre, Henri. 1971 [1967]. *Everyday Life in the Modern World.* Translated from the French by Sacha Rabinovitch. New York: Harper & Row.

Lerner, Richard and Christie Buehrig. 1975. "The Development of Racial Attitudes in Young Black and White Children." *Journal of Genetic Psychology* 127 (Sept.): 45.

Lesse, Stanley. 1973. "Oh God! Who Created Heaven and Earth and Even Psychiatrists and Psychologists, Please Protect Us from Well-Meaning but Confused 'Experts'—or—The Current Confusion Over Homosexuality." (editorial) *American Journal of Psychotherapy* 27 (April): 151.

Levitt, Eugene and Albert Klassen. 1974. "Public Attitudes toward Homosexuality: Part of the 1970 National Survey by the Institute for Sex Research." *Journal of Homosexuality* 1 (Fall): 32.

Lewin, Kurt. 1948. *Resolving Social Conflicts: Selected Papers on Group Dynamics, 1935–1946*, edited by Gerturd Lewin. New York: Harper.

Lewis, Helen. 1971. *Shame and Guilt in Neurosis.* New York: International Universities.

Lifton, Robert. 1956. "'Thought Reform' of Western Civilians in Chinese Communist Prisons." *Psychiatry* 19 (May): 189.

———. 1961. *Thought Reform and the Psychology of Totalism: A Study of "Brainwashing" in China.* New York: Norton.

Loney, Jan. 1972. "Background Factors, Sexual Experiences, and Attitudes toward Treatment in Two 'Normal' Homosexual Samples." *Journal of Consulting and Clinical Psychology* 38 (1): 61.

Lourié, Anton. 1949. "The Jews as a Psychological Type." *American Imago* 6 (March): 126.

Lukács, Georg. 1975 [1922]. *History and Class Consciousness: Studies in Marxist Dialectics.* Translated from the German by Rodney Livingstone. Cambridge, Mass.: MIT Press.

Lyman, Stanford. 1972. *The Black American in Sociological Thought: A Failure of Perspective.* New York: Putnam.

——— and Marvin Scott. 1970. *A Sociology of the Absurd.* New York: Appleton-Century-Crofts.

Maass, E. 1958. "Integration and Name Changing among Jewish Refugees from Central Europe in the United States." *Names* 6 (Summer): 6.

MacDonald, A. P. 1974. "The Importance of Sex-Role to Gay Liberation." *Homosexual Counseling Journal* 4 (Oct.) 169.

Maliver, Bruce. 1970 [1965]. "Anti-Negro Bias among Negro College Students." In *Black Americans and White Racism: Theory and Research*, edited by Marcel Goldschmid. New York: Holt, Rinehart and Winston.

Mann, Michael. 1973. *Consciousness and Action among the Western Working Class*. London: Macmillan.

Mannoni, Dominique. 1964 [1948]. *Prospero and Caliban: The Psychology of Colonization*. Translated from the French by Pamela Powesland. New York: Praeger.

Marcuse, Herbert. 1955. *Eros and Civilization: A Philosophical Inquiry into Freud*. New York: Knopf, Vintage Books.

———. 1966. *One-Dimensional Man: Studies in the Ideology of Advanced Industrial Society*. Boston: Beacon Press.

———. 1969. "Repressive Tolerance." In *A Critique of Pure Tolerance*. edited by Robert Wolff, Barrington Moore, and Herbert Marcuse. Boston: Beacon Press.

———. 1970 [1960]. *Reason and Revolution: Hegel and the Rise of Social Theory*. Boston: Beacon Press.

Marrus, Michael. 1971. *The Politics of Assimilation: A Study of the French Jewish Community at the Time of the Dreyfus Affair*. Oxford: Clarendon.

Marx, Gary. 1967. *Protest and Prejudice: A Study of Belief in the Black Community*. New York: Harper & Row.

Marx, Karl. 1967. "Economic and Philosophic Manuscripts (1844)." In *Writings of the Young Marx on Philosophy and Society*, translated from the German and edited by Loyd Easton and Kurt Guddat. Garden City, N.Y.: Doubleday.

———. 1971. *Early Texts*. Translated and edited by David Mclellan. Oxford: Blackwell.

———. 1973 [1939]. *Grundrisse: Foundations of the Critique of Political Economy*. Translated from the German by Martin Nicolaus. New York: Random House, Vintage Books.

——— and Friedrich Engels. 1975 [1844]. *The Holy Family, or Critique of Critical Criticism: Against Bruno Bauer and Company*. Translated from the German by Richard Dixon and Clemens Dutt. Moscow: Progress.

Maslow, Abraham and Béla Mittelmann. 1951 [1941]. *Principles of Abnormal Psychology: The Dynamics of Psychic Illness*. New York: Harper.

McCarthy, John and William Yancey. 1971. "Uncle Tom and Mr. Charlie: Metaphysical Pathos in the Study of Racism and Personal Disorganization." *American Journal of Sociology*. 76 (Jan.): 648.

McCord, William, John Howard, Bernhard Friedberg, and Edwin Harwood. 1969. *Life Styles in the Black Ghetto*. New York: Norton.

McKelvey, B. 1970. "Cities as Nurseries of Self-Conscious Minorities." *Pacific Historical Review* 39 (Aug.): 367.

McKenzie, Robert. 1973. "The Shelby Iron Company: A Note on Slave Personality after the Civil War." *Journal of Negro History* 58 (July): 348.

Meenes, Max. 1943. "A Comparison of Racial Stereotypes of 1930 and 1942." *Journal of Social Psychology* 17 (May): 332.

Memmi, Albert. 1963 [1962]. *Portrait of a Jew*. Translated from the French by Elisabeth Abbott. London: Eyre & Spottiswoode.

———. 1968. *Dominated Man: Notes toward a Portrait*. New York: Orion.

———. 1969. *The Colonizer and the Colonized*. Translated from the French by Howard Greenfield. Boston: Beacon Press.

———. 1973 [1966]. *The Liberation of the Jew*. Translated from the French by Judy Hyun. New York: Viking.

Merleau-Ponty, Maurice. 1968 [1948]. *Sense and Non-Sense*. Translated from the French by Hubert Dreyfus and Patricia Dreyfus. Evanston, Ill.: Northwestern University Press.

Meyer, Michael. 1967. *The Origins of the Modern Jew: Jewish Identity and European Culture in Germany, 1749–1824*. Detroit, Mich.: Wayne State University Press.

Middleton, Russell and John Moland. 1959. "Humor in Negro and White Subcultures: A Study of Jokes among University Students." *American Sociological Review* 24 (Feb.): 65.

Mitchell, Roger. 1969. *The Homosexual and the Law*. New York: Arco.

Moan, Charles and Robert Heath. 1972. "Septal Stimulation for the Initiation of Heterosexual Behavior in a Homosexual Male." *Journal of Behavior Therapy and Experimental Psychiatry* 3: 23.

Moore, Barrington. 1967 [1966]. *Social Origins of Dictatorship and Democracy: Lord and Peasant in the Making of the Modern World*. Boston: Beacon Press.

Morland, J. Kenneth. 1962. "Racial Acceptance and Preference of Nursery School Children in a Southern City." *Merrill-Palmer Quarterly of Behavior and Development* 8 (Oct.): 279.

Mosse, George, ed. 1966. *Nazi Culture: Intellectual, Cultural, and Social Life in the Third Reich*. New York: Grosset & Dunlap.

Murphy, John. 1972. "Queer Books." In *Out of the Closets: Voices of Gay Liberation*, edited by Karla Jay and Allen Young. New York: Douglas.

Myers, Henry and Leon Yochelson. 1948. "Color Denial in the Negro: A Preliminary Report." *Psychiatry* 11 (Feb.): 44.

Myrdal, Gunnar. 1964. *An American Dilemma*. New York: McGraw-Hill.

Newby, Idus. 1965. *Jim Crow's Defense: Anti-Negro Thought in America, 1900–1930*. Baton Route: Louisiana State University Press.

Newton, Huey. 1972. *To Die for the People: The Writings of Huey P. Newton*. New York: Random House.

Niederland, William. 1964. "Psychiatric Disorders among Persecution Victims: A Contribution to the Understanding of Concentration Camp Pathology and Its After-Effects." *Journal of Nervous and Mental Disease* 139 (Nov.): 458.

Nietzsche, Friedrich. 1966 [1886]. *Beyond Good and Evil: Prelude to a Philosophy of the Future*. Translated from the German by Walter Kaufmann. New York: Random House, Vintage Books.

———. 1969 [1967]. *On the Genealogy of Morals*. Translated from the German by Walter Kaufmann. New York: Random House, Vintage Books.

———. 1971 [1960]. *Joyful Wisdom*. Translated from the German by Thomas Common. New York: Frederick Ungar.

———. 1971 [1892]. "Thus Spoke Zarathustra: A Book for All and None." Translated from the German by Walter Kaufman. In *The Portable Nietzsche*. New York: Viking.

Noel, D. L. 1964. "Group Identification among Negroes: A Empirical Analysis." *Journal of Social Issues*. 20 (April): 76.

Norton, Rictor. 1974. "The Homosexual Literary Tradition: Course Outline and Objectives." *College English* 35 (March): 674.

Oliver Brachfeld, F. 1972 [1951]. *Inferiority Feelings in the Individual and the Group*. Westport, Conn.: Greenwood.

Ovesey, Lionel. 1969. *Homosexuality and Pseudohomosexuality*. New York: Science House.

Panken, Shirley. 1973. *The Joy of Suffering: Psychoanalytic Theory and Therapy of Masochism*. New York: Jason Aronson.

Parker, Seymour and Robert Kleiner. 1970 [1964]. "Status Position, Mobility, and Ethnic Identification of the Negro." In *Black Americans and White Racism:*

Theory and Research, edited by Marcel Goldschmid. New York: Holt, Rinehart and Winston.

————. 1966. *Mental Illness in the Urban Negro Community*. New York: Free Press.

Parkes, James. 1969. *Antisemitism*. Chicago: Quadrangle.

Pauly, Ira. 1969. "Adult Manifestations of Male Transsexualism." *Transsexualism and Sex Reassignment*, edited by Richard Green and John Money. Baltimore: The Johns Hopkins University Press.

Pelcovits, N. A. 1947. "What about Jewish Anti-Semitism? A Prescription to Cure Self-Hatred." *Commentary* 3 (Feb.): 118.

Piccone, Paul. 1975. "Reading the Grundrisse: Beyond 'Orthodox' Marxism." *Theory and Society* 2 (Summer): 239.

Piers, Gerhart and Milton Singer. 1971 [1953]. *Shame and Guilt: A Psychoanalytic and a Cultural Study*. New York: Norton.

Pinard, Maurice. 1971. *The Rise of a Third Party: A Study in Crisis Politics*. Englewood Cliffs, N. J.: Prentice-Hall.

Pinderhughes, Charles. 1973. "Racism and Psychotherapy." In *Racism and Mental Health: Essays*, edited by Charles Willie, Bernard Kramer, and Bertram Brown. Pittsburgh, Pa.: University of Pittsburgh Press.

Pinkney, Alphonso. 1969. *Black Americans*. Englewood Cliffs, N. J.: Prentice-Hall.

Plummer, Kenneth. 1975. *Sexual Stigma: An Interactionist Account*. London: Routledge & Kegan Paul.

Porter, Judith. 1971. *Black Child, White Child: The Development of Racial Attitudes*. Cambridge, Mass.: Harvard University Press.

Poussaint, Alvin. 1972. *Why Blacks Kill Blacks*. New York: Emerson Hall.

Powdermaker, Hortense. 1943. "The Channeling of Negro Aggression by the Cultural Process." *American Journal of Sociology* 48 (May): 757.

Powell, Gloria. 1973. "Self-Concept in White and Black Children." In *Racism and Mental Health: Essays*, edited by Charles Willie, Bernard Kramer, and Bertram Brown. Pittsburgh, Pa.: Univ. of Pittsburgh Press.

Pulzer, P. G. J. 1964. *The Rise of Political Anti-Semitism in Germany and Austria*. New York: Wiley.

Radke, Marian, Helen Trager, and Hadassah Davis. 1949. "Social Perceptions and Attitudes of Children." *Genetic Psychology Monographs* 40: 439.

Radke-Yarrow, Marion and Bernard Lande. 1953. "Personality Variables and Reactions to Minority Group Belonging." *Journal of Social Psychology* 38 (Nov.): 270.

Ransford, H. Edward. 1970. "Skin Color, Life-Chances, and Anti-White Attitudes." *Social Problems* 18 (Fall): 177.

Rath, R. and R. G. Sircar. 1960. "Inter-Caste Relationship as Reflected in the Study of Attitudes and Opinions of Six Hindu Caste Groups." *Journal of Social Psychology* 51 (Feb): 8.

Raven, Simon. 1963 [1960]. "Boys Will Be Boys: The Male Prostitute in London." In *The Problem of Homosexuality in Modern Society*, edited by Hendrik Ruitenbeek. New York: Dutton.

Reade, Brian. 1971 [1970]. *Sexual Heretics: Male Homosexuality in English Literature from 1850 to 1900*. New York: Coward-McCann.

Rechy, John. 1964. *City of Night*. New York: Grove Press.

Reich, Wilhelm. 1970 [1946]. *The Mass Psychology of Fascism*. Translated from the German by Vincent Carfagno. New York: Farrar, Straus & Giroux.

————. 1971 [1934]. "What is Class-Consciousness?" Translated from the German by Anna Bostock. *Liberation* 16 (Oct.): 25.

Reik, Theodor. 1962. *Jewish Wit*. New York: Gamut.

———. 1962 [1941]. *Masochism in Sex and Society*. Translated from the German by Margaret Beigel and Gertrud Kurth. New York: Grove Press.

Reiss, Albert. 1963 [1961]. "The Social Integration of Queers and Peers." In *The Problem of Homosexuality in Modern Society*, edited by Hendrik Ruitenbeek New York: Dutton.

Riesman, David. 1970 [1948]. "A Philosophy for 'Minority' Living." In *Zionism Reconsidered: The Rejection of Jewish Normalcy*, edited by Michael Selzer. London: Macmillan.

Riordan, Michael. 1975. "Capital Punishment: Notes of a Willing Victim." *Body Politic* 17 (Jan.–Feb.): 15.

Rooney, Elizabeth and Don Gibbons. 1966. "Societal Reactions to 'Crimes Without Victims'." *Social Problems* 13 (Spring): 108.

Rosen, David H. 1974 [1973]. *Lesbianism: A Study of Female Homosexuality*. Springfield, Ill.: Thomas.

Rosen, Ephraim and Ian Gregory. 1966. *Abnormal Psychology*. Philadelphia: Saunders.

Rosenberg, Morris. 1965. *Society and the Adolescent Self-Image*. Princeton, N.J.: Princeton University Press.

——— and Roberta Simmons. 1971. *Black and White Self-Esteem: The Urban School Child*. Washington, D.C.: American Sociological Association.

Rosenman, Stanley. 1956. The Paradox of Guilt in Disaster Victim Populations." *Psychiatric Quarterly Supplement* 30: 220.

Ross, H. Laurence. 1971. "Modes of Adjustment of Married Homosexuals." *Social Problems* 18 (Winter): 388.

Ruitenbeek, Hendrik. 1974. *The New Sexuality*. New York: New Viewpoints.

Ryan, William. 1971. *Blaming the Victim*. New York: Pantheon.

Sachar, Howard. 1958. *The Course of Modern Jewish History*. Cleveland: World Publishing.

Sagarin, Edward. 1969. *Odd Man In: Societies of Deviants in America*. Chicago: Quadrangle.

———. 1973, "The Good Guys, the Bad Guys, and the Gay Guys." *Contemporary Sociology* 3 (Jan.):3.

Saghir, Marcel and Eli Robins. 1973. *Male and Female Homosexuality: A Comprehensive Investigation*. Baltimore: Williams & Wilkins.

Salzman, Leon. 1959. "Masochism: a Review of Theory and Therapy." In *Individual and Family Dynamics*, edited by Jules Musserman. New York: Grune & Stratton.

Sarason, Seymour. 1973. "Jewishness, Blackness, and the Nature-Nurture Controversy." *American Psychologist* 28 (Nov.): 965.

Sarnoff, Irving. 1951. "Identification with the Aggressor: Some Personality Correlates of Anti-Semitism among Jews." *Journal of Personality* 20 (Sept. 1951– June 1952): 214.

Sartre, Jean Paul. 1960. *Critique de la raison dialectique (précédé de Question de méthode)*. Paris: Gallimard.

———. 1966 [1943]. *Being and Nothingness: An Essay on Phenomenological Ontology*. Translated from the French by Hazel Barnes. London: Methuen.

———. 1968 [1960]. *Search for a Method*. Translated from the French by Hazel Barnes. New York: Random House, Vintage Books.

———. 1973 [1946]. *Anti-Semite and Jew* Translated from the French by George Becker. New York: Schocken.

Savitz, Leonard. 1973. "Black Crime." In *Comparative Studies of Blacks and Whites in the United States*, edited by Kent Miller and Ralph Dreger. New York: Seminar.

Sawyer, Ethel. 1973. "Methodological Problems in Studying So-Called 'Deviant' Communities." In *The Death of White Sociology*, edited by Joyce Ladner. New York: Random House.

Schofield, Michael. 1965. *Sociological Aspects of Homosexuality: A Comparative Study of Three Types of Homosexuals*. London: Longmans.

Schorsch, Ismar. 1972. *Jewish Reactions to German Anti-Semitism, 1870–1914*. New York: Columbia University Press.

Schutz, Alfred. 1973 [1970]. "Interpretive Sociology." In *On Phenomenology and Social Relations*, edited by Helmut Wagner. Chicago: Univ. of Chicago Press.

—— and Thomas Luckmann. 1973. *The Structures of the Life-World*. Translated from the German by Richard Zaner and H. Tristram Engelhardt. Evanston, Ill.: Northwestern University Press.

Scott, Robert. 1976 [1969]. *The Making of Blind Men: A Study of Adult Socialization*. New York: Russell Sage.

Seiden, Morton. 1967. *The Paradox of Hate: A Study in Ritual Murder*. South Brunswick, N. J.: Yoseloff.

Selznick, Gertrude and Stephen Steinberg. 1969. *The Tenacity of Prejudice: Anti-Semitism in Contemporary America*. New York: Harper & Row.

Simmons, J. L. 1965. "Public Stereotypes of Deviants." *Social Problems* 13 (Fall): 228.

Singer, L. 1962. "Ethnogenesis and Negro-Americans Today." *Social Research* 29 (Winter): 424.

Socarides, Charles. 1968. *The Overt Homosexual*. New York: Grune & Stratton.

Sontag, Susan. 1966. "Notes on Camp." In *Against Interpretation and Other Essays*. New York: Farrar, Straus & Giroux.

Stampp, Kenneth. 1971. "Rebels and Sambos: The Search for the Negro's Personality in Slavery." *Journal of Southern History* 39 (Aug.): 370.

Steakley, James. 1975. *The Homosexual Emancipation Movement in Germany*. New York: Arno.

Stember, Charles, ed. 1966. *Jews in the Mind of America*. New York: Basic Books.

Sterling, Eleonore. 1958. "Jewish Reactions to Jew-Hatred in the First Half of the Nineteenth Century: Notes on How the Jews Pictured Themselves." *Leo Baeck Institute Year Book* 3: 408.

Stern, Paul. 1964. *The Abnormal Person and His World: An Introduction to Psychopathology*. Princeton, N. J.: Van Nostrand.

Stevenson, Harold and Edward Stewart. 1958. "A Developmental Study of Race Awareness in Young Children." *Child Development* 29 (Sept.): 408.

Stonequist, Everett. 1937. *The Marginal Man: A Study in Personality and Culture Conflict*. New York: Scribner.

Strange, Jack. 1965. *Abnormal Psychology: Understanding Behavior Disorders*. New York: McGraw-Hill.

Strassman, Harvey, Margaret Thaler, and Edgar Schein, 1956. "A Prisoner of War Syndrome: Apathy as a Reaction to Severe Stress." *American Journal of Psychiatry* 112 (June): 1,001.

Suinn, Richard. 1970. *Fundamentals of Behavior Pathology*. New York: Wiley.

Szasz, Thomas. 1970. *The Manufacture of Madness: A Comparative Study of the Inquisition and the Mental Health Movement*. New York: Harper & Row.

————. 1971. "The Sane Slave: An Historical Note on the Use of Medical Diagnosis as Justificatory Rhetoric." *American Journal of Psychotherapy* 25 (April): 228.

Teal, Donn. 1971. *The Gay Militants*. New York: Stein and Day.

Thomas, Alexander and Samuel Sillen. 1972. *Racism and Psychiatry*. New York: Brunner-Mazel.

Thompson, Norman, Boyd McCandless, and Bonnie Strickland. 1971. "Personal Adjustment of Male and Female Homosexuals and·Heterosexuals." *Journal of Abnormal Psychology* 78 (2): 240.

Tocqueville, Alexis de. 1956 [1840]. *Democracy in America*, edited by Richard Heffner. New York: New American Library.

Trent, Richard. 1957. "The Relation between Expressed Self-Acceptance and Expressed Attitudes toward Negroes and Whites among Negro Children." *Journal of Genetic Psychology* 91 (Sept.): 30.

Tripp, C. A. 1975. *The Homosexual Matrix*. New York: McGraw-Hill.

Troiden, Richard. 1974. "Homosexual Encounters in a Highway Rest Stop." In *Sexual Deviance and Sexual Deviants*, edited by Erich Goode and Richard Troiden. New York: Morrow.

Udry, J. Richard, Karl Bauman, and Charles Chase. 1971. "Skin Color, Status, and Mate Selection." *American Journal of Sociology* 76: 732.

Ullman, Leonard and Leonard Krasner. 1969. *A Psychological Approach to Abnormal Behavior*. Englewood Cliffs, N. J.: Prentice-Hall.

Waite, Richard. 1968. "The Negro Patient and Clinical Theory." *Journal of Consulting and Clinical Psychology* 32 (4): 429.

Waldman, Roy. 1971. *Humanistic Psychiatry: From Oppression to Choice*. New Brunswick, N. J.: Rutgers University Press.

Ward, Susan and John Braun. 1972. "Self-Esteem and Racial Preference in Black Children." *American Journal of Orthopsychiatry* 42 (July): 646.

Warren, Carol. 1974. *Identity and Community in the Gay World*. New York: Wiley.

Wax, Darold. 1966. "Negro Resistance to the Early American Slave Trade." *Journal of Negro History* 51 (Jan.): 1.

Weaver, Edward. 1955. "How Do Children Discover They Are Negroes?" *Understanding the Child* 24 (Jan.): 108.

Weber, Max. 1968 [1920]. *Economy and Society: An Outline of Interpretive Sociology*. Edited by Guenther Roth and Claus Wittich. Translated from the German by Fischoff et al. New York: Bedminster.

Weinberg, Martin. 1970. "The Male Homosexual: Age-Related Variations in Social and Psychological Characteristics." *Social Problems* 17 (Spring): 536.

———— and Alan Bell, eds. 1972. *Homosexuality: An Annotated Bibliography*. New York: Harper & Row.

———— and Colin Williams. 1974. *Male Homosexuals: Their Problems and Adaptations*. New York: Oxford University Press.

Weissbach, Theodore and Gary Zagon. 1975. "The Effect of Deviant Group Membership upon Impressions of Personality." *Journal of Social Psychology* 95 (April): 265.

Wellman, Barry. 1971. "Social Identities in Black and White." *Sociological Inquiry* 41 (Winter): 57.

Wellmer, Albrecht. 1971. *Critical Theory of Society*. Translated from the German by John Cumming. New York: Herder and Herder.

White, Robert. 1964. *The Abnormal Personality*. New York: Ronald.

White, William. 1926. *The Meaning of Disease: An Inquiry in the Field of Medical Philosophy*. Baltimore: Williams & Wilkins.

1975. "Who Could They Possibly Mean?" *Body Politic* 20 (Oct.): 10.

Williams, Colin and Martin Weinberg. 1971. *Homosexuals and the Military: A Study of Less Than Honorable Discharge.* New York: Harper & Row.

Williams, Robert and Harry Byars. 1969. "Negro Self-Esteem in a Transitional Society." *Personnel & Guidance Journal* 47 (Oct.): 123.

Winks, Robin. 1971. *The Blacks in Canada: A History.* Montreal: McGill-Queen's University Press.

Wirth, Louis. 1964. *The Ghetto.* Chicago: Univ. of Chicago Press.

—— and Herbert Goldhamer. 1944. "The Hybrid and the Problem of Miscegenation." In *Characteristics of the American Negro*, edited by Otto Klineberg. New York: Harper.

Wolfgang, Marvin and Bernard Cohen. 1970. *Crime and Race: Conceptions and Misconceptions.* New York: Institute of Human Relations.

—— and Marc Riedel. 1973. "Race, Judicial Discretion, and the Death Penalty." *Annals of the American Academy of Political and Social Science* 407 (May): 119.

Woodward, C. Vann. 1974 [1955]. *The Strange Career of Jim Crow.* New York: Oxford University Press.

Wyne, Marvin, Kinnard White, and Richard Coop. 1974. *The Black Self.* Englewood Cliffs, N. J.: Prentice-Hall.

Yancey, William, Leo Rigsby, and John McCarthy. 1972. "Social Position and Self-Evaluation: The Relative Importance of Race." *American Journal of Sociology* 78 (Sept.): 338.

Young, Ian. 1975. "Pigs & Fishes." *Body Politic* 18 (May–June): 16.

Young, Jock. 1975. "Working-Class Criminology." In *Critical Criminology*, edited by Ian Taylor, Paul Walton, and Jock Young. London: Routledge & Kegan Paul.

Zborowski, Mark. 1969. *People in Pain.* San Francisco: Jossey-Bass.

Zola, Irving. 1965 [1963]. "Observations on Gambling in a Lower-Class Setting." In *Blue-Collar World: Studies of the American Worker*, edited by Arthur Shostak and William Gomberg. Englewood Cliffs, N. J.: Prentice-Hall.

INDEX

Sex role: 113, 132, 147; male, 36, 56, 99, 114, 152; female, 35–36, 98, 152
Sexuality: and objectification, 41, 61, 113–114, 136; inferiorized people and, 43–46, 86, 109; and preference, 106, 112–114
Sieg des Judentums über das Germanentum, Der, 88
Simmons, Roberta, 68
Singer, L., 131
Sipple, Oliver, 147
Smell, 43
Socarides, Charles, 37
Social construction of identity, *see* Identity
Social control, *see* Cultural transmission, Domination
Social order, *see* Problem of order
Sociology, interpretive, 4
Stampp, Kenneth, 84, 138
Stein, Gertrude, 25
Stember, Charles, 49
Stereotype, *see* Composite portrait of the inferiorized person
Stevenson, Harold, 107
Stewart, Edward, 107
Stöcker, Adolf, 19
Stonewall Rebellion, 26–27, 123
Structure of life limitations, 4, 7–8, 28–29, 58–60, 70–71, 77–78, 127–128, *see* Domination, Phenomenology
Subjectivity, *see* Desubjectivization, Dialectic
Subordination, *see* Domination, Inferiorization
Symonds, John Addington, 25

T

Therapy, *see* Psychiatry, Psychology
Tocqueville, Alexis de, 69
Total institution, 8, 73, 86
Toward a Critique of Hegel's Philosophy of Law, 126
Transsexualism, 101, 113
Treason, 46, 47–48, 98
Treitschke, Heinrich von, 19
Trent, Richard, 65
Trial, The, 116

U

Ulrichs, Karl, 25
Urbanization, 2, 22–24, 25–27

V

Visibility and identity, 14–15, 97, *see* Overvisibility

W

Warren, Carol, 12, 91, 123
Washington, Booker T., 22, 88
Weber, Max, 131
Weinberg, Martin, 15, 27, 63, 67, 92, 114
Weininger, Otto, 88
Weisman, Carol, 66, 67
Weissbach, Theodore, 50
Wellman, Barry, 62
Wellmer, Albrecht, 119
Whitman, Walt, 25
Wilde, Oscar, 25
Williams, Colin, 15, 27, 63, 67, 92, 114
Williams, Gertrude, 60
Wirth, Louis, 94
Withdrawal: 4, 31; social, 93–97; psychological, 97–99; *see* Closetry
Witchhunt, 15, 20, 21, 26, 29, 44, 45, 88, *see* McCarthyism, Nazism, Racism, Scapegoating
Women, 3, 9, 35–36, 72, 98, 101, 135, *see* Patriarchy
Working class, 9, 58, 63, 78, 110, 120, 124, 127–129

Y

Yancey, William, 68
Young, Jock, xi

Z

Zagon, Gary, 50
Zborowski, Mark, 72
Zionism, 20
Zola, Irving, 104